LAST SEASONS IN HAVANA

Last Seasons in
HAVANA

The Castro Revolution *and the* End *of* Professional Baseball *in* Cuba

CÉSAR BRIOSO

University of Nebraska Press

LINCOLN & LONDON

Library of Congress Cataloging-in-Publication Data
Names: Brioso, César, 1965– author.
Title: Last seasons in Havana: the Castro Revolution and the
end of professional baseball in Cuba / César Brioso.
Description: Lincoln: University of Nebraska Press, [2019] |
Includes bibliographical references and index.
Identifiers: LCCN 2018018103
ISBN 9781496205513 (cloth: alk. paper)
ISBN 9781496213778 (epub)
ISBN 9781496213785 (mobi)
ISBN 9781496213792 (pdf)
Subjects: LCSH: Baseball—Cuba—History—20th
century. | Baseball—Social aspects—Cuba. | Castro,
Fidel, 1926–2016. | Cuba—History.
Classification: LCC GV863.25.A1 B753 2019 |
DDC 796.357097291/0904—dc23
LC record available at https://lccn.loc.gov/2018018103

Set in Questa by E. Cuddy.

For my smart and talented cello-playing son, Daniel. For my loving and supportive wife, Karen, the best social media director any author could have. And for my mom, María Luisa. The courage she showed by returning to Cuba in 1980 to bring her family to the United States still leaves me in awe.

CONTENTS

ILLUSTRATIONS

In the months after Fidel Castro came to power in Cuba, his government began rounding up *batistianos*, supporters of Fulgencio Batista. The deposed Cuban dictator had fled the country during the early morning hours of January 1, 1959. The Fortaleza de San Carlos de la Cabaña, an eighteenth-century fortress that stands along the eastern ridge of Havana harbor, became the prison of choice for those apprehended in Havana. My uncle, René Higinio Brioso, became a prisoner there on April 14. He was not a Batista supporter. In fact, he had actively participated in actions designed to topple Batista's corrupt and repressive regime, and like many Cubans welcomed Castro as a hero when he triumphantly entered Havana after Batista's ouster. But none of that mattered.

In one step among the many he took to consolidate power, Castro had installed new directors in the Sindicato de Omnibus Aliados (Allied Bus Union). Those directors accused more than fifty bus drivers, including my uncle, of being Batista sympathizers. So René was taken into custody, and for more than a month he heard the daily sounds of firing squads in the courtyard of La Cabaña and wondered when his name might be called by the guards. Fortunately, he was eventually released unharmed.

But while René was still imprisoned, a family reunion revealed the depths of the divisions being sown by Castro's revolution. As was the family's annual custom, they gathered at my great-grandmother Conchita's house in Havana on May 10, the Saturday before Mother's Day. Enrique, one of René's uncles and a Castro supporter, made a stunning pronouncement: "I wish I was in charge at La Cabaña so I could take a .50-caliber gun and gun down every prisoner there," he said, "rrrah, rrrah, rrrah, rrrah, with a machine gun and kill everybody there." Enrique said this in front of his brother, René's father (my grandfather), knowing his nephew was still at La Cabaña.

My grandfather, René Isaac Brioso, was one of eleven siblings, five of whom became Communists after the revolution. "There were lots of fights when we got together after the revolution," my father, César, once told me. "It hit a point that . . . they didn't talk to us, complete separation." Such was the intensity of the political differences that divided families, friends, and neighbors in postrevolutionary Cuba. Those differences tore through the fabric of every level of Cuban society, including the country's national sport, baseball.

Baseball in pre-Castro Cuba was in the midst of a golden age. The Cuban League, which had been founded in 1878, just two years after the formation of the National League in the United States, was thriving under the auspices of Organized Baseball. Cuban teams had come to dominate the annual Caribbean Series tournament. And Havana had joined the highest levels of Minor League baseball, fielding the Havana Sugar Kings of the Class Triple-A International League. Confidence was high that Havana might one day have a Major League team to call its own.

Away from the baseball diamond, however, events portended seismic changes for Cuba. In 1952, Fulgencio Batista had overthrown the democratically elected but corrupt administration of president Carlos Prío Socarrás. In the years that followed, anti-Batista sentiments rose. Amid growing unrest, a young radical named Fidel Castro became a leading voice for political dissent at the University of Havana. He moved from words to action, leading a failed attack on the Moncada Barracks in 1953 that resulted in his imprisonment on the Isle of Pines. But after a shortened prison sentence and brief exile in Mexico, Castro returned to Cuba, managing to make his way into the Sierra Maestra Mountains with a band of rebels. For years, they waged a successful guerrilla war that eventually overthrew Batista.

My father was nineteen during the triumph of the revolution. He had grown up as a fan of Almendares, one of the four teams in the Cuban League. His uncle, Raúl, had taken him to games at El Gran Stadium of Havana during the late 1940s and early 1950s. Throughout the first half of the twentieth century, players from the Major Leagues, Minor Leagues, and Negro leagues had come to Cuba to play in the country's winter baseball league. And my father had watched some of the Cuban League's top players: Negro leagues stars such as Monte Irvin and Ray Dandridge, Cuban stars such as Roberto Ortiz and Willy Miranda, and American players such as All-Star pitcher Max Lanier and future Hall of Fame manager Tommy Lasorda. In the working-class neighborhood of Luyanó, my father lived around the corner from Almendares star third baseman Héctor Rodríguez and played pick-up baseball games with his sons.

But professional baseball became one of the many victims of Castro's Communist revolution. His rise to power forever altered Cuba's future and changed the course of a sport that had become ingrained in the island's culture for almost a century. "I lost interest in the game," my father once told me. "I lost the tradition, and I lost a lot of players that I knew when I followed the game. All these good American players, they were gone too. Everything changed."

ACKNOWLEDGMENTS

Multiple cellphone voice messages had gone unreturned when I decided to contact Pepe Lacayo at Radio Marti in Miami. I had been trying desperately to reach Orlando Peña, hoping he would agree to an interview for this book. Lacayo, who hosts a nightly sports talk show that includes Peña, graciously agreed to help hook me up with the Cuban Baseball Hall of Fame pitcher. But he also warned me: it would depend on the mood of El Guajiro (a Cuban colloquial term of endearment that means country bumpkin and Peña's nickname). I called Lacayo at the appointed hour. He corralled Peña and brought him to the phone. I made my pitch, explaining I was writing a book about the final seasons of professional baseball in Cuba. And I made sure to mention my father was an *almendarista*, a fan of Almendares, the Cuban League team for which Peña had played six winter league seasons. Come by the station when you are in town, he told me. I was in.

On my next visit to Miami, I found the station that transmits in Spanish to Cuba, amid the many blocks of a sprawling industrial park area near Miami International Airport. Once I managed to get through security, Lacayo introduced me to Peña, who was in a room preparing for the night's radio show. What ensued was less an interview than Peña holding court and telling stories for about an hour and a half. It was great. When the conversation concluded, Peña suddenly invited me to appear on the show *Al duro y sin guantes*, which translates roughly as "playing catch barehanded." Thus, I made my Spanish-language radio debut on Cuban airwaves.

The other almost twenty interviews I conducted for this book may not have been nearly as eventful but they were no less enjoyable. And I want to thank all the former players and others who agreed to share their memories of Cuba. Most often, I tracked down my subjects by phone. Sometimes they found me. That was the case with Jorge Maduro, the son of Cuban baseball entrepreneur Bobby Maduro, who built Havana's El Gran Stadium and owned the Cienfuegos club of the Cuban League and the Havana Sugar Kings of the Class Triple-A International League. Jorge introduced himself after my appearance on a panel at the Society for America Baseball Research convention in Miami. We arranged to talk on the phone. His stories about his father and his own memories of Cuba in the 1940s and 1950s were invaluable in writing this story. Maduro introduced me to another Miami radio personality, Pepe Campos, who put me in touch with Cuban Baseball Hall of Fame pitcher Pedro Ramos late in the writing process, for which I will always be grateful.

Another unexpected interview came when a gentleman named Al López-Chávez introduced himself to me at a book signing in Miami. The New Jersey resident winters in South Florida. He happened to see that I would be presenting my first book on Cuban baseball history and decided to attend. Al showed me a photo on his phone of himself as a young child on the field at El Gran Stadium with Almendares star player Roberto Ortiz and told me he had served as a batboy for the Sugar Kings after the team was forced to move from Havana to Jersey City, New Jersey, in the middle of the 1960 season. Al, who still counts Cuban Baseball Hall of Famer Cookie Rojas as a friend, shared his experience with the relocated team and was a joy to talk to.

And another completely out-of-the-blue connection was made by David Caveda, who reached out to me because he had come across my blog about Cuban baseball history. Turned out he and I attended high school together in Hialeah, Florida, (although we didn't know each other at the time) and his father was a childhood friend of Cuban Baseball Hall of Fame pitcher Luis Tiant. I had given up hope of talking to Tiant, who played in the final season of the Cuban League. I was thrilled to be able to include his voice in this book.

I am also grateful for the help of my friend and former *USA Today* colleague Bob Kimball, who once again offered his services in back-reading my chapters. And the book was greatly facilitated by online access to the archives of *The Sporting News, New York Times,* and *Washington Post. The Sporting News* covered the Cuban League of the 1950s in remarkable detail. The *New York Times* covered the Castro Revolution on a daily basis with staff writers based in Havana. I also was able to access crucial articles from the Cuban newspaper *Diario de la Marina* thanks to the University of Florida's online searchable PDF database. Thank you to everyone who helped make this book possible.

The House That Bobby Built

O pening nights for the Havana Sugar Kings often were elaborate affairs, replete with celebrities, foreign ambassadors, and other dignitaries. One year, beloved Cuban child actor Rolando Ochoa might serve as master of ceremonies. The next International League season might open with French actor Maurice Chevalier throwing out the ceremonial first pitch. But this particular opening night included something entirely different, unbeknownst to the vast majority of fans packed into El Gran Stadium in Havana.

As fans streamed through the gates, Joaquín Cordero stood outside the stadium, handing out tickets to fifty to sixty men who joined the crowd, sitting scattered throughout the highest row of the grandstand. They paid little attention to the baseball game on the field. Instead their eyes remained transfixed on a building beyond the outfield fence, awaiting a signal from a rooftop flashlight that would indicate the assassination of Cuban dictator Fulgencio Batista had succeeded. Upon seeing the signal, they were to leave the stadium, retrieve the cache of arms stored in a building across the street, and storm the nearby police armory. If everything went as planned, they could begin restoring deposed democratically elected president Carlos Prío Socarrás to power.

The men awaiting their signal at El Gran Stadium were members of AAA (Triple A), the Asociación de Amigos Aureliano (Association of Friends of Aureliano), so named for Aureliano Sánchez Arango. The former lawyer and university professor had served as minister of education and then as foreign minister under Prío, who was elected president of Cuba in 1948. Batista, who had served as Cuba's elected president from 1940 to 1944, won a seat in the Cuban Senate the same year Prío was elected president and chose to mount another presidential campaign in 1952. Facing certain electoral defeat, Batista staged a bloodless coup d'etat on March 10, three months before the election. Batista, former head of the Cuban Army, took over the military headquarters at Camp Columbia without firing a shot, and Prío fled Cuba. While in exile in Miami, Florida, Prío started supplying arms through the AAA Movement to anti-Batista efforts back home in Cuba.

Among those efforts was a plot to assassinate Batista, planned to coincide with a season-opening game of the Sugar Kings, according to conspirator René Brioso, who was Cordero's nephew. "The arms were in a building that was [beyond] right field of the stadium," René recalled years later. "[Prío] had rented apartments in a tall building that was eight or nine floors high. . . . He gave the money to buy tickets for all us who were organized because it was believed we could kill Batista that night."[1]

René was no stranger to political activism. Born in 1928 in the sugar mill town at Central Niágara, he became involved with the Partido Auténtico (Authentic Party) in 1951. As a conductor and then a bus driver for Omnibus Aliados, René worked to keep Communists from controlling the bus drivers' union. His first anti-Batista action came the year after Batista's coup, helping to organize a strike that shut down bus service throughout Havana. Those involved had to meet clandestinely at night at Havana's famed Colón Cemetery out of fear of being arrested. Once Batista assured there would be no reprisals, the drivers returned to work and bus service resumed the next day without incident.

The latest action in which René was involved, however, was far more dangerous. The night of the Sugar Kings' opening game, Batista was supposed to attend a party. "We were going to intercept him on the road," René said. "There was a conspiracy, and one of the guys who was with us was with the police. He worked [as a dispatcher] in the radio section in the police station, where the motorcycles were kept, the motor pool. That station, the motor pool, was close to the stadium. And when he received the news by radio that they had killed Batista, he was supposed to go to the roof of the building and signal us with a flashlight. There were about sixty of us. They gave us the tickets so we could enter and sit in the last row of the stadium, not low, but high up because from there you could see the police station motor pool."[2]

Because the conspirators didn't know when the signal might come and because of the grave nature of what that signal would mean, it would have been difficult to focus on the game, let alone enjoy it. By the end of the game as the vast majority of fans celebrated victory, the several dozen conspirators were left to wonder what went wrong. "The time passed and passed and passed, and we never saw a light [signal]," René said. "The Sugar Kings game ended, and we left, and then we got the news that [Batista] didn't take the route he was expected to take to the party he was going to, or wherever he was going. We knew he was going there, but then he took a different route. He didn't go by the route we were expecting, where people were holed up waiting to kill him, to assassinate him. That's how that ended."[3]

Although the plot was abandoned, the seeds of Cuba's latest revolution continued to be sown among multiple groups resisting the Batista regime. One was led by a young radical named Fidel Castro. His failed attack on the Moncada Barracks on July 26, 1953, had launched the 26th of July Movement. Despite imprisonment on Cuba's Isle of Pines, Castro continued to coordinate revolutionary activities via correspondence. One day, he would transform Cuba, as well as the sport that had become so ingrained in the country's culture.

The inaugural game of the Sugar Kings' existence opened to great fanfare. Ribbons adorned all the box seats. Cuban, American, and Canadian flags draped the front of the press box. A highly choreographed first pitch included a pair of foreign ambassadors and the president of a United States–based Minor League. A new era dawned for baseball in Cuba on Tuesday, April 20, 1954. El Gran Stadium would play host to the first game of Cuba's entry in the Class Triple-A International League. Roberto "Bobby" Maduro had built the stadium in 1946 to be the new, modern home of the Cuban League, the country's professional winter circuit. But Maduro's stadium was about to become home to Havana's fledgling Minor League team, which he owned as well.

In almost every measurable way, El Gran Stadium was a superior baseball facility to its predecessor, La Tropical, which had housed the Cuban League from 1930 to 1946. Built in Havana's working-class El Cerro neighborhood, El Gran Stadium was about half the distance from La Tropical to downtown Havana. It seated more than thirty-five thousand fans, fifteen thousand more than the previous stadium had. Unlike La Tropical, with its space for a soccer field and Olympic track, as well as beer gardens and a dance hall, El Gran Stadium was designed specifically for baseball. Eight light towers allowed for night games.

But upgrading the Cuban League's accommodations wasn't Maduro's only goal when he and Miguel "Miguelito" Suárez, his partner in La Compañía Operadora de Stadiums, built El Gran Stadium with backing from the Bacardi Rum Company. Maduro's ultimate goal was to bring a Major League team to Havana, and the Sugar Kings were the next step in accomplishing that aspiration. The team's motto alluded to just that: "Un paso más y llegamos" ("One more step and we're there"). Maduro would celebrate the Sugar Kings' first game in keeping with the significance of such an accomplishment. The Havana daily newspaper *Diario de la Marina* proclaimed the preparation for opening night "gives the impression that what will be witnessed will be a spectacle superior to the World Series."[4]

Indeed, a festive atmosphere permeated the stands before the scheduled 8:30 p.m. start time. Throughout the stadium, twenty-three thousand roaring fans waved white handkerchiefs. The raucousness subsided only when Monsignor Alfredo Müller, the

Catholic archbishop of Havana who had presided over the benediction of El Gran Stadium when it opened in 1946, blessed a Sugar Kings banner during a ceremony at home plate.

Players from the Toronto Maple Leafs stood along the first base line. Sugar Kings players flanked the third base line, debuting their home-white flannels with "Cubanos" in red script across the chest ("Sugar Kings" would appear only on road gray uniforms throughout the team's existence). After the ceremony, Rolando Ochoa, a child actor of radio, film, theater, and television, presented the team with a large sack of sugar with a crown, which would be the team mascot, symbolizing "los Reyes de Azúcar"—the Sugar Kings.

Then came the elaborate opening-pitch ceremony. U.S. ambassador Arthur Gardner, wearing a dark suit, would play the role of umpire, donning a chest protector and mask. Canadian ambassador Harry Scott would throw the first pitch, to Roberto Fernández Miranda, Cuba's director of sports, stationed behind home plate. And International League president Frank Shaughnessy would stand in the batter's box. But first, Scott made a show of calling Fernández to the mound to get their signs straight. Gardner then walked out to break up the mound conference while exaggeratedly gesturing that they no longer delay the game. The only thing not as easily choreographed was Scott's pitch, which was so off the mark it struck a photographer in the head as he positioned himself near home plate to capture the proceedings.

The pregame festivities complete, home plate umpire Augie Guglielmo yelled out, "Play ball!" And when Havana starting pitcher Emilio Cueche threw the first pitch, the inaugural season of the Sugar Kings was officially under way. The Maple Leafs were considered one of the strongest teams in the International League, boasting former Negro leagues star Sam Jethroe, Cuban League star Héctor Rodríguez, and future New York Yankees catcher Elston Howard. But the Sugar Kings were never in danger of losing their first game in the circuit.

Havana batters hit Toronto starting pitcher Ed Blake early,

scoring runs in four consecutive innings starting in the second frame. Cueche, Havana's Venezuelan-born starting pitcher, was the "undisputed hero of the night," going three for four and driving in the first run of the game in the second inning on a rocket shot to right field. Cueche also scored once.[5] After scoring a run in both the third and fourth innings, the Sugar Kings broke the game open with three runs in the fifth, one scoring on a single by Cueche. Havana rapped fifteen total hits and beat Toronto 7–2.

Traditionally, Cuban baseball fans had been largely divided by their allegiance between Habana or Almendares, the "Eternal Rivals" of the Cuban League. But on that night, fans "witnessed the birth of a mystical new national baseball," René Molina wrote in the next day's *Diario de la Marina*. "Before now, the Creole people were divided into habanismo and almendarismo. . . . That traditional division has allowed us to experience unforgettable moments. . . . However, it must be accepted that last night a new, different horizon was seen in the crowd that packed the stadium, a unanimous reaction, a collective sense of support for the team that represents the country."[6]

Long before opening night, Bobby Maduro was confident Havana could support not only a Triple-A team but also a Major League team. "In many ways, Havana is a big-league town," Maduro said in 1953 as he was lobbying to have the Cuban capital admitted into the International League. "Its new stadium seats 35,000. The players can stop here at first-class hotels, where American meals are served at all times, and almost everyone speaks English."[7] And it was with Havana's potential in mind that Maduro pursued his plan to bring a Major League team to Cuba.

Born in Havana on June 27, 1916, Roberto Maduro de Lima came from a family of Sephardic Jewish origin, having migrated from the Netherlands to the Caribbean. Maduro's paternal grandfather S.E.L. Maduro founded Curacao's oldest company in 1837. Maduro's father Salomón Mozes Levy Maduro was born in Curacao in 1890 and moved the family to Cuba in 1914 as the country's sugar industry expanded following independence from Spain. The Maduro family was not observant and converted to Catholicism after migrating to Cuba.[8]

"Momón" Maduro worked as a sugarcane planter for the American Sugar Refining Company in Cunagua, in Camagüey Province. In 1926, Momón went into the insurance business, eventually working his way up to president of the Compañía Cubana de Fianzas, the Cuban Fidelity Company. As was common in wealthy Cubans families, Bobby was sent to school in the United States, attending the Asheville School in North Carolina and then studying engineering at Cornell University.[9] But after completing his sophomore year, he left Cornell in 1936 to help his father operate the family sugar plantation following the death of an uncle.[10]

When he wasn't studying abroad or working in the family businesses—which included insurance, cattle, and the Flecha de Oro bus line—Bobby Maduro played first base for the Vedado Tennis Club's amateur baseball team, los Marqueses, the Marquis(es).[11] Maduro's early baseball experience no doubt sparked his lifelong passion for the sport. That passion drove him to build a baseball stadium, buy Cuban League and Minor League teams, help launch a countrywide youth baseball system known as los Cubanitos, and aspire to bring a Major League team to Havana. "When I was a boy, to be able to share in my father's dream, which was that the Sugar Kings could become a Major League franchise, it's an extraordinary memory," Maduro's son Jorge said. "That's what consumed him."[12]

Jorge Maduro was the fourth of eight children born to Bobby and his wife, Isolina Olmo Fernández Garrido, who was known as "Fufila." They were married on January 28, 1940, and by the time Jorge was born on July 22, 1947, the Cuban League had completed its first season at El Gran Stadium. It remains perhaps the most memorable season in league history thanks to a dramatic three-game series to determine the championship. Almendares had to win thirteen of its final fourteen games, including that season-ending series against Habana. Almendares pitcher Max

Lanier, a two-time All-Star with the St. Louis Cardinals, won the decisive game on one day's rest, igniting a wild celebration that spread through the streets of Havana and across Cuba. "As far as I'm concerned," Almendares catcher and league MVP Andrés Fleitas recalled years later, "it was one of the greatest series, one of the greatest championships Cuba has ever seen."[13]

It was a spectacular way to christen the new stadium Bobby Maduro had built with key help from others, such as Miguelito Suárez, promoter Emilio de Armas, and the Compañía Ron Bacardi S.A. "The stadium always looked as if Bobby was the owner," recalled Maduro's longtime friend Rafael "Ralph" Ávila, who went on to preside over the Los Angeles Dodgers' successful Latin American scouting program for more than twenty years during the 1980s and 1990s. "Bobby was the one with the idea, . . . but in reality, if you went to the stadium, everything was advertisements for Bacardi. Since I also worked for Bacardi, I know that 51 percent of the action in the stadium were Bacardi's. That's why in the stadium there was only signage for Bacardi and Hatuey [the company's beer brand]."[14]

Born on March 25, 1930, in Camagüey, Ávila started working for Bacardi at age sixteen during the construction of the Cervecería Modelo brewery in the Havana suburb of El Cotorro. He worked in everything from bottling to sales to public relations. He also organized internal company baseball tournaments, managed the amateur Bacardi team, and helped organize the Liga Intermunicipal de Béisbol Amateurs Libre, a winter amateur league commonly known as the Liga de Quivicán. And Ávila, whose son Al would go on to become general manager of the Detroit Tigers in 2015, would play a role in a future revolution that would forever alter the course of Cuba's history.

Unlike Almendares and Habana, which had been members of the Cuban League since it was founded in 1878, the Cienfuegos Base Ball Club had a shorter, less storied, and more sporadic history. The franchise first played during the issue-plagued 1926–27 season but withdrew from the league on November 13 as it struggled to pay travel costs. Cienfuegos did not participate in the 1927–28 season but returned to action for 1928–29 before disappearing again after the 1930–31 season.

During the early half of the twentieth century, it was not uncommon for teams to join the league for brief periods before withdrawing, never to return. The league finally stabilized with four teams—Almendares, Habana, Cienfuegos, and Marianao—beginning with the 1943–44 season. Cienfuegos had become a fixture in 1939 under the control of Luis Oliver and Francisco Curbelo, who immediately sold the team to Florentino Pardo Galí. Under his ownership, the Elefantes (Elephants) won their first Cuban League championship in 1945–46, the league's final season at La Tropical.

After Cienfuegos finished third, third, and last in subsequent seasons, Bobby Maduro chose to enter the realm of team ownership following the 1948–49 season. Together with Emilio de Armas and Luis Parga, Maduro bought the team in 1949, agreeing to pay annual installments of $10,000. Each member of the Cienfuegos triumvirate brought specific qualities to bear: Maduro was one of the owners of El Gran Stadium; De Armas was a financial advisor to the Cuban League; and Parga was owner of the Casa Tarín sporting goods store, which ran concessions for Wilson baseballs used by the league.

In his seminal work on Cuban baseball history, Roberto González Echevarría explained the significance of the new Cienfuegos ownership group: "With this clout Cienfuegos could counter that of the ten owners of Almendares, which . . . belonged to powerful Cuban families such as the Sanguilys, Mendozas, and Menocals; Marianao's newly acquired financial and political power; and Habana's financial stability under Miguel Ángel [González]."[15]

Almendares enjoyed great success after a group of wealthy Vedado Tennis Club members bought the club in 1944. The Alacranes (Scorpions) won six championships in the first eleven seasons under the direction of engineer Mario Mendoza (team president) and doctors July Sanguily (treasurer) and Juan Portela (secretary). In that same time period, Habana won four times under the ownership of Miguel Ángel González. He had played or managed (or, some seasons, did both) for the Leones (Lions) since 1910 and bought controlling interest in the team from the widow of previous owner, Abel Linares, in the early 1940s. González paid her $30,000 in December 1946 to become sole owner.[16]

Marianao had its new ownership group in place starting in 1948, when Alfredo Pequeño and José Rodríguez took control of the club and changed the mascot from the Monjes Grises (Gray Monks) to the Tigres (Tigers). Marianao had won the championship in 1922–23, its first season in the league, but had only captured one other title since, in 1936–37. For much of their existence, Marianao and Cienfuegos were also-rans to Almendares and Habana. With new ownership groups, however, the Tigers and Elephants would both go on to enjoy success previously reserved for the league's Eternal Rivals. But before Cienfuegos would reach those heights, Maduro set his sights on the Havana Cubans, a team in the Class B Florida International League, which was run by longtime Washington Senators scout Joe Cambria.

Carlo Cambria was born in Messina, Italy, on July 5, 1890. His father, Giovanni, a shoemaker, immigrated to the United States that same year, settling in Boston. In 1893, Giovanni arranged to have Carlo and his two older brothers, Pasquale and Giovanni, brought to the United States, where Carlo's name was Americanized to Joseph Carl Cambria after he arrived in New York on August 2. Young Joseph loved baseball and went on to play semipro ball in Massachusetts towns such as Boston, Roxbury, Lowell, and Medford. He joined the professional ranks, signing with Newport of the independent Rhode Island State League in 1909. The *Newport Daily News* described Cambria as "a dark, pleasant-looking player from Medford way."[17]

In 1911, Cambria joined the Berlin (Ontario) Green Sox of the Class D Canadian League, where he played two seasons before a broken leg ended his playing career. But after serving in the U.S. military during World War I, Cambria returned to baseball, this time running amateur and semipro teams. He bought his first professional team, the Hagerstown Hubs of the four-team, Class D Blue Ridge League, in December 1929. In 1932, Cambria bought the Baltimore Black Sox, which competed in Cum Posey's East-West League before briefly joining Gus Greenlee's new Negro National League in 1933. That same year, Cambria purchased the Albany Senators of the Class Double-A International League for $7,500 and immediately made an estimated $40,000 by selling off its players.[18]

During this time, Cambria established a working agreement with Washington Senators owner Clark Griffith and began signing Cuban talent. The first was Ysmael "Mulo" Morales, purchased from Cuban-American baseball promoter Alex Pompez in 1932.[19] As manager of the Cincinnati Reds in 1911, Griffith had signed Armando Marsans and Rafael Almeida. They were the first two Cuban-born players to play in the Major Leagues during the modern era (since 1900). While Cambria was signing players for Griffith during the 1930s, he continued buying, running, and selling several Minor League teams until he was forced to sell the Class D Salisbury Indians after the 1940 Eastern Shore League season. Baseball commissioner Kenesaw Mountain Landis had ruled that no Major League scout could operate a Minor League club.[20]

Over parts of three decades beginning in the 1930s, "Papa Joe," as he became known in Cuba, signed as many as four hundred Cuban players. Cambria "was an extraordinary person. He helped and signed many Cuban players. He had an extraordinary eye for scouting players," recalled Evelio Hernández, who pitched in the Cuban League from 1954 to 1959.[21] "To most of us, he was like a father. If we have any problems, well, we go to Papa Joe," said Julio Bécquer, who was signed by Cambria for the Washington Senators in 1951. "He was a short guy, kind of stocky, smile on his face all the time, and he was just a great human being."[22]

Not everyone agreed with Bécquer's assessment. Cambria had a reputation for signing Cuban players at rock-bottom prices, typically offering them seventy-five dollars a month. Cuban sports writer Jess Losada of *Carteles* magazine "acidly referred to him as the Christopher Columbus of baseball, denoting his thirst for and taking of the island's treasures."[23]

Camilo Pascual serves as an example of Cambria's frugality, as well as the high regard in which he was held by Cuban players. The future Major League All-Star turned down a $4,000 offer from the Brooklyn Dodgers to sign with Washington for $175 in 1952. "He signed everybody," recalled Cuban pitcher Orlando Peña, who played fourteen seasons in the Majors from 1958 to 1975. "He didn't give bonuses to anybody. He wouldn't even give away shoes."[24]

By the early 1940s, Cambria had become a ubiquitous presence in Havana, operating out of a room at the American Club at 309 Paseo de Martí in the heart of the city. He owned rental properties, an apartment building, several bars, and a restaurant called Triple-A that sat beyond the center field scoreboard at El Gran Stadium. One biographer described Cambria as a "fat little Italian who walked around in the baggy white linen suit with an untucked shirt with fake pearl buttons and a Panama hat. A cigar was ever-present in his mouth. . . . He cut an impressive figure traveling to big events in a limousine."[25]

Early efforts to bring Minor League baseball to Cuba had fizzled. The Class B Southeastern League first attempted to expand into Havana in 1929, but the plans fell through when a second expansion team in Florida failed to materialize in either Miami or St. Petersburg. The Great Depression short-circuited a second attempt in 1931. But Minor League baseball finally came to Havana in 1946. On December 6, 1945, the executive committee of the National Association, Minor League baseball's governing organization, qualified the Class C Florida International League as a new Minor League circuit.

The league previously had been denied admission because of

a general policy against admitting any city in Cuba or Mexico for the 1946 season. But in a statement reversing that stand, the committee ordered that "Havana be given permission to enter the National Association for the purpose of playing professional baseball in Havana, Cuba, under the rules and regulations of the National Association on strict probation, from month to month, until they have satisfied the membership of the National Association that they are operating and working under said rules."[26]

Baldomero "Merito" Acosta, who in 1918 became the only player in Cuban League history to execute an unassisted triple play, became president of the new Havana Cubans franchise. Aside from a stellar Cuban League career, he also had played for Clark Griffith's Washington Senators from 1913 to 1918. Acosta, who had been a part owner of Marianao in the Cuban League, owned a 25 percent share of the Havana Cubans. George P. Foster, an American and longtime resident of Cuba, owned 50 percent, and Cambria owned 25 percent.[27] Former Minor League and Cuban League infielder Oscar Rodríguez managed the team, which would play the 1946 season at La Tropical. With the installation of a 420,000-watt lighting plant, the stadium could finally host night games, and Acosta predicted that as many as 25,000 fans would attend the team's inaugural game on April 17.[28]

The Cubans won their Florida International League debut 5–4 against the Miami Beach Flamingos and continued winning. Havana finished with a 76–41 record, winning the pennant by 7 games over the Tampa Smokers despite having to forfeit 17 victories for using too many veteran players. Because the Cubans had turned the race into a runaway, the league instituted a split-season format for qualifying for the playoffs "for the purpose of boosting gate receipts by some $25,000."[29] Havana drew the West Palm Beach Indians in the first round of the playoffs. Tampa, which had won the second half, was paired against Miami Beach. But the plan backfired when the Indians eliminated first-half champs Havana, three games to two. Acosta shrugged off the first-round defeat: "It's too bad that we couldn't win, but it wasn't in the cards. We lost."[30]

Even before the season had ended, Griffith increased his stake in the Havana ownership group, buying Foster's twenty thousand shares on July 18. Foster sold out because of an undisclosed dispute with Acosta.[31] Washington and Havana already had a working agreement, and it was cemented by Griffith becoming the Cubans' vice president. In 1947, the team moved from La Tropical to the new El Gran Stadium, finishing in first place with a 105-45 record. Havana's winning ways continued as the team finished in first place the next three seasons. The Cubans won the playoffs in back-to-back seasons (1947 and '48) and won at least 100 games twice (105 in 1947 and 101 in 1950). Havana topped two hundred thousand in attendance in each of its first four seasons at El Gran Stadium.

But the Cubans' stay in the Florida International League was not without its issues. One such incident came in August of 1947, when Cambria was investigated for using $9,000 in "scouting expenses" to pay "under-the-table money" to three players—catcher Mario Díaz and pitchers Rafael Rivas and Ray Martínez—thus exceeding the Class C monthly team payroll limit of $2,000. Brooklyn Dodgers president Branch Rickey and Montreal Royals general manager Mel Jones filed a complaint after the three players had been purchased from Havana for $20,000. The trio refused to accept their $250-per-month salary offers to play for the Royals because they could "get more money in Havana."[32]

League president Wayne Allen demanded Cambria appear in his office to explain the expenses or risk expulsion from the league. In Havana, Cambria insisted he knew nothing about salary violations. But on August 16, Allen fined the Cubans $500, the largest fine in league history, for violating the league's salary rules. Allen announced the penalty included sanctions against Cambria, who was the team's treasurer. Years later, Bécquer defended how Cambria operated. "If you go to his office you would always see seven or eight or 10 players around him all the time," he said. "He helped many, many, many players."[33]

Before the 1950 season began, a rift within the Havana Cubans was revealed during a March 16 meeting attended by Merito Acosta, Joe Cambria, and former Major League player Ossie Bluege, who represented the Washington Senators. At the meeting, prominent Havana lawyer Dr. Antonio Casuso was named president, supplanting Acosta. Feelings ran so hot that law enforcement became involved. Acosta accused Cambria and Bluege of "illegal assembly of a corporation," a charge police passed on to the courts. Bluege required a police escort to get him past Acosta's supporters on his way to catch a plane to Orlando, Florida. On March 23, George Trautman, president of the National Association, recognized Clark Griffith as the principal owner of the team.[34]

Prior to the April 3 season opener, Florida International League president Phil O'Connell met with the warring factions and was assured by Acosta and Cambria that their court battle would not interfere with the season. "I did not delve into the ownership," O'Connell said. "All I wanted was assurance that the legal sparring would not affect the team." Asked about the meeting, Acosta said, "I told O'Connell that I refuse to recognize any agreements, or deals, made by the new directors."[35]

Despite the ongoing front-office court battle, the Cubans continued their success on the field. Havana would go on to finish first in the league with a 101-49 record. But August brought a stunning turn when a Cuban court voided the March 16 vote that ousted Acosta and restored him as president of the team. Jimmy Burns explained the ruling in *The Sporting News*: "Clark Griffith of Washington and Joe Cambria of Havana owned 32 of the 43 shares with an aggregate value of $43,000. But the minority stock of 11 shares was divided between Acosta and ten associates, while Griffith and Cambria held $31,800. The other $200 was vested equally with Calvin Griffith and Ossie Bluege of the Senators' organization. That gave them only four votes to Acosta's 11. Under an old Cuban law, each stockholder was entitled to a vote so the March 16 election . . . was voided."[36]

Griffith vowed to take the case to the Cuban Supreme Court,

while Acosta said he would retake control of the franchise once court documents were filed with the Florida International League and the National Association. Acosta also promised to release Havana manager Oscar Rodríguez upon his official reinstatement despite the fact Rodríguez appeared to be on his way to leading the Cubans to their fifth pennant. In the playoffs, Havana swept Tampa in three games in the first round but lost to the Miami Sun Sox four games to one in the finals.

Despite the court ruling, Acosta never regained the presidency of the Cubans, although he maintained a 20 percent stake in the team. By December of 1950 it was Cambria who fired Rodríguez. Cuban baseball legend Adolfo Luque, whose 705 career managerial victories is second only to that of Miguel Ángel González (846) in Cuban League history, took over as manager. But the Cubans' winning ways were over. Havana finished fifth under Luque's direction in 1951 and fifth in 1952 under manager Fermin Guerra.

Equally concerning, attendance, which had dipped below 200,000 to 168,419 in 1950, plummeted to 83,051 in 1951 and 81,468 in 1952. "Many things," Bobby Maduro responded when asked what caused the decline. "At first, the Cubans tired of their team winning the pennant every year. It did not help when Merito Acosta was ousted as president by Cambria and Clark Griffith. . . . And in recent seasons, the fans have revolted against the use of older Cuban players, instead of youngsters."[37] And yet, Maduro had hope for the future of Minor League baseball in Cuba.

Joe Cambria's tenure running the Havana Cubans was a contentious one, marked by ill will and criticism at home and abroad, as well as threats of expulsion from the Florida International League. Aside from grousing about the continued rumors of the Cubans circumventing the league payroll limit, other team owners complained about not receiving their requisite share of gate receipts from games played in Havana. Terms such as "unethical administration" and "too much superiority" were bandied about. According to *Miami Herald* writer Barney Waters, *Información* columnist Llillo Jiménez believed that "Miami Beach's Sam Shapiro has instigated the entire anti-Havana crusade and that he has turned [Miami Sun Sox president Harry] Traber against the Cubans."[38]

Some of the criticism within Cuba came from amateur baseball circles, whose players lost their amateur status after signing with Cambria. "We have a lot of trouble with the Havana club," said Pedro Montesino Sánchez of Cuba's National Amateur League. "They are taking our best material, and if a young player doesn't prove experienced enough, he is sent back, unable to play pro or amateur ball. My idea is to either pass a rule making a two-year amateur career in Cuba a prerequisite to a pro contract or for the Americans to come here and sign some of the promising players themselves."[39]

But perhaps Cambria's biggest mistake came when the Cubans' business manager failed to renew the team's lease with Maduro for the use of El Gran Stadium prior to the start of the 1953 season. Maduro had notified Cambria that the Cubans could not play in the stadium until a contract for the season was signed. And because La Tropical also was unavailable, the Cubans were forced to play their April 15 opener in Key West and were facing the possibility of playing all their games that season in Florida. If this was a power play by Maduro, it worked. On May 4, Maduro bought the Havana team from Clark Griffith for a reported $40,000. "I am the sole owner of the club," Maduro said in announcing the purchase. "I will take an active role in handling the team's business affairs."[40]

Maduro named Armando Llano as general manager. He also retained former playing legend Armando Marsans, who had replaced Guerra, as manager and Faustino Lavilla as public relations director. Ousted former team president Merito Acosta retained his 20 percent interest in the club but was not given an active role in the management of the team. Cambria surrendered his position as business manager but remained connected to the team as a scout. The league officially approved the sale on May 6 at a special meeting in Miami, where the league's directors "made it obvious that they were welcoming the Cuban sportsman into the fold," according to Jimmy Burns's account in *The Sporting News*.[41]

But Burns's story contained one disturbing note about Maduro, writing that "he did not care to discuss it at great length, and does not want to stir up a controversy, but Maduro frankly said that Havana has too many Negroes [six] on its roster."[42] Such a comment would have been out of character for someone who helped black Cubans reach the Majors and completely at odds with how veteran Cuban sportswriter Fausto Miranda eulogized Maduro upon his death in 1986: "The dreamer and enthusiast dedicated more than half a century of his 70 years to the enlargement of baseball 'without borders and without prejudices,' as he said himself."[43]

Maduro's first and only season in charge of the Havana Cubans was the worst in the franchise's eight-year history as the team limped along to a 63-67 record and a fourth-place finish. Attendance cratered to just 23,460. Yet, Maduro insisted that Havana could support a second team as the Florida International League began exploring the possibility of expanding to eight clubs for the 1954 season. "I think another team there," Maduro said in August of 1953, "would help stimulate interest in baseball."[44]

By November, Maduro had turned instead to the idea of Havana hosting a Class Triple-A team, and submitted a proposal to International League president Frank Shaughnessy to consider the Cuban capital. "Our Florida circuit gives us only Class B ball," Maduro said. "The Triple-A International League offers the same brand of ball we give the fans during the winter time in the Cuban Winter League. That's the kind of baseball the Cubans like. If the International League takes the opportunity of having Havana as a new franchise, I am sure they wouldn't regret the move. I believe we could average 12,000 per game for Triple-A ball."[45]

At a January 12, 1954, meeting at the Commodore Hotel in New York, Havana and Richmond, Virginia, were formally admitted into the International League, replacing Baltimore, which became an American League city with the relocation of the St. Louis Browns; and Springfield, Massachusetts. The Havana entry would be called the Sugar Kings, the nickname chosen through a contest held by one of the radio stations in Cuba. Maduro tabbed Regino Otero to manage the club. Otero had played thirteen seasons in the Cuban League between 1936 and 1953, mostly with Cienfuegos, and was considered the best fielding first baseman of his era.

As part of joining the league, Maduro agreed to guarantee the round-trip airfares for all the clubs between Richmond and Havana. "We will draw at least 300,000 admissions for the season," Maduro declared.[46] In order to be released from the Florida International League, Maduro paid $4,000 to each team in the league. The Cubans' departure left the future of the circuit in doubt with just four cities—Miami, St. Petersburg, Tampa, and West Palm Beach—in place for the 1954 season. The league managed to operate that season, adding a team in Tallahassee, Florida, but folded after the season.

Maduro had only three months to put everything in place before the April 20, 1954, International League season opener. By early March, CMQ-TV had secured the television rights and Union Radio had acquired rights to air the games throughout Cuba. Maduro and Otero set out to build the Sugar Kings' roster by scouring Major League training camps in Florida. Unlike the Cubans with strong ties to the Washington Senators, the Sugar Kings were not affiliated with a specific Major League team during their first season and had to draw players from several organizations, including the Senators, Cincinnati Reds, and Pittsburgh Pirates. Maduro secured a working agreement with the FIL's West Palm Beach team, managed by former Cuban League star player Gilberto Torres, who played for the Senators in the 1940s.

After acquiring Puerto Rican catcher Joe Montalvo from Sacramento of the Pacific Coast League in early March, the Sugar Kings added another catcher in Cuban-born Rafael Noble from the New York Giants. Noble was a Cuban League veteran, having played with Cienfuegos since the 1946–47 season, and would occupy the number four spot in the batting order. "Noble really likes to hit at our stadium," Maduro said. "Records show that every year he has played in the Cuban Winter League he has had luck at the plate in our park. Last season, he was the home run king of the loop" with 10 home runs in 60 games.[47]

As March progressed, the Sugar Kings added future Senators first baseman Julio Bécquer, former Chicago Cubs second baseman Bob Ramazzotti, Venezuelan third baseman Luis "Camaleón" García, and Cuban shortstop Juan Delís. "At least at the start of the season, I believe we'll be in pretty good shape at those positions," Otero said.[48] Ángel Scull, Clint Hartung, and Ray Coleman would round out the starting outfield. The pitching staff included former Senators and Cuban League stalwarts Julio Moreno and Raúl Sánchez, as well as former Almendares hurler Vicente López.

Heading into the season opener, Otero understood the magnitude of what he would be undertaking as manager of the Sugar Kings. "I know that I carry an extraordinary responsibility on my shoulders," he said, "perhaps the most difficult in baseball at this moment, because I go out to debut as manager in Cuba with a team that marks the entrance of our homeland in such a category as high as Triple-A. And because I work for demanding fans who know baseball and like to win."[49]

For his part, Maduro was brimming with confidence. "I'm counting on a 20,000 crowd for the opener," he said. "So far, all the field boxes at the Stadium have been sold for the entire season, while about 400 reserve seats also have been purchased. With radio and TV rights bringing a fair figure, and an average crowd of at least 4,000 fans per game, the Havana team should do all right in its first season in the International League."[50] His optimism belied the turmoil Maduro had to be experiencing with his family. As he was taking the next step in his ultimate goal for baseball in Cuba, Maduro also was dealing with the despair of watching his second-oldest son battle leukemia.

2

Winds of Change

C onnections between baseball and revolution in Cuba date to the late nineteenth century, when the sport was first introduced on the island. The American Civil War raged on and Cuba remained within the stranglehold of Spanish colonial rule when Nemesio Guilló brought the first baseball and bat to his native Cuba in 1864. The son of a wealthy Cuban family, Guilló was born in Havana in 1848. He, his brother Ernesto, and Enrique Porto had been sent to the United States to study at Springhill College in Mobile, Alabama, in 1858. The day after returning to their homeland six years later, the trio started to play baseball games in El Vedado district of Havana.

Cuban baseball historian Roberto González Echevarría described the scene: "At first the game consisted in hitting fungos, which became a hit, or a double according to where it struck. . . . Groups of players began to be organized with other boys returning from the United States. They wore drill pants, white shirts, and a tie that was red or blue according to the 'camp.'"[1] By 1868, the Guilló brothers were among the founding members of the Habana Base Ball Club, which in 1878 became one of the original teams in the Liga General de Base Ball de la Isla de Cuba (General League of Cuban Baseball).

It was not long after its introduction into Cuba that baseball became ingrained in what it meant to be Cuban, as evident by a proliferation of baseball-related publications. The sport quickly surpassed bullfighting, horse racing, and cockfighting as the most popular sport on the island. The March 12, 1882, edition of *El Base Ball* proclaimed that "baseball . . . has con-

tributed much to redeeming us from such degrading specta-
cles" as bullfights.[2] Editors of *El Pitcher* concurred, writing in
1888, "We categorically reject the bullfight."[3] But choosing baseball over bullfighting had a deeper meaning than merely an
appeal to a more refined Cuban sensibility. "Baseball," according to historian Louis A. Pérez Jr., "became a means by which
Cubans disaffected from Spain could give one more expres-
sion to their discontent."[4]

Cuban discontent boiled over on October 10, 1868, when Carlos Manuel de Céspedes freed thirty-seven slaves from his La
Demajagua sugar plantation near the town of Manzanillo in
eastern Cuba. "Citizens," Céspedes's voice boomed, "up until
now you have been my slaves. From this moment on, you are
as free as I am. To win its independence and freedom, Cuba
needs every one of its sons."[5] What became known as "El Grito
de Yara," the "Cry of Yara," launched Cuba's Ten Years' War
against Spain, the first of three major conflicts against the
Spanish Crown.

Beginning as an insurrection waged by fewer than 150 fighters, their ranks swelled to 12,000 within the first month.[6] The
mixed army of blacks, whites, and mixed-race soldiers came
to be derisively called "Mambi" by the Spanish. It was the same
pejorative white Spanish troops had used earlier against black
rebels in Santo Domingo in the Dominican Republic. Derived
from African origins, the label suggested the rebels were "ban-
dits and criminals." But in Cuba, "it was assumed by the blacks
themselves as a badge of honour."[7]

Although the bloody war was fought in Cuba's easternmost
province of Oriente, it reverberated throughout the island,
inspiring a young student at the Havana Municipal School for
Boys named José Martí, who would go on to become the most
revered leader in Cuba's history. As a sixteen-year-old, Martí
published "Abdala," a dramatic poem, in *La Patria Libre* newspaper on January 13, 1869. The provocative allegory of Cuban
independence brought Martí to the attention of Spanish officials in Havana, and he was arrested in October 1869. Branded

a subversive, Martí was sentenced to six years of hard labor in the stone quarry at San Lázaro in Havana. After six months, he was granted clemency and placed under house arrest on the Isle of Pines, a large island off Cuba's southern coast, before being deported to Spain on January 15, 1871.[8]

From there, Martí would eventually travel to Mexico, Guatemala, Venezuela, and the United States, using his considerable skills as a journalist, poet, orator, activist, and politician to rally the Cuban people in his homeland and abroad to the cause of independence from Spain. In the United States, Martí found a country where "one can breathe free because liberty is the basis, the shield, the very essence of life."[9] He understood the cause of Cuban independence needed the "sympathy" of the United States, but he also recognized the threat American expansionism posed for that cause. "I lived in the monster," Martí wrote, "and know its entrails."[10]

As he continued to champion Cuban independence, Martí eventually settled in New York, where he worked as a freelance journalist for various U.S. and Latin American newspapers. In the pages of *La Nación*, he once noted how baseball had taken hold in American society: "In every neighborhood there is a baseball game. Children . . . in New York like baseball and pistols more than they like books. . . . They go into the streets and hide from the police to play baseball in the courtyards."[11]

In the months following Martí's exile, baseball continued to spread across Cuba despite the war and periodic bans by Spanish officials. By April 1871, Esteban Bellán, who had learned to play baseball while studying at New York's Fordham University between 1863 and 1868 (known then as St. John's College), became the first Cuban-born player to reach a Major League circuit, playing for the Troy Haymakers of the National Association. Bellán and Ernesto Guilló were among the participants in the first recorded organized baseball game in Cuban history on December 27, 1874, when Habana traveled to Matanzas to play the local team at Palmar de Junco. Habana beat Matanzas

51–9. Bellán played catcher and scored seven runs, and Guilló played right field and scored three times.

The Ten Years' War finally ended the same year the Cuban League was formed. By the time the governments of Spain and Cuba reached a peace accord, through the Pact of Zanjón, on February 10, 1878, the war had taken the lives of approximately fifty thousand Cubans and two hundred thousand Spanish soldiers.[12] The short-lived peace did not give Cuba independence, but rebels were offered the promise of future reforms and freedom for slaves who had fought in the Mambi army. Abolition of slavery remained a contentious issue despite black Cubans serving with distinction in the war effort. Many among Cuba's white elite feared the island becoming a "Haiti-style black republic."[13]

Less than seven months after the war's end, on December 20, representatives of the Habana, Almendares, and Matanzas baseball clubs convened at number 17 Calle de Obrapía in Havana to establish the Cuban League. The league's first game was played on December 29. Under Esteban Bellán's direction, Habana beat Almendares 21–20 in the season opener and went on to win the inaugural Cuban League championship, compiling a 4-0-1 record. The winning team received a silk banner denoting the "Championship of 1878," and each player was awarded a silver medal with the inscription "Isla de Cuba Base Ball Championship, 1878."[14] Among Habana's players was second baseman Emilio Sabourín, who would become one of several "patriot ballplayers" to take up the cause of independence from Spain.

In the years since his exile, Martí had become the apostle of Cuba's independence movement. A pair of impassioned speeches in November 1891 sparked revolutionary zeal in the Cuban communities of Tampa and Key West in Florida, and solidified Martí's place as the movement's leader. In his first Florida speech, Martí embraced the notion of racial unity (Cuba had officially abolished slavery in 1886). "Should we fear the black man, the generous black man, the black brother?" Martí asked. "Let others fear him. I love him."[15]

In January 1892, Martí met with Cuban exile leaders in Key West to form the Partido Revolucionario Cubano (Cuban Revolutionary Party).[16] He launched Cuba's third and final war against Spain on February 24, 1895, ordering the revolution to begin simultaneously in four locations in the island's easternmost province, Oriente—Bayate, Ibarra, Guantanamo, and Baire. This became known as "El Grito de Baire," the "Cry of Baire."[17] Determined to join the fight despite having no military experience, Martí ignored the urgings of General Máximo Gómez that he stay safely behind the front lines. Instead Martí rushed headlong into battle on May 19, 1895, only to be ambushed and shot in the chest, dying instantly. Martí's martyrdom at Dos Ríos would galvanize the Cuban people to the cause of independence.

Across the island on the day of Martí's death, the Cuban League disbanded without crowning a champion. Rain had forced umpires Antonio Utrera and Vicente Quesada to call a game at Almendares Park between Habana and Almendares in the fourth inning, sparking a riot among angry fans. Given the political climate in Cuba, Spanish authorities decreed the suspension of baseball. The 1894–95 Cuban League season concluded with Habana holding a four-game lead over Almendares, the only other team in the league (Matanzas had withdrawn from competition). The ongoing war would force cancellation of the next two seasons and limit the 1897–98 season to just fourteen games.[18]

Perhaps no Cuban baseball pioneer best illustrates the ties between the sport and revolutionary activities during Cuba's fight against Spain than Emilio Sabourín. The son of French surveyor Claudio Esteban and a Cuban mother, Sabourín was born in Havana on September 2, 1853. He was sent to finish his studies in Washington. Upon returning to Cuba in 1868, Sabourín worked in the customs office and played baseball in his spare time.[19] Sabourín embarked upon his professional baseball career in the months after the conclusion of the Ten Years'

War. He played seven seasons with Habana between 1878 and 1887. But his greatest success came as Habana's manager, leading the team to three league championships in six seasons from 1889 to 1894.

Sabourín's Habana club began defense of its inaugural Cuban League championship in November 1879, months after the start of La Guerra Chiquita, Cuba's Little War. Launched by revolutionary leaders who had not signed the Pact of Zanjón, Cuba's second war against Spain officially began on August 26, 1879. The appropriately named insurgency ended in defeat by September 1880. Both of Cuba's first two conflicts against Spain apparently made an impression on the young Sabourín, whose conspiratorial activities began as a teenager. He and other boys would buy weapons and ammunition discarded by Spanish soldiers, repair them, and send them to insurgents.[20] Sabourín and his older brothers eventually joined Cuba's War of Independence.

An active participant in the early days of the war, Sabourín helped raise funds for the insurrection, no doubt through his baseball connections.[21] At the time, it was common for Cuban exiles living in Florida cities such as Tampa, Ybor City, and Key West to organize baseball games, proceeds of which would be funneled to Cuba for the war effort. Perhaps Sabourín's riskiest activity involved providing haven to José Lacret Morlot at his home, the headquarters of the Habana club. The Mambi general of French descent had returned to Cuba hidden aboard a U.S. steamship.[22]

But Sabourín's activities against the colonial government eventually were discovered. Accused of supplying arms and munitions to the rebels, Sabourín was arrested on December 15, 1895.[23] On February 29, 1896, Spanish captain general Valeriano Weyler presided over the trial at the Fortaleza de San Carlos de la Cabaña, the eighteenth-century fortress along the eastern ridge of Havana harbor. Weyler—known as "El Carnicero" (the Butcher) for forcing hundreds of thousands of Cubans into camps, where tens of thousands died of starvation or disease— asked for the death penalty. A Spanish war council rejected the death penalty but sentenced Sabourín to twenty years.[24] After spending one year at La Cabaña, Sabourín was deported to serve out the remainder of his sentence in the Hacho Castillo in the African penal colony of Ceuta in Spanish Morocco. While imprisoned he contracted double pneumonia and died on July 5, 1897, at age forty-three.

Among the hundreds of prisoners crammed into the presidio along with Sabourín was Afro-Cuban revolutionary leader Juan Gualberto Gómez, who helped tend to Sabourín, as he lay dying in his prison cot, his emaciated body wracked with fever. "I still remember with sincere emotion," Gómez wrote years later. "He called me; he took my hand in his, and he told me 'Juan, this will end . . . and soon.'" With that, Sabourín, pulled a photograph of his wife and children from under his pillow. "Look, at what I leave." Gómez helped Sabourín return the picture to its hiding place, and "a few hours later he expired." Of his cellmate, Gómez concluded, "Emilio Sabourín deserves the affection of his countrymen. He was not only an enthusiastic defender of this sport [baseball] . . . but also a passionate lover of the national freedoms. To defend them, he suffered and died."[25]

Sabourín was not the only Cuban baseball player to fight for Cuban independence or to give up his life for the cause. Alfredo Arango, who played for Almendares from 1885 to 1887, was a colonel in the Cuban army.[26] Ricardo Cabaleiro, who played for Habana, Almendares, and Matanzas from 1890 to 1895, was killed in action in 1897 while serving as a captain in the Cuban army.[27] Juan Manuel Pastoriza, who played for the Fe, Almendares, and Aguila de Oro teams from 1889 to 1895, was charged with conspiracy and shot in La Jata, Guanabacoa, in 1896.[28]

With the War for Independence still raging, intervention by the United States would alter the course of the conflict and impact Cuba's future well into the next century. Violent pro-Spanish demonstrations had broken out in Havana in January 1898. Fearing a breakdown of order in the capital, U.S. consul Fitzhugh Lee requested that Washington send a battleship to

Cuba to protect American interests.[29] Lee's telegraphic coded message went out on January 24. In Key West, Florida, members of the USS *Maine*'s baseball team were ashore playing a game when the order came for everyone to board immediately for the ninety-mile journey across the Florida Straits. The *Maine* arrived in Havana at 10 a.m., on January 25, steaming past the Castillo de los Tres Reyes del Morro, a sixteenth-century fortress guarding the entrance to Havana harbor.[30]

For months, yellow journalism newspapers in the United States—led by William Randolph Hearst's *New York Journal* and Joseph Pulitzer's *New York World*—had been publishing sensational pro-Cuba stories to boost circulation and whip up American support for U.S. intervention on the island. When an artist complained in 1897 about the absence of fighting in Havana, Hearst reportedly sent a cable saying, "You furnish the pictures, and I'll furnish the war."[31] Later, Hearst turned a jailed Cuban activist into a cause célèbre. Upon arranging to break Evangelina Cisneros out of the Casa de Recogidas prison and smuggling her to New York, the *Journal* trumpeted the rescue under banner headlines: "Evangelina Cisneros Rescued by the Journal. An American Newspaper Accomplished at a Single Stroke What the Red Tape of Diplomacy Failed Utterly to Bring About in Many Months."[32]

On February 15, the *Journal* and the *World* were handed their biggest story when a pair of explosions wracked the Maine, sinking her and sending more than 260 sailors to their deaths. All but one member of the baseball team that had won the navy championship were among the casualties. Some of those players had been scouted by the Major Leagues. The team had been scheduled to play a series of exhibitions against Cuban competition before the sinking took the lives of players, such as second baseman and team captain Bill Gorman, third baseman C. H. Newton, and African American pitcher William Lambert, who was one of twenty-three black sailors who perished that day. Only right fielder John Bloomer was among the eighty-eight survivors.[33]

The *Journal* and *World* seized on the story. Headlines in the February 16 editions of the *Journal* blared, "Crisis Is at Hand" and "Cabinet in Session; Growing Belief in Spanish Treachery." The next day, both newspapers placed the blame squarely on Spain. One headline in the *World* asked, "Maine Explosion Caused by Bomb or Torpedo?" The *Journal* declared, "Destruction of the War Ship Maine Was the Work of an Enemy," complete with an engraving that depicted a Spanish mine planted beneath the ship. Even Theodore Roosevelt, the U.S. assistant secretary of the navy, agreed, writing in his diary that the Maine "was sunk by an act of dirty treachery."[34]

Years later, the sinking of the Maine would be proven to be a terrible accident, but in the immediate aftermath, U.S. public opinion—fueled by the press—demanded justice for the fallen sailors. "Remember the Maine, to hell with Spain!" became the rallying cry that propelled America into the war. On April 25, 1898, the United States declared war on Spain, and what had been Cuba's War for Independence was suddenly the Spanish-American War, waged not only in Cuba but also in Puerto Rico and the Philippines.

On July 1, U.S. troops numbering approximately three thousand men fought the only significant land battle in Cuba, outside Santiago de Cuba against just one thousand Spanish troops. U.S. forces included Roosevelt's regiment of Rough Riders, described as a colorful collection of "millionaires, paupers, shyster lawyers, cowboys, quack doctors, farmers, college professors, miners, adventurers, preachers, prospectors, socialists, journalists, insurance agents, Jews, politicians, Gentiles, Mexicans, professed Christians, Indians, West Point graduates, Arkansas wild men, baseball players, sheriffs and horse-thieves."[35]

After more than three years of fighting between Cuba and Spain, U.S. forces liberated Cuba in less than three weeks. The Treaty of Paris officially ended the war on December 10, 1898. But liberation from Spain didn't mean independence for Cuba. Under the Teller Amendment to the United States' declaration of war, America could not annex Cuba, but José Martí's fears of American control of his homeland came to pass. The United States would occupy and rule the island under a military dictatorship from 1898 to 1902.

Cuba held its first postcolonial elections in 1900. Its first constitution was adopted in 1901. But the Platt Amendment, introduced by Senator Orville Platt of Connecticut, allowed the United States "to intervene for the preservation of Cuban independence [and] the maintenance of a government adequate for the protection of life, property, and individual liberty."[36] The United States would in fact intervene in Cuban affairs from 1906 to 1909, in 1912, and again from 1917 to 1923. Although the Platt Amendment was eventually repealed in 1934, "it had," historian Richard Gott wrote, "the baneful effect on Cuba's political development during the first three decades of the Republic and clouded U.S.-Cuba relations until the end of the twentieth century."[37]

Cuba took its first steps as fledgling republic when it narrowly ratified the country's first constitution—including the Platt Amendment—by a 15–14 vote on June 12, 1901.[38] But Cuba's democracy was tumultuous as a pattern emerged in the early decades of "independence": suspect election, followed by public rebellion, leading to U.S. intervention, only to see the sequence repeat itself with another suspect election. Early presidential administrations also were marred by racial unrest. Although slavery had been abolished more than two decades earlier and black Cubans had been instrumental in the country's struggle for independence, "white supremacy was the official mood in the early years of the republic," according to Gott. "Black Cubans provided the bulk of the solidarity in the independence war, and reaped no rewards."[39]

In addition to being marked by racial strife, the early decades of the republic also saw an economic boom thanks largely to Cuba's sugar, tobacco, and mining industries. But the boom times ended after World War I. Sugar prices plunged and the Cuban banking system collapsed. Cuba suddenly needed financial rather than military assistance from the United States. As a result, "Cuba had become a [U.S.] colony in all but name."[40]

The 1924 Cuban election was as fraudulent as previous ones, but Gerardo Machado took office in May 1925. With Cuba's economy languishing, Machado turned his government into a dictatorship. In 1928, he extended his term another six years without bothering to hold elections, sparking the formation of multiple opposition groups. Among those opposed to Machado was Cuban baseball player Martín Dihigo. Proficient at playing almost any position and equally adept as a pitcher, Dihigo would be enshrined in the Hall of Fame in Cooperstown, New York, in 1977. Dihigo joined the Cuban League in 1922 and quickly became a star. He batted .300 or higher in seven of eight seasons between 1924 and 1930, including three seasons in which he hit over .400. And he was the Cuban League's most valuable player in 1927–28, leading Habana to the league championship. But Dihigo's vocal opposition to Machado's dictatorship "put him in a difficult situation and his life in constant danger in Cuba."[41]

Dihigo's situation apparently became so untenable that he had to leave Cuba in the middle of the 1931–32 Cuban League season. He had only ten official at bats for Almendares. Some sources even suggest he had already fled the country, questioning whether he played at all that season. Regardless, Dihigo declared he would not return to Cuba until the "tyrant Machado has left."[42] In fact, Dihigo did not return to his homeland until the 1935–36 season, playing instead in Puerto Rico, Venezuela, the Dominican Republic, and the United States in the Negro leagues during his exile from Cuba.

The 1932–33 season concluded in a tie between Almendares and Habana, the league's Eternal Rivals. But a planned play-off series never materialized amid growing unrest during the Machado regime. The ongoing political turmoil would later force cancellation of the 1933–34 Cuban League season. Opposition to Machado came to a head in July 1933. A general strike paralyzed the city, leading to bloody conflicts with police. With the Cuban capital on the brink of civil war, Machado resigned on August 12, and fled the country. Carlos Manuel de Céspedes Quesada, the namesake son of the 1868 independence leader, was appointed as interim president.[43]

The establishment of a provisional government, however, did little to quell revolutionary fervor in the streets of Havana. On September 4, soldiers mutinied against the officers' corps at the Camp Columbia military base on the outskirts of Havana. Among the mutineers in what became known as the "Revolt of the Sergeants" was Fulgencio Batista, a stenographer sergeant who later would propel himself into the Cuban presidency.

Born on January 16, 1901, in Banes, a rural community in Oriente Province, Batista joined the Cuban army as a private in 1921. He worked his way up to sergeant and became a tribunal stenographer in 1932. Batista was one among several sergeants to lead the revolt against the officers' corps but quickly maneuvered himself into position as the head of the army.[44] On September 10, Batista's junta installed Ramón Grau San Martín, a wealthy doctor and professor who had supported a radical student group at the University of Havana, as Cuba's next president.[45]

Meanwhile, the deposed former army officers had taken refuge on September 8 at Havana's Hotel Nacional, an elegant, fourteen-story, twin-towered landmark built on a high bluff overlooking the city's famed Malecón coastal highway. The Nacional had opened in 1930, and its guest book would include a star-studded list of actors, athletes, and mobsters. But for nearly a month, some three hundred armed former military leaders occupied the opulent hotel.[46]

The Nacional came under attack from the Batista-led army during the early morning hours of October 2. The barricaded officers repelled the initial assault. A second assault later that morning proved more effective as soldiers "unleashed a barrage of artillery fire against the hotel." After a ceasefire, negotiations, and another ferocious volley of artillery fire, the deposed officers finally surrendered by 4 p.m.[47]

The victory came at a heavy cost. As many as one hundred of Batista's soldiers and paramilitary men died and another two hundred were wounded. Despite the heavy losses, it was a political victory for Batista, who suddenly was "the most powerful man in the country."[48] Batista further consolidated his power on January 14, 1934, ousting Grau as president. The United States instantly recognized the Batista-installed provisional government led by Carlos Mendieta, who became "the first of a succession of six stooge presidents manipulated by Batista until he ran for president in 1940."[49]

Fidel Castro was barely seven years old at the time Batista first became the power behind the Cuban government in 1933. Born on August 13, 1926, Fidel Alejandro Castro Ruz spent his childhood on the large Manacas family estate in Birán, a municipality in the Mayarí region in Oriente Province. It was an area steeped in Cuba's revolutionary tradition, located about twenty-five miles east of Dos Ríos, where José Martí was martyred in 1895. The region also was emblematic of the U.S. money that poured into Cuba in the years after the island was free of Spanish control. Following the Spanish-American War, U.S. investments exceeded $1.6 billion.[50]

After the prosperous period of the "Dance of the Millions," when sugar prices skyrocketed during World War I, the world sugar market cratered, devastating Cuban banks. Into the breach stepped U.S. companies, gaining monopolies in Cuban railroads, sugarcane production, and other industries. The Mayarí region, with its fertile soil ideal for sugarcane, tobacco, and livestock, may have seen the most pervasive U.S. presence and control of anywhere in Cuba, as foreign banks controlled as much as 80 percent of the country's sugar production.[51]

Castro's father, Ángel Castro Argiz, had served as a soldier in the defeated Spanish army in Cuba in 1898. But after returning home to the Galicia region of Spain, Ángel Castro emigrated to Cuba as American influence on the island expanded. After making his way to Mayarí, the elder Castro began leasing land from the United Fruit Company—probably around 1910—and using the money he made from sugar sales to buy up parcels of his own land, gradually becoming an affluent Oriente landowner. In time, Manacas grew into a twenty-six-thousand-acre operation.[52]

Fidel was a natural athlete in his youth and developed an early interest in baseball. He once organized a team in Birán with equipment his father had allowed him to order. Castro preferred pitching, although he lacked control with his fastball. And the game could bring out his infamous temper. "When his side was not winning," Castro biographer Tad Szulc wrote, "Fidel would simply halt the game and go home."[53] In the fall of 1941, Castro was sent by his parents to study at Colegio de Belén, an exclusive Jesuit preparatory school in Havana, where he excelled at track, ping pong, baseball, and basketball. He was named Cuba's "outstanding collegiate athlete" during his third year at Belén.[54]

Castro's time at Belén coincided with Cuba's first real period as a functioning democracy. After being led by a series of Batista's puppet presidents, Cuba adopted a new constitution on October 10, 1940. It included a host of progressive rights: universal suffrage, free elections, maximum work hours, minimum wages, pensions, workers' compensation, the right to strike, and a wide range of other civil liberties, including freedom of speech, a free press, and freedom of association.[55]

With the new constitution came the presidential election of 1940, which pitted Fulgencio Batista, retired as commander of the army, against Ramón Grau San Martín, who had returned from exile. After running the country from behind the scenes at Camp Columbia for seven years, Batista became Cuba's legitimately elected president. He tallied more than 800,000 votes to Grau's 575,000 in a campaign that was "fairly conducted, certainly among the most honest in the nearly four decades of the republic's history."[56]

Batista became president during an economic boom time that coincided with World War II. Cuba capitalized on the war-induced collapse of sugar production in Europe and Asia as the value of raw sugar production increased from $110 million to $251 million. Governing as a social democrat, Batista allowed organized labor to grow, spent money on social programs, and welcomed Communists to participate in the government.

After his four-year term ended, Batista retired to Daytona Beach, Florida, having amassed a personal fortune through graft.[57] Prime Minister Carlos Saladrigas ran to continue the policies of the Batista administration. But after a decade of repeated and failed presidential bids, Grau won the 1944 election overwhelmingly. He received more than one million votes, sweeping five of six provinces.

The Auténtico victory "raised enormous popular expectations," but those expectations would be dashed. "Embezzlement, graft, corruption, and malfeasance of public office permeated every branch of national, provincial, and municipal government," historian Louis A. Pérez wrote. "The public trust was transformed into a private till. Politics passed under the control of party thugs, and a new word entered the Cuban political lexicon: *gangsterismo*. Violence and terror became extensions of party politics and the hallmark of Auténtico rule."[58]

Castro graduated from Belén in the spring of 1945, having cared little about politics during those four years. But as Grau's government moved to the right and became marred by corruption and chaos, and after Castro entered law school at the University of Havana, his ambivalence toward politics would change.

The University of Havana was a breeding ground for Cuban nationalism, anti-imperial sentiment, and political gangsterism. Fidel Castro had to maneuver among the violent student groups on campus.[59] In 1947, he aligned himself with Senator Eduardo "Eddie" Chibás, a popular anti-Grau voice who broke ranks with Grau's administration and launched the Partido del Pueblo Cubano. It became known as the Ortodoxo party, so named for keeping orthodoxy with the ideals of the 1930s, such as economic reform, social justice, and public honesty.[60]

While Chibás gave voice to the Cuban people's grievances against Grau, Castro moved to bolster his revolutionary bona fides. In the summer of 1947, he joined an abortive invasion designed to topple Dominican Republic dictator General Rafael Trujillo. Castro spent the next year leading student demonstrations, denouncing Grau's corrupt administration, and finding himself the target of accusations and death threats.

Political assassinations were common during Grau's four-year term from 1944 to 1948. When the president of the Federación Estudiantil Universitaria (FEU; University Student Federation) was assassinated on February 22, 1948, Castro was charged with murder, arrested, but eventually released for lack of evidence.[61] He again found himself accused of murder in June after a university police sergeant was shot dead in front of his house. But a witness identifying Castro as the assassin later retracted his statement, saying he had been bribed by police.[62]

Another of Castro's forays into revolutionary activity came in Bogota, Colombia, where he participated in urban anti-government rioting. On April 9, Jorge Eliécer Gaitán, leader of Colombian Liberal Party, was shot and killed in front of his office. The crowd instantly lynched the assassin, and the streets of Bogota erupted into violence. El Bogotázo was Castro's "real baptism" as a revolutionary. Afterward, Castro returned to Havana and devoted himself to Chibás's presidential campaign, to no avail. When votes for the June 1 elections were tallied, Carlos Prío Socarrás, Grau's labor secretary, crushed Chibás, who finished third, ahead of only Communist candidate Juan Marinello. The Liberal Party's Ricardo Nuñez Portuondo finished second.[63]

Inaugurated on October 10, Carlos Prío Socarrás came into office having vowed to end corruption and gangsterism. But violence and government malfeasance continued largely unabated. Prío himself accumulated "an enormous bounty of personal wealth and made little progress in reducing the power of armed political gangs."[64]

Prío's education minister, Aureliano Sánchez Arango, became a frequent target for Chibás. The senator and failed presidential candidate now hosted a radio show on CMQ, which also broadcast Cuban League games throughout the island. Chibás used his show to rail against Prío's government and Sánchez Arango.[65] In July 1951, Chibás told *Alerta* magazine he had "overwhelming, truthful, and sensational proof," and requested CMQ give him an hour of airtime, "to demonstrate that this administration of Carlos Prío is the most corrupt the republic has ever had."[66]

During an hour-long show on CMQ on July 29, Chibás only delivered old charges and unverified new allegations. The embarrassing episode damaged Chibás's reputation. On August 5, after his radio broadcast cut off and went to a Café Pilon commercial, Chibás continued exhorting into his microphone despite being off the air: "People of Cuba. Rise up and walk! People of Cuba, wake up! This is my last loud knock!" Moments later, a shot rang out in the studio, and Chibás's .38 Colt dropped to the floor.[67]

The self-inflicted shot had done considerable damage: a punctured colon, perforated intestine, and fractured vertebra. Friends rushed Chibás to a nearby hospital. Before going into surgery, he implored his associates: "I'm going to die, but the [Ortodoxo] party has to unite now more than ever." Chibás lingered for another ten days before complaining of stomach pain just before midnight on August 15. Surgery discovered a hemorrhage, and at 1:55 a.m., Chibás "passed into myth."[68] Chibás's death left a political vacuum in Cuba that both Fulgencio Batista and Fidel Castro would eventually fill.

Chibás's death sparked feelings of "mass disillusionment[,] . . . cynicism, resignation, and indifference" among the Cuban populace and left Prio's government "substantially weaker."[69] The corruption and gangsterism that permeated Cuba's political system also engendered anger among the military's junior officers, who approached Batista to determine whether he would support a coup d'état. Batista, who had been living in Daytona

Beach, Florida, since leaving office in 1948, had declared himself a candidate to succeed Prio. With Chibás dead, Grau once again would be his primary opponent.[70]

But having calculated that he might not win, Batista acted three months ahead of the scheduled 1952 elections. In the early morning hours of Sunday, March 10, Batista arrived at the Camp Columbia military base outside Havana and had the senior officers arrested as they lay sleeping.[71] The bloodless coup took all of one hour and seventeen minutes and was essentially over by 2:40 a.m. Historian Louis A. Pérez's description of the ease with which Prío was toppled is chilling:

> Military roadblocks sealed access to and from the capital. Army units occupied local radio stations and continued normal programming without, however, broadcasting news. Later that morning, city residents awoke amidst rumors of a coup; when they turned to radio broadcasts, they heard only uninterrupted music. Telecommunication service to the interior was interrupted. Sites of potential protest demonstrations against the coup passed under military control. Opposition press offices were closed. Local headquarters of various unions and the Communist party were occupied, and union leaders and political opponents were detained and arrested. The university was closed. Constitutional guarantees were suspended; congress was dissolved.[72]

Prío abandoned the presidency without a single shot being fired. He gathered his family, left the presidential palace, and boarded a plane for Miami.[73] Batista declared himself Cuba's head of state, and the United States quickly recognized his government. In describing Cuban reaction to the coup, the Spanish-language *Reader's Digest* circulated in Cuba described a populace "too disillusioned by a long succession of corrupt, inefficient governments . . . to care for anything more than a hard hand at the helm."[74]

The coup left the Auténtico and Ortodoxo parties largely in disarray, and militant anti-Batista groups began to form. Castro, who had aligned himself with Chibás and Auténtico, abandoned any idea of a political remedy to Batista and embraced armed insurrection. He and like-minded young radicals leased a farm in Siboney and began gathering men and munitions in preparation for an ill-conceived assault on the Moncada Barracks outside Santiago. The facility, the second-largest barracks in the country behind Camp Columbia, was first built to house Cuba's Rural Guard during U.S. occupation after 1898.[75]

The year 1953 was the centennial of José Martí's birth, and in the early morning hours of July 26, Castro led a force of approximately 165 rebels on an attack on the Moncada Barracks, as well as a diversionary strike against the barracks at Bayamo. At Moncada, Castro and the bulk of the rebels attacked the barracks while his younger brother Raúl led a smaller force on an assault of the Palace of Justice. A third group targeted the hospital. Despite the element of surprise, Castro's forces were overwhelmed by superior firepower. Raúl's unit managed to seize the palace but was forced to withdraw. Fidel's brother escaped into the woods before eventually being captured. Fidel ordered a retreat and escaped into the hills and was captured a few days later.[76]

Other members of the offensive were not nearly as fortunate as the Castro brothers. Of the more than 160 rebels nearly half were captured, tortured, and executed. In the end, only 26 rebels survived.[77] Castro and the other survivors were put on trial in September, with Castro acting as his own attorney. During the trial in October, Castro delivered his famous two-hour speech that became the manifesto for his future revolution. "Condemn me, it does not matter," Castro declared. "History will absolve me." All 26 prisoners were found guilty. Raúl Castro was sentenced to thirteen years. Fidel was sentenced to fifteen. The rebels were jailed on the Isle of Pines.[78] Despite the total and disastrous failure of the Moncada attack, Castro's 26th of July Movement was born.

3

Golden Age

The secret meetings to save the Cuban League began in April 1947. The league that had been founded in 1878 and survived wars, economic downturns, and political upheaval was facing perhaps its greatest threat. So Cuban baseball officials gathered in Havana to plan their strategy. It was decided the best course of action would be to take their case once again directly to the lords of the baseball. As a result, Bobby Maduro joined a group of Cuban baseball dignitaries dispatched to the United States. Along with Habana team owner and manager Miguel Ángel González and Almendares part owner Dr. July Sanguily, they went to meet with baseball commissioner A. B. "Happy" Chandler and George Trautman, president of the National Association. Their mission? Bring the Cuban League into the good graces of Organized Baseball.[1]

The Cuban League had become collateral damage in Organized Baseball's war against the Mexican League. Beginning in 1946, Mexican League president Jorge Pasquel had lured players to jump their Major League contracts with the promise of exorbitant salaries for playing in Mexico. Chandler responded to the threat by declaring that all "jumpers" would be ineligible to play in Organized Baseball for at least five years. The list included Cuban players Roberto Ortiz (Washington Senators), Roberto "Tarzán" Estalella and René Monteagudo (Philadelphia Phillies), and Napoleón Reyes and Adrián Zabala (New York Giants). Chandler also ruled any players, managers, or coaches who had participated in games with or against ineligible players would be banned as well. This included Cuban baseball icon Adolfo Luque, who had played twenty seasons in the Majors and twenty-one seasons in the Cuban League. He also had managed in the Cuban League since 1919. But Luque, who had served as New York Giants pitching coach, committed the cardinal sin of managing ineligibles in Mexico. And because many Cubans had played with or against "jumpers" in Mexico and Cuba, the Cuban League essentially became an outlaw circuit.

As early as October 1946, Sanguily had pleaded Cuba's case before the Major League meetings during the World Series. He and other Cuban team owners offered to bar twelve ineligible jumpers, such as Max Lanier, Danny Gardella, and Sal Maglie, from ever playing in the Cuban League. They asked only that Cuban players who had not played in Mexico be given temporary forgiveness. "I came within an inch of winning," Sanguily explained. "I had the American League on my side. . . . In the National League, [Brooklyn Dodgers president] Branch Rickey was on my side, and after Sam Breadon of the [St. Louis] Cardinals asked some questions, he, too, lined up with us. But then Lou Perini of the [Boston] Braves made a speech against us, and the men were in a hurry to get to series business, and nothing was done."[2]

Under Chandler's edict, Cuban players had a choice: continue playing winter ball with the Cuban League and risk losing their eligibility to play in the Majors, or join the rival, Organized Baseball–sanctioned league operating simultaneously at La Tropical for the 1946–47 season. Most remained in the Cuban League, which went on to experience perhaps the greatest finale in league history. Meanwhile the rival Federación Nacional de Béisbol faded into obscurity with an abridged season, a truncated playoff series, and $100,000 in losses as Cuban fans maintained their loyalty to the traditional winter league.

Despite outdueling the rival National Federation, the Cuban League faced an untenable situation. It could not expect to thrive without ready access to American players while also facing possible defections by Cuban players wanting to preserve their eligibility to play in Organized Baseball. No one understood this better than González. "We need ball players," González told the St. Louis Star-Times.[3] He had played seventeen seasons in the Majors and served as the St. Louis Cardinals' third base coach for thirteen seasons. But González was ruled ineligible for stocking his Habana team with jumpers, such as former Cardinals players Lou Klein and Fred Martin, and not divesting himself of ownership in his Cuban League team. González, like Sanguily, was willing to cut loose Klein, Martin, and other jumpers on his Habana club if it would mean an accord with Organized Baseball.[4]

Efforts by González and the rest of the Cuban delegation to the United States paid off by the end of April. Sanguily and Chandler reached an agreement to remove the Cuban League's designation as an outlaw circuit. The pact also was the precursor to a larger plan to bring all of Latin America under the umbrella of Organized Baseball. For Cuba, the deal meant the Cuban League would no longer be off-limits to players from Organized Baseball. In return, the Cuban League would release all ineligible players and refrain from signing players banned by Chandler.

The commissioner, in turn, would guarantee Cuban teams access to Triple-A players. Of the ineligible players, coaches, and managers, only González would be permitted to remain in the Cuban League as owner and manager of the Habana club.[5] The Major-Minor League Executive Council tentatively approved allowing the Cuban and Venezuelan winter leagues into Organized Baseball at a May 12 meeting in Columbus, Ohio. Final approval was deferred to another meeting in Chicago on the eve of the 1947 All-Star Game.[6]

Organized Baseball officially welcomed the Cuban League into the fold on July 11, recognizing it as an unclassified minor league within the National Association. A mail vote of members had agreed to allow players with four years or less of professional experience to participate in the Cuban League (previously players with more than two years' experience were barred from playing). Organized Baseball also agreed to provide the

Cuban League with thirty-two players, eight per team. "The National Association is happy to co-operate with the Cuban Winter League in their expressed desire to accept the National Association rules and standards of play," Trautman said. "The new agreement affords us the opportunity to work in greater harmony with our good neighbors from the south."[7]

The pact stipulated that Cuban League teams were required to provide players with living expenses, such as first-class room rent, meals, and laundry; and had to formally request a player's services through the National Association.[8] All "jumpers" remained barred from playing, but Organized Baseball gave "favorable consideration" to twelve Cuban players if they applied for reinstatement before October 20. Trautman ruled that those players—Andrés Fleitas, Antonio "Tony" Castaño, Agapito Mayor, Salvador Hernández, Gilberto Valdivia, Antonio "Mosquito" Ordeñana, Oliverio Ortiz, Antonio "Pollo" Rodríguez, Armando Roche, Ramón Roger, Jorge "Cocoliso" Torres, and Daniel Doy—were not guilty of jumping their contracts but were ineligible for "various lesser violations," essentially guilt by association for playing with or against ineligible players.[9]

This new era of harmony between the Cuban League and Organized Baseball was not completely without discord in its early stages. Cubans and other players barred from participating in the Cuban League formed their own league, the ill-fated Liga Nacional, which competed directly against the Cuban League in the winter of 1947–48. But declining ticket sales, financial troubles, legal battles, and player defections plagued the Liga Nacional throughout the winter. In the end, the Liga Nacional suffered a similar fate as did the National Federation, finishing its lone season of existence before its scheduled conclusion. With its latest native competition vanquished, all that remained for the Cuban League was working to have ineligible Cuban players reinstated by Organized Baseball.

Several of the same officials who had successfully brought the Cuban League back into good standing with Organized Baseball presided over the next critical stage for baseball in Latin America. Sanguily, González, former Marianao owner Eloy García, Cienfuegos part owner Florentino Pardo Galí, Cuban League president Rafael Inclán, and league official Emilio de Armas led the proceedings at an April 12, 1948, meeting in Havana. Along with representatives from Puerto Rico and Panama, the delegates established the Caribbean Professional Baseball Confederation. Venezuela eventually joined, and the Confederation reconvened in Havana during a two-day gathering on August 21–22 to establish the rules for an annual Caribbean Series that would pit the champions of the leagues from the four participating countries.

The series, set to debut in Havana on February 20, 1949, would open with teams representing Cuba and Venezuela facing off and the Panamanian and Puerto Rican champions matched against each other. Cuba, Puerto Rico, and Venezuela would conclude their respective winter leagues by February 18, earlier than usual, to accommodate the series schedule. Each team would play twice against the others in a round-robin tournament scheduled to end on February 26. "The players who come to the Caribbean Conference will do so on their own volition. We are serving as a clearing house," said Robert Finch, public relations director for the National Association. "Baseball in these four countries is on the up and up. The baseball men do what they say they will."[10] The Confederation also set host cities for the next three Caribbean Series: San Juan, Puerto Rico, in 1950; Caracas, Venezuela, in 1951; and Panama City, Panama, in 1952.

But revolution—this one in Venezuela—threatened to derail the inaugural Caribbean Series before it ever began. Rómulo Gallegos became the country's first democratically elected president, in December 1947. But the Venezuelan military overthrew Gallegos's government on November 24, 1948. The resulting political upheaval disrupted the Venezuelan League's schedule, sending players from Organized Baseball back to the United States. After league play finally resumed on December 18, Venezuelan League

44

officials promised to finish the season and participate in the Caribbean Series.[11] Those assurances were reiterated in early February 1949, when Rafael Inclán announced the inaugural Caribbean Series would go on as planned at El Gran Stadium.[12]

Having successfully won its revolution-interrupted winter league season, Cerveceria Caracas represented Venezuela. Mayaguez, which finished four games ahead of Ponce and Santurce, represented Puerto Rico. Because Panama's season had not finished on time, Spur Cola earned the right to represent the isthmus by holding a half-game lead over Carta Vieja. Almendares, having won the 1948–49 season by 8 games over Habana, represented Cuba. "Almendares and Habana were the two best teams," Negro leagues star and Almendares outfielder Monte Irvin recalled years later. "They were always fighting for the championship. It was like the Yankees and Boston or Brooklyn and the Giants. It was a very intense rivalry."[13]

Managed by Fermin Guerra, Almendares's roster included Cuban stalwarts, such as catcher Andrés Fleitas, MVP of the dramatic 1946–47 season; veteran pitcher Conrado Marrero, who had been a legendary hurler in the Cuban amateur league; and left-handed pitcher Agapito Mayor, who had teamed with Max Lanier to deliver the Scorpions' come-from-behind championship in 1947. Among the American players were catcher Mike Sandlock, credited with helping Don Newcombe become a better pitcher early in his career; outfield Al Gionfriddo, famous for robbing Joe DiMaggio of a home run in the 1947 World Series; and first baseman Kevin Connors, a Minor Leaguer in the Dodgers farm system who would go on to become far more famous as Hollywood actor Chuck Connors.

The Scorpions also included former Negro leagues stars Sam Jethroe, of the Cleveland Buckeyes; and Irvin, a former Newark Eagles outfielder and future Hall of Famer who had signed with the New York Giants. Almendares had given Guerra his first Cuban League championship in only his second season as manager. Pitcher Morris Martin, who would go on to a ten-year Major League career, was the league's MVP after compiling a 9-2 record. Jethroe led the league with 32 stolen bases. Irvin clubbed a league-leading 10 home runs in 72 games while driving in 53 runs, second-best in the league.

Cuba made an emphatic statement to begin the inaugural Caribbean Series, beating Venezuela 16–1 in the second game of the tournament as Marrero limited Cerveceria Caracas to four hits. The Cuban entry went on to win all six of its games. Mayor compiled a 3-0 record, winning twice in relief and once as a starter. Gionfriddo led all hitters with a .533 batting average. Third baseman Héctor Rodríguez had 11 hits for a .458 average. Irvin batted .389 and led the series with 2 home runs and 11 runs batted in. "We won everything that year," Irvin said.[14]

The series, however, was something of a financial disappointment. Only fifty-five thousand fans attended the six-day tournament, generating $65,000 in gate receipts. Still, Trautman was effusive in his praise. "The first Caribbean Series will be remembered for many years to come as the realization of the dreams of baseball leaders of Cuba, Panama, Puerto Rico, and Venezuela," he said. "This 1949 series has proven the possibility of using the game as the best good neighbor policy to tighten friendship ties. Cuba can consider itself proud of the work it has done in this series and there is no doubt there never has been a more delightful host."[15]

Irvin also received some individual post-series praise. Guerra, who aside from managing Almendares in the Caribbean Series was a catcher with the Philadelphia Athletics, endorsed Irvin's chances of succeeding as he was about to join the New York Giants' Jersey City farm team. "Monte is 28 years old now, but that doesn't make any difference," Guerra said. "He is a hustler, a team man, and carries enough punch in his bat to settle himself in the International League."[16]

Irvin, who would make his Major League debut with the Giants on July 8, 1949, was among the many Negro leagues players to benefit after Jackie Robinson broke baseball's modern-era color barrier. Born on February 25, 1919, in Haleburg, Alabama,

Monford Merrill Irvin joined the Newark Eagles of the Negro National League in 1937 and distinguished himself as one of the best players in the Negro leagues. Many within black baseball believed Irvin was the best choice to integrate the game. "Monte was the choice of all Negro National and American League club owners to serve as the No. 1 player to join a white major league team," said Effa Manley, who owned the Newark Eagles. "We all agreed, in a meeting, he was the best qualified by temperament, character ability, sense of loyalty, morals, age, experiences and physique to represent us as the first black player to enter the white Majors since the Walker brothers back in the 1880s. Of course, Branch Rickey lifted Jackie Robinson out of Negro ball and made him the first, and it turned out just fine."[17]

Robinson's historic 1947 season with the Brooklyn Dodgers began with spring training in Cuba as a member of the Dodgers' Class Triple-A Montreal Royals team. Before Robinson used exhibition games in Havana to prepare himself to reach the Majors, African American teams and individual players had been coming to Cuba for decades. The ironically named Cuban X-Giants (the team had no Cuban players on its roster) were the first to barnstorm the island for a series of exhibition games in 1900. And dozens of individual African American players—such as future Hall of Famers Oscar Charleston, Cool Papa Bell, Pop Lloyd, Josh Gibson, Buck Leonard, Satchel Paige, Mule Suttles, Jud Wilson, Smokey Joe Williams, and Rube Foster—had played in the Cuban League throughout the first half of the twentieth century. But none of those players had any hope of playing in Major League Baseball. They were barred because of the color of their skin.

After Robinson, however, African American players such as Irvin, Jethroe, Hank Thompson, Joe Black, Don Newcombe, and others could play in Cuba with Major League aspirations. "We could not aspire to become Major Leaguers [before Robinson] because we thought the tone of the country would never change," Irvin said. "In fact, we were sure of that. But then after [World War II], I knew there was a good chance. And then when they gave Jackie Robinson the chance to play and he succeeded, then it made it easier for all of us who came after him."[18]

Irvin's experience typified that of most African American ballplayers in Cuba, both before and after Robinson broke baseball's color barrier. "We were treated very well in every way," Irvin said. "We were given an apartment, shown around the city, taken to the beach, taken places, that type of thing. It was wonderful. . . . It was the best place to play. The salaries were good. You could make about $1,500 a month. You could never make more than $200 a month in the Negro leagues."[19]

Integration came in time for Irvin to enjoy a ten-year Major League career. But for many, such as future Hall of Fame third baseman Ray Dandridge, the breakthrough came too late. Dandridge began playing in the Negro leagues in 1933, becoming a star third baseman with the Newark Eagles before playing in the Mexican League. He played in Cuba nearly every winter, beginning in 1937, mostly with Marianao. Nicknamed "Talúa" by Cuban fans, Dandridge was perhaps the greatest fielding third baseman of his time. In Cuba, it was said of the bow-legged Dandridge that a train could pass through his legs but never a ground ball. After integration, the New York Cubans of the Negro American League sold the thirty-five-year-old player-manager to the New York Giants, who assigned him to their Class Triple-A Minneapolis Millers team. Despite his age, Dandridge earned Rookie of the Year honors after hitting .362 in 99 games. He batted over .300 in three of his four seasons with the Millers, but Dandridge's playing days ended in 1953 with him having never reached the Majors.

Before Jackie Robinson, only white Cubans—Esteban Bellán, Armando Marsans, Rafael Almeida, Merito Acosta, Adolfo Luque, Miguel Ángel González, Fermín Guerra, Gilberto Torres, and Roberto Ortiz among them—or Cubans of distant African descent who had light skin, such as Roberto "Tarzán" Estalella and Tomás de la Cruz, had been allowed to reach the Majors. Organized Baseball was off-limits to some of the greatest Cuban ballplayers of the first half of the twentieth century, including future Hall of Famers Martín Dihigo, Cristóbal Torrente, and José Méndez. Robinson's elevation to the Majors finally opened the door for black Cubans. After Orestes Miñoso, who made his Major League debut with the Cleveland Indians on April 19, 1949, almost two dozen black Cuban players would begin playing in the Majors throughout the 1950s.

Born on November 29, 1925, in El Perico, Matanzas, Miñoso would be given the nickname "Minnie" while playing in the Majors, where he became a nine-time All-Star. In his autobiography, Puerto Rican–born Hall of Famer Orlando Cepeda said that Miñoso "is to Latin ballplayers what Jackie Robinson is to black ballplayers. As much as I loved Roberto Clemente and cherish his memory, Minnie is the one who made it possible for all us Latinos. Before Roberto Clemente, before Vic Power, before Orlando Cepeda, there was Minnie Miñoso. Minnie is the one who made it possible for all us Latins. . . . He was the first Latin player to become a superstar."[20]

Among the other black Cubans to debut in the Majors during the 1950s were pitcher Miguel "Mike" Cuellar, who went on to win 20 games four times and compile 185 victories and a 3.14 career-earned run average in fifteen Major League seasons, and two-time All-Star infielder Antonio "Tony" Taylor. By 1959, Cubans—both black and white—easily represented the largest contingent of Latin American–born players in the Majors. That trend continued throughout the 1960s, but with the pipeline of talent cut off after 1961, Cuba would not be able to maintain that distinction.

In the aftermath of the pact with Organized Baseball, veteran catcher Salvador Hernández, who had played two seasons in Mexico, was reinstated for the 1948–49 season. But several other Cuban players—Tony Castaño, Pedro "Natilla" Jiménez, Sandalio Consuegra, Cocoliso Torres, Roberto Ortiz, Roberto Estalella, Adrián Zabala, René Monteagudo, Santiago Ullrich, and Napoleón Reyes—remained ineligible for the season. "I'd gladly swim the Mexican Gulf, back to the States," *The Sporting News* quoted one of the unnamed player as saying, "if I ever know there is a chance to be reinstated."[21] Adolfo Luque, who had managed in the Mexican League, also remained barred.

After the 1948–49 Cuban League season concluded, *America Deportiva*, a weekly sports publication in Havana, excoriated Chandler for not lifting the ban. "Latin American baseball has suffered a deep humiliation this winter when High Baseball Commissioner Albert B. Chandler refused to reinstate its best ball players even to play only in their country's winter league.... By eliminating the native stars ... Chandler didn't make a wise move, and instead of tightening the friendly feeling between each Latin America country and Organized Ball, he dug a deeper hole.... He could be a great man around these shores, but instead, he has caused a lot of bitterness."[22]

Everything changed once U.S. courts refused to reinstate Max Lanier, Fred Martin, and Danny Gardella, who had sued Major League Baseball the following summer. On April 5, 1949, Chandler, no longer facing the specter of legal action, reinstated every player who had been suspended for jumping to the Mexican League, calling it "a fair thing to do."[23] The news was hailed in Cuba. "Many congratulations on your generous gesture," Almendares owner Mario Mendoza cabled the baseball commissioner. "Receive the blessing of five million Cuban fans." His fellow Almendares owner agreed. "Your generosity in lifting the ban creates a climate of understanding and sympathy among thousands of Cuban fans," Sanguily wrote. "My sincere congratulations."[24]

But Luque's reinstatement came too late to secure a managerial job for the 1949–50 Cuban League season, so Miguel Ángel González hired his former longtime rival as an assistant coach on his Habana team. Just before the start of the winter season, Chandler declared that Cuban-born Major Leaguers, regardless of service time, could play in the Cuban League, allowing players such as Roberto Ortiz, Napoleón Reyes, and René Monteagudo to again play in their homeland. *Diario de la Marina* columnist

Eladio Secades declared that Chandler's decision "will forever kill any ill feelings against Organized Ball in all Latin American countries"; *El Mundo* sports editor Sergio Varona wrote, "The Commissioner's gesture will never be forgotten"; *Alerta* sports editor Fausto Miranda opined that Chandler "will never know how much good his decision has done"; and an editorial in *El Cristo* proclaimed, "Now everybody loves Organized Baseball."[25]

With baseball peace restored, the Cuban League flourished under the pact with Organized Baseball during the 1950s. Even Batista's 1952 coup had little impact on the sport. Throughout the decade, a steady flow of North American talent augmented the rosters of the league's four teams: Almendares, Habana, Cienfuegos, and Marianao. Players who would go on to careers in the Majors, such as Tom Lasorda, Joe Black, Wilmer "Vinegar Bend" Mizell, Hoyt Wilhelm, Ken Boyer, Brooks Robinson, Bill Virdon, and Don Zimmer, developed their skills in Cuba early in their professional careers.

Zimmer came to the island in the winter of 1951 thanks to the league's insistence on quality performances from its imported players. It was play well or go home. Cienfuegos shortstop Gene Mauch, who had already played for the Brooklyn Dodgers, Pittsburgh Pirates, Chicago Cubs, and Boston Braves, was struggling (he would finish the 1951–52 Cuban League season batting just .178). So Zimmer went from a paltry Minor League salary to making, in his words, "I want to say $700 or $800 a month— which, I thought I was a millionaire."[26]

The Cincinnati, Ohio, native was a twenty-year-old shortstop in Brooklyn's Minor League system and was "up to [his] tookus" in snow during the off-season when the call came from the Dodgers' scouting director. "I was a very young kid, just coming out of Class A ball in the Eastern League," Zimmer said. "In those days, well, if you didn't play good, they'd send you home. And I don't think Mauch was playing too good. I was home in Cincinnati in the snow. Al Campanis called me one day and said, 'Do you want to go to Cuba to play the rest of the winter in the Cuban League?' I said, 'Yeah, my goodness.' I got on an airplane with my wife the next day."[27]

Zimmer would be joining Cienfuegos to replace the struggling Mauch, but there was some question about whether the Elephants would be willing to sign a mere Class A ballplayer. "We had a guy that owned the club, Bobby Maduro, and they wanted Major League players or top Triple-A players," Zimmer said. "Here I just come out of the Eastern League, Class A ball. And when they looked at a press guide, they said, 'No, we can't have anybody out of Class A ball.' And Campanis said to Maduro, 'Take him on my recommendation.' And that's how I wound up in Cuba."[28]

Zimmer and his pregnant wife, Jean—who went by her childhood nickname, "Soot"—flew to Miami and then on to Havana, where they were put up at Club Náutico, a group of luxury apartments on the beach where Cuban League teams housed American players each winter. "It was just absolutely gorgeous," Zimmer said, "an apartment building, like condos, right on the ocean in a private gated area."[29] The compound was about fifteen to twenty minutes from El Gran Stadium. And with each team in the league playing only about four games a week, there would be plenty of down time to enjoy Havana's amenities. "Beautiful casinos" and the Oriental Park Racetrack in Marianao were readily within reach. "At that time, I thought it was heaven," Zimmer said. "Havana, Cuba, oh, my goodness."[30]

Zimmer's manager with Cienfuegos was future Hall of Famer Billy Herman. A career .304 hitter in his fifteen-year Major League career from 1931 to 1947, Herman was in his second winter as Cienfuegos's manager. His roster also included former Negro leagues pitcher Joe Black, of the Baltimore Elite Giants. Under Herman's tutelage, Black showed good form early on, besting future Hall of Fame knuckleballer Hoyt Wilhelm for a 2–1 victory against Habana on December 10. Black would go on to lead the league with a 15-6 record, 78 strikeouts, and a 2.42 ERA that winter. "Herman was the first one who ever told me how to set up hitters for my best pitches," Black said. "I learned how to pitch the way a kid learns to read. The letters on the page look like hen tracks until they suddenly run together and make sense one day. That's how it was with me and pitching after I listened to Herman for a couple of weeks."[31]

Zimmer returned to Cuba to play with Cienfuegos the following winter. But with Humberto "Chico" Fernández, a future inductee in the Cuban Baseball Hall of Fame, taking over at shortstop, Zimmer was traded to Marianao for pitcher Sandalio Consuegra. The trade worked out for both teams. Zimmer's numbers improved from his first winter, batting .272 with 7 home runs and 33 RBIs in 70 games, and Fernández, who went on to play eight seasons in the Majors, established himself as an everyday starter in his second season in the Cuban League. But Cienfuegos stumbled badly, finishing in last place, 16 games behind league champion Habana, and Herman was fired midway through the 1952–53 season. The move would lead to Campanis becoming the team's manager the following season. Years later as vice president of the Los Angeles Dodgers, Campanis would be fired for an infamous 1987 *Nightline* interview in which he said blacks "may not have some of the necessities to be a field manager or general manager."[32]

The other significant managerial move in 1952–53 was Almendares hiring Bobby Bragan as its manager. The former Dodgers catcher and infielder had been among those involved with a petition to keep Jackie Robinson from reaching the Majors during spring training in March 1947. When confronted by Branch Rickey, the Birmingham, Alabama, native told the Dodgers president, "I'd rather be traded" than play with Robinson. Bragan wasn't traded and eventually came around on Robinson, saying that playing with him "was the greatest thing that ever happened to me."[33]

Bragan's playing career had ended in 1948, and he became the first American to manage a team in the Cuban League. In managing Almendares for four seasons, Bragan led the Scorpions to league titles in 1953–54 and 1954–55. More importantly, according to Ralph Ávila, Bragan and Campanis introduced

modern baseball to the Cuban League. "Al Campanis direct-
ing Cienfuegos and Bobby Bragan managing Almendares were
the people who brought baseball, modern baseball [to Cuba],"
Ralph Ávila said. "We played good baseball, but we played prim-
itive baseball. Get a clean base hit, start running and whoever
scored more runs won and whoever pitched better won. We
didn't play the fundamentals of baseball, but we learned them
when Bobby Bragan and Al Campanis were, in reality, the ones
who brought modern baseball to Cuba."[34]

A twin-engine Douglas DC-3 carrying a three-kilowatt plant took
off from Havana's Rancho-Boyeros Airport on the morning of
September 29, 1954. It climbed to an altitude of eight thousand
feet and began circling over the Florida Straits, some fifty miles
from Matanzas. From that flight pattern off of Cuba's northern
coast, the plane served as a relay station, picking up a broadcast
signal from Miami. The signal was "rebroadcast to a receiver
on a hill at Matanzas, being relayed to Hershey and thence to
Havana as well as to television outlets along the island."[35] When
New York Giants starter Sal Maglie threw his opening pitch,
Cuban fans were watching Game 1 of the World Series in the
first direct television broadcast from the United States to Cuba.

The historic television event, carried on Channel 6 in Havana,
was possible because Goar Mestre, president of CMQ, Cuba's
largest television network, chartered the DC-3. To aid the broadcast, Channel 4 in Havana was silenced to prevent interfer-
ence with the Miami station that was transmitting the signal
to the plane. Cuban announcers Cuco Conde, Gabino Delgado,
and Jess Losada called the action as Maglie surrendered two
first-inning runs to the Cleveland Indians but settled down to
pitch six consecutive scoreless frames. Cuban fans watching
the game were familiar with Maglie, who had pitched in Cuba
earlier in his career. He had a 9-6 record with Cienfuegos, when
the Elephants won the 1945–46 Cuban League championship.
And Maglie led the outlaw Liga Nacional with a 14-9 record for
the Cuba and Alacranes teams in 1947–48.

Maglie left Game 1 of the World Series with the score tied at 2-all. The Giants won when Dusty Rhodes hit a three-run home run against Indians starter Bob Lemon in the bottom of the tenth inning. The broadcast "proved satisfactory in all respects," but there were anxious moments as the game went into extra innings. "The length of the game afforded some uneasy moments," *The Sporting News* reported. "The plane had been in the air four hours and 20 minutes and there was some fear that it would run out of gas, but Dusty Rhodes's homer enabled the telecast to be completed without interruption."[36] The same procedure was used the following year to televise the 1955 World Series. That year, Cuban fans watched live as native son Edmundo "Sandy" Amorós made a Series-saving catch in Game 7, snaring Yogi Berra's sliced drive down the left field line as the Dodgers went on to win their only World Series while based in Brooklyn.

It's not surprising Cuba would have been involved in a television innovation. "Cuba," author Manuel Márquez-Sterling wrote, "was the first Latin American country to have television, and the first to televise baseball games."[37] Cuba became the second country behind the United States to have a national TV network when CMQ-TV expanded into a seven-station network in 1954. It had regular color broadcasting by 1957.[38] Regular TV broadcasts began in Cuba when Union Radio TV (Channel 4) officially launched on October 24, 1950. CMQ-TV was officially inaugurated on March 11, 1951. And three more channels— CMBF-TV (Channel 7), CMBA-TV, Telemundo (Channel 2), and TV Caribe (Channel 11)—were established by 1953.[39] "1950s Cuba," Márquez-Sterling wrote, "was an early and voracious adopter of telecommunications technology."[40]

The final month of the Sugar Kings' inaugural 1954 season produced a whirlwind of activity. As Havana chased a berth in the International League playoffs, it secured a working agreement with the Cincinnati Reds to provide the team with players for the 1955 season. The deal was the culmination of Maduro's close friendship with Reds general manager Gabe Paul. "Gabe is the only major leaguer who was of real help to me when I finally got my franchise," Maduro said. "I am very much indebted to him."[41]

The Sugar Kings closed out the regular season with eleven victories in their final twelve games. Havana concluded its home schedule on September 4 at El Gran Stadium by beating Richmond 2–1. Despite the late-season surge and playoff implications, a sparse crowd of 1,845 fans watched the home finale, in which Jim Melton tossed a six-hit gem for his thirteenth victory. Even with the light turnout, Havana drew an estimated 296,000 fans, second only to Toronto in home attendance. The regular season concluded in Rochester with a four-game series against the Red Wings, with Maduro and his oldest son, Roberto Jr., in attendance. The Sugar Kings swept the Red Wings, finishing with a 15-7 record against their easiest opponent, including an 8–3 mark in games played in Rochester. Melton punctuated the sweep with a 12–2 victory in the September 12 finale to improve the ace's record to 14-9.

But Maduro and son failed to see the Sugar Kings clinch a playoff spot. Havana finished the regular season tied with the Syracuse Chiefs for fourth place and the final postseason berth. A one-game playoff would determine which team would continue onto the playoffs. League rules called for a coin flip to determine the home team. With the Sugar Kings in Rochester and Syracuse having finished its season at home, Maduro agreed to have the game played in Syracuse, New York, to avoid the possibility of a three-thousand-mile round-trip. Had the Sugar Kings won the toss, the game would have been played in Havana and the winner would have had to immediately fly to Toronto to begin the playoffs. League president Frank Shaughnessy instituted a coin flip to determine which club would bat last. The Sugar Kings won the right to be designated as the home team, but it didn't help. The Chiefs opened the game with five runs in the first inning, clubbed eighteen hits, and won 13–4 to advance to the postseason.[42]

Despite failing to reach the playoffs, the Sugar Kings' inaugural season was a success by almost any measure. But instead of being able to fully enjoy his achievements, Maduro carried a heavy heart throughout the season. His twelve-year-old son, Felipe, had spent much of the season battling leukemia before succumbing to the decease on August 22. The more than one thousand people who attended the funeral included International League president Frank Shaughnessy, as well as "members of president Batista's cabinet, officials in industry, newspapermen, executives of the Cuban Winter League, players and laborers from the Maduro industries."[43]

Described as "an ardent fan," Felipe was the second of eight children—Roberto Jr., Felipe, Adela, Jorge, Beatriz, Rosario, Alberto, and Isabel—born to Maduro and his wife, "Fufila." The obituary that ran in *The Sporting News* touted Felipe as a second baseman for the LaSalle School and a "fine tennis player" prior to his illness. It also described him as "a rabid reader of the *Sporting News* and was considered an excellent judge of talent, despite his age. Only a few days before his death, Felipe told his father what would have to be done to convert the Sugar Kings into pennant contenders next season."[44]

Jorge Maduro was seven years old when his older brother died. He remembers Felipe as loving baseball and joining their father on road trips. "I remember later when they realized what he had and that there wasn't a cure, they took him to New York to see Joe DiMaggio," Jorge said. "I have a photo in my house of Felipe looking at Joe DiMaggio with these incredible eyes and there's a photo of Marilyn Monroe behind the sofa where they were talking, Joe DiMaggio and my brother. . . . I remember Felipe when he was near the end in his room, in an oxygen tent. It was something very sad, very difficult. . . . Later when he died it was incredible, the church and the funeral, etc. It was a very difficult moment for my father and my mother." [45]

Batista's 1952 *golpe de estado* (coup d'état) had paved the way for the Cuban president to renew ties with mobster Meyer Lansky, who had made his early fortunes during Prohibition. After the repeal of Prohibition in 1933, Lansky moved to Cuba in 1937 to "reorganize and professionalize gaming rooms" at Oriental Park racetrack and the Gran Casino Nacional.[46] But World War II temporarily halted Lansky's ventures in Cuba. "We stopped when the war broke out," Lansky explained during his 1951 testimony before the U.S. Senate Kefauver Committee hearings into organized crime. "You see, because after that, there weren't any boats at sea. And at that time, you didn't have enough planes; and you couldn't live from the planes coming from Miami. You can't live from the Cuban people themselves."[47]

Following World War II, Meyer Lansky orchestrated a mob conference at Havana's Hotel Nacional to discuss plans for controlling casino gambling in Havana. Running December 22–26, 1946, the gathering included the biggest names in organized crime, including Vito Genovese, Albert Anastasia, Frank Costello, Santo Trafficante, and Lucky Luciano. The entertainment for the event? Frank Sinatra. Luciano, who had been living clandestinely in Havana, had been deported from the United States to his native Sicily following a commuted prison sentence. Two months after the conference, syndicated Scripps-Howard columnist Robert Ruark revealed that Sinatra had vacationed in Havana with Luciano. "They were seen together at the race track, the gambling casino, and at special parties," Sinatra's FBI files quoted Ruark's February 20, 1947, *Washington Daily News* column.[48]

Alerted to Luciano's presence in Havana, the United States began pressuring the Cuban government to deport Luciano back to Italy by threatening to withhold shipments of legal narcotics as long as he remained in Cuba.[49] Cuban authorities arrested Luciano on February 22, and by March 20, the mobster was bound for Sicily aboard the Turkish freighter *Bakir*.[50] Lansky eventually sailed to visit his friend in June 1949, under the watchful eye of New York and federal law enforcement officers. Lansky and his wife "had approval of the State Department to sail," the *New York Times* quoted one officer. "But we were just wondering who might come to see them off." [51]

The following year, the Kefauver Committee hearings shined

a spotlight on the mob's operations in the United States and eventually forced the closures of Lansky's casinos in Florida and New York. Another outgrowth of the hearings was an indictment against Lansky and a subsequent three-month prison sentence for gambling operations in Saratoga Springs, New York, in 1953. Upon his release from jail, Lansky refocused his sights on Havana. "As soon as he got out," Lansky's FBI files quoted a January 9, 1958, *New York World-Telegram* article, "he started for new fields to conquer and picked Havana as the greenest pasture of all—the lush shade of green peculiar to tourist dollars."[52]

After taking power in 1952, Batista was looking to "clean up" Cuban casinos after complaints started coming into the U.S. embassy in Havana about crooked gaming practices, particularly at the Sans Souci nightclub. In March 1953, a *Saturday Evening Post* exposé documented use of "razzle"—shills prodding tourists to double down on bets on crooked dice games—by Havana casinos. One of the "suckers" was a Los Angeles lawyer and sponsor of Vice President Richard Nixon's senatorial expense fund.[53] The exposé prompted Cuba to deport thirteen U.S.-born card dealers at the Sans Souci and Tropicana.[54] Lansky ran a legitimate operation at the Montmartre, and during the winter of 1953–54, Batista offered Lansky a $25,000 per year retainer to become the president's gambling czar.[55]

Lansky's ambitions dovetailed perfectly with those of Batista. Gambling "became the centerpiece of [Batista's] ambitious program to put Havana firmly in the center of the American tourist map."[56] During the 1950s, American entertainers such as Eartha Kitt, Nat King Cole, Dorothy Dandridge, and Ella Fitzgerald headlined Havana casinos and nightclubs such as the Tropicana. Among the many American tourists who enjoyed the Havana nightlife were the players who came every winter to play in the Cuban League. "The most popular place was the Tropicana," remembered Bill Virdon, who batted .340 with 6 home runs and 54 RBIS for Habana during the 1954–55 season. "Yes, we did go. Yes, we did enjoy it." Virdon, who went on to play twelve Major League seasons, mostly with the Pittsburgh Pirates, and manage the Houston Astros for eight seasons, had also played in Havana as a member of the Rochester Red Wings. "I didn't see any difference [in Cuba] than when I go to Las Vegas these days or back years ago," Virdon said. "A lot of action, a lot of people, everything under control."[57]

With Batista again in control after his coup, Lansky looked to expand his operations in Havana. He convinced Batista to pass Hotel Law 2074, which allowed for gambling in hotels worth more than $1 million, and "then proceeded to build the only hotels that qualified."[58] In 1956, Lansky began building the lavish Riviera Hotel near Calle Paseo along El Malecón. Built at a cost of $14 million, the Riviera opened on December 10, 1957, and included 440 air-conditioned rooms, a casino, a night club, and other amenities. The Havana Hilton would open the following March, and plans were on the drafting boards for the $15 million Montecarlo, which would include 676 rooms, a swimming pool, cabanas, a night club, and a casino.[59] "Havana," Batista once declared, "will become the Monte Carlo of the Caribbean."[60]

4

"This Was a Shipwreck"

Fidel Castro joined his twenty-five Moncada conspirators at Presidio Modelo on the Isle of Pines on October 17, 1953. Despite their crimes, Castro and his cohorts were spared incarceration at Havana's infamous La Cabaña fortress. Instead they found themselves confined to Cuba's largest and most modern prison. As political prisoners, they were segregated from common criminals and enjoyed special privileges. Castro quickly set to work building the prison's library and educating fellow rebels. But the special treatment abruptly ended on February 12, 1954. With Fulgencio Batista visiting the prison to dedicate a new power plant, Castro convinced prisoners to join in singing the July 26 revolutionary hymn. An irate Batista ordered the men punished, and Castro was placed in solitary confinement.[1]

In the aftermath of the Moncada attack, Batista immediately suspended constitutional guarantees for ninety days. On August 6, 1953, Batista issued Law of Public Order No. 997, which sought to suppress attacks "against the national dignity, peace, public confidence, stability of the Government, the economy, and the credit of the nation."[2] The decree established fines and jail sentences for those found guilty of "spreading false reports and malicious propaganda by publications, radio, television, motion pictures, or word of mouth."[3] And Cuban authorities were given the power to shut down publications, radio and television stations, or theaters from ten to sixty days. In addition to blanket censorship, Batista outlawed the Communist Party on October 31.

The regime lifted censorship and restored constitutional guarantees on October 24. A week earlier, Batista had announced that general elections would finally be held on November 1, 1954. But the *New York Times* reported that there was little enthusiasm for Batista's decision to hold elections. "The average Cuban views the proposed elections with apathy," R. Hart Phillips wrote from Havana. "The lack of outstanding political figures makes the choice of an opposition Presidential candidate difficult. . . . The greater part of both the Autentico and Ortodoxo parties representing the only real opposition to the Government are split into schisms. There is no leadership on the horizon at present sufficiently strong to weld them into a party with any possibility of victory against General Batista."[4]

Since being deposed by Batista's *golpe*, Carlos Prío Socarrás had been living in exile in the United States, helping to fund and arm anti-Batista operatives in Cuba. Prío's activities caught up with him on December 4, 1953, when the former Cuban president was indicted for conspiring to ship arms to Cuba in violation of the U.S. Neutrality Act. Despite declaring his innocence for months, Prío pleaded no contest in U.S. federal court and was fined $9,000 on September 7, 1954, less than a month before the Cuban election. "I am glad that American justice has recognized the exceptional circumstances of this case by accepting this extraordinary plea," Prío said in a written statement. "My case is now closed; but the fight for Cuba's freedom shall go on, consistent, of course, with the laws of the United States."[5]

While Prío was working outside the law to oust Batista, former Cuban president Ramón Grau San Martín was weighing whether to run for president against Batista. Grau announced on October 3 that he would run as Batista's sole opponent. But he abruptly withdrew from the race on October 30, accusing the government of rigging the election. "We have become convinced," Grau's statement declared, "there exists a well-directed plan to convert the coming elections into a common farce in order to perpetuate the present usurpers of power."[6] Running unopposed, Batista won easily. Figures issued by military authorities had the count at 1,220,389 votes for Batista and 177,423 for Grau.[7]

Buoyed by his six-to-one margin of victory, Batista promised he would decree full amnesty for political prisoners to "contribute to the return of harmony in the Cuban family."[8] With the return of constitutional guarantees, including freedom of the press, the public campaign for amnesty continued to build leading up to and after Batista was sworn in as president on February 24, 1955. By May, the Chamber of Representatives and Senate finally approved a bill that freed all political prisoners except those involved in Communist activities, and Batista signed the bill into law on May 6. On Sunday, May 15, Castro walked out of Presidio Modelo having served less than two years of his fifteen-year sentence. "As we leave the prison," Castro declared, "we proclaim that we shall struggle for [our] ideas even at the price of our existence."[9]

The most lopsided trade in Cuban League history transpired in the first month of the 1953–54 season when Marianao traded right-handed pitcher Camilo Pascual to Cienfuegos. Born on January 20, 1934, the Havana native had made his Cuban League debut the previous season, posting a 1-0 record with a 3.52 ERA in 15⅓ innings. That season, Pascual benefited from the tutelage of Marianao manager Adolfo Luque. "When I was a very, very young age, I always fooled around, trying to throw a curve," Pascual said. "And [when I made the] reserve squad my first manager was Adolfo Luque. And you know, he worked with me a lot in the bullpen and he really helped me develop the curve ball."[10]

But Pascual got knocked around in his only outing with the Tigers in the 1953–54 season. He surrendered two runs on a walk and three hits without recording an out. Officially, the nineteen-year-old Pascual was traded to Cienfuegos for twenty-five-year-old catcher Rafael Fernández, who had not played in the league for four years and did not play again. Ralph Ávila, however, says there was more to the trade than the players who were exchanged. According to Ávila, Marianao owner Alfredo

Pequeño traded Pascual to Cienfuegos to pay off a debt to the Casa Tarín sporting goods store.

Luis Parga, one of the Cienfuegos co-owners, also owned Casa Tarín, which provided equipment to teams in the league. "Club Marianao owed Parga money, so we would joke with Camilo and we would say that Camilo was traded for a dozen bats," Ávila said. "To pay off that debt Club Marianao had with Casa Tarín—who were the same owners of Club Cienfuegos—that's when the trade happens that sends Camilo . . . from Marianao to Cienfuegos."[11] After the trade, Pascual showed what a mistake the trade had been. With the Elephants, he went 4-5 with a stellar 1.95 ERA to finish the 1953–54 season, a hint of his future greatness.

But Cienfuegos was unable to reap the benefits of the trade the following season. Pascual, who had signed with the Washington Senators as an amateur free agent in 1952, made his Major League debut on April 15, 1954, and went 4-7 with a 4.22 ERA in his rookie season. The Senators, seeking to protect their star signee, barred Pascual from participating in the 1954–55 Cuban League season. He was not the only Cuban player prevented from playing in Cuba that winter by his Major League club. Chicago White Sox general manager Frank Lane prohibited outfielder Orestes "Minnie" Miñoso and pitchers Sandalio Consuegra and Miguel "Mike" Fornieles from playing winter ball as well.

Under baseball rules, native Latinos were exempt from the three-player limit on those with more than forty-five days' Major League experience participating in winter ball. But individual Major League owners were forbidding certain Latin stars from playing. The impact of the absent natives was certainly felt in the Cuban League, where the attendance decline for the 1954–55 season was "nothing short of alarming."[12] During the Caribbean Series in Caracas, Venezuela, Dr. July Sanguily expressed his concern to National Association president George Trautman at the Caribbean Confederation's executive meeting. The Almendares owner insisted that Latino players be allowed to play in their native lands without restrictions. "Without that, we cannot survive," Sanguily said. "There will be more and more major leaguers developed in our country, by our winter baseball within the next few years. . . . All we ask is that they be permitted to come back and play for us after their season in the States. If we cannot get that, we shall die."[13]

Delegates from countries in the Caribbean Confederation presented their complaints to baseball commissioner Ford Frick during a July 18, 1955, meeting in New York. Cuba was represented by Cuban League president Dr. Arturo Bengochea, Almendares general manager Monchy de Arcos, Marianao owner Alfredo Pequeño, and Habana owner Miguel Ángel González. De Arcos pointed to five Almendares players—Willy Miranda, Carlos Paula, José Valdivielso, Lino Donoso, and Román Mejías—who belonged to Major League clubs. "If we are deprived of the services of these players, we are forced to throw up the sponge," De Arcos told Frick. "Certainly, if American players want to come to Cuba and play for the salaries available, fine. We will take them. But our native players must be guaranteed to us."[14]

The three-hour conference produced several proposals, which were to be discussed at the baseball meetings in Chicago on August 1, and the Caribbean delegates were instructed to return to Frick's headquarters on August 12. At the subsequent meeting with Frick, the Caribbean Confederation reached a final agreement with the commissioner. Under the revised rules, every Latino player could play winter ball in his country and each Caribbean team was permitted a total of four Major League players, including Caribbean natives. The Caribbean players could have unlimited Major League experience, but nonnatives could not have played more than two years in the Majors.

The agreement meant a dozen Cuban-born Major Leaguers, including Miñoso, Pascual, Consuegra, Miranda, and Pedro Ramos could participate in the 1955–56 season without objection from their respective Major League clubs. The players, clad in their Major League uniforms, joined Bengochea on the mound for the ceremonial first pitch for the league's opening game. With Pascual back and Ramos enjoying a stellar rookie campaign, Cienfuegos finally ended the string of supremacy by Almendares and Habana. The Eternal Rivals had come to dominate the league. From 1947 to 1955, nine consecutive pennants had been won by either the Scorpions or Lions. But both clubs would begin to fade as the 1950s wound down, beginning with the 1955–56 season.

Under manager Oscar Rodríguez, who had led the Havana Cubans to back-to-back Florida International League championships (1947 and 1948), Cienfuegos won its first Cuban League title since 1946. Despite a remarkable season by pitcher Wilmer "Vinegar Bend" Mizell, Habana finished tied for second with Marianao, 6 games behind Cienfuegos. Mizell, coming off of two years of military service and preparing to return to the St. Louis Cardinals, set a league record with 206 strikeouts in 179 innings. Almendares finished a distant fourth, 10 games behind Cienfuegos.

Pascual went 12-5 with a league-leading 1.91 ERA. Elephants outfielder Ultus Álvarez led the Cuban League with 10 home runs. Ramos earned Rookie of the Year honors by leading the league with a 13-5 record to go along with a 3.11 ERA. Ramos was coming off of his Major League rookie season, in which he went 5-11 despite a respectable 3.88 ERA for the Washington Senators. At age seventeen, the Pinar del Rio native had signed in 1953 with Joe Cambria for a reported $150 bonus.[15] "Camilo and Pedro, they were extraordinary," recalled Almendares catcher Evelio Hernández. "Camilo had very good velocity, a very good curve. He was a very intelligent pitcher, very good control. And Pedro Ramos had that Vaseline ball that he threw. He threw a pitch that moved. He had Vaseline on his head on the back of his cap. He would get that on his hands and he would throw and his ball would move."[16]

Ramos gave the pitch a different name. "What happened was that every so often, I would wet my fingers, and they would say it was a spitball," Ramos recalled. "And I would say, 'No, that's a Cuban palmball. It was a spitball, but instead of a spitball, I would say it was a Cuban palmball. I changed the name."[17] That was in keeping with the maverick personality of a player who would come to be known as the Cuban Cowboy because of his affinity for dressing in black, lace-trimmed Western outfits. "I was born in the country and liked those clothes. I liked Western movies," Ramos said. "Our [Senators] catcher Clint Courtney, when we went to Kansas City [in 1957 or 1958], we went to a Country Western store, and I saw a cowboy outfit, and I bought spurs, cowboy outfit, cowboy hat, everything. And I kept dressing like that. They asked Yogi Berra when I went to the Yankees—because the Yankees would dress in shirt and ties and that sort of thing—they asked him if I would still dress like a cowboy. Berra responded that, 'I don't care how he dresses. I just want him to get outs.'"[18]

Upon his release from prison and return to Havana, Castro immediately began reconstituting the 26th of July Movement. He met with followers, gave speeches, and lashed out against the Batista regime in the press. But his stay in Havana was brief. As he continued his anti-Batista activities, Castro began to fear for his safety and started moving from home to home of various friends, never staying in the same place on consecutive nights. Convinced he would be killed if remained in Cuba, Castro boarded Mexican Aviation Flight 566 for Veracruz on July 7, 1955. "I am leaving Cuba because all doors of peaceful struggle have been closed to me," Castro declared in a message left behind on the pages of *Bohemia* magazine. "I believe the hour has come to take rights and not to beg for them, to fight instead of pleading for them. I will reside somewhere in the Caribbean. From trips such as this, one does not return or else one returns with the tyranny beheaded at one's feet."[19]

Castro reached Mexico City on July 8, joining his brother Raúl and other followers in the Mexican capital. Within weeks of arriving, Raúl Castro introduced Fidel to a twenty-seven-year-old Argentine named Ernesto Guevara at a dinner to celebrate the second anniversary of the Moncada attack. Guevara had grown up in Argentina during the nationalist era of General Juan Perón. Before coming to Mexico, Guevara spent nine months in Guatemala, where he witnessed the toppling of Jacobo Arbenz's democratically elected government by a CIA-backed invasion. The experience aroused a powerful distrust of the United States in Guevara, who found a kindred spirit in Castro. The amateur revolutionary described Castro as "a young man, intelligent, very sure of himself, and of extraordinary audacity. I think there is a mutual sympathy between us."[20]

Guevara eventually came to be known to his new Cuban comrades as "Che," a word with a meaning similar to "Hey, buddy" commonly used by Argentines. With Guevara on board, Castro began gathering more followers he could mold into a guerilla force that would return to Cuba and attempt to overthrow Batista. Castro traveled to the United States hoping to raise money for his invasion. But funds were difficult to come by at first as other anti-Batista groups were already organizing inside Cuba, where tensions and violence were on the rise. By May 1956, Castro's group rented a farm about twenty miles south of Mexico City, where they gathered arms and conducted training exercises. Finally, he wrangled enough funds from deposed president Carlos Prío Socarrás to purchase the *Granma*, a small motor yacht, from an American living in Tuxpan, on Mexico's Gulf Coast.[21]

On November 26, the *Granma* set sail for the twelve-hundred-mile voyage across the Gulf of Mexico to Eastern Cuba. Built to carry just twenty-five passengers, the yacht was laden with eighty-two armed men. Before leaving Tuxpan, Castro sent a coded message to Frank País, informing the leader of the 26th of July Movement in Santiago de Cuba that the *Granma* would make landfall in Oriente Province on November 30. The plan was for País to launch an attack on the National Police and Maritime Police headquarters that would coincide with the landing of Castro's invasion force. Instead, a voyage that should have taken five days was delayed by more than two days by foul weather and rough seas.[22]

As País launched his attack at 7 a.m., the *Granma* was foundering near Grand Cayman Island, only three-quarters of the way to Oriente. The uprising failed. País managed to escape but most of his twenty-eight-man force were killed or captured and later executed. And the Batista regime was now expecting Castro's expedition, which finally ran aground at 4:20 a.m. on December 2. "This wasn't a landing," Guevara would later say. "This was a shipwreck."[23] Hours after coming ashore, they came under fire on the ground and from the air. Military authorities immediately declared victory, claiming aircraft had "annihilated 40 members of the supreme command of the revolutionary 26th of July Movement . . . among them its chief, Fidel Castro."[24]

In fact Castro survived, and his guerilla force fled into the Sierra Maestra, Cuba's largest mountain range, which runs east to west across Oriente Province in southeast Cuba. There they were aided by local peasants. On December 5, the rebels' fourth night in Cuba, they ran into a devastating ambush by Batista's Rural Guard at Alegría de Pío. Guevara sustained a superficial bullet wound in the shoulder. Three rebels were killed, twenty-one were executed within a day or two, twenty-two were caught and imprisoned, and another nineteen disappeared. Only sixteen survived the ambush, including Castro, his brother Raúl, Guevara, and Camilo Cienfuegos.[25]

When Orestes Miñoso returned to Cuba after the 1956 Major League season, his luggage included twenty-seven suitcases, two trunks, a Cadillac El Dorado, and a new contract offer from the Chicago White Sox. Miñoso was coming off of another fine season in Chicago, having batted .316 with 21 home runs and 88 RBI. Cuban fans revered Miñoso, who was immortalized in Enrique Jorrín's popular 1954 cha-cha-chá, "Miñoso al bate" (Miñoso at bat). The lyrics spoke to Miñoso's hitting skills, proclaiming how the ball "dances the cha-cha-chá" whenever he comes to the plate. "He was a marvel, a tremendous player," said Marianao shortstop José Valdivielso. "And if he was a tremendous ballplayer, as a person, he was indisputably a gentleman on and off the field."[26]

In returning to Cuba for the 1956–57 Cuban League season, Miñoso was about to lead his Marianao club to new heights. The Tigers had not won a pennant in the twenty seasons since the legendary Martín Dihigo managed the team to the 1936–37 championship while earning league MVP honors. Since signing with Marianao in 1945, Miñoso had played his entire Cuban League career with the Tigers, missing only two winter seasons. In that time, Marianao finished no higher than second (twice), third six times, and last three other seasons.

But Marianao came into the 1956–57 season with a loaded roster for Napoleón Reyes, who had managed the team since 1954. Aside from Miñoso, the Tigers had first baseman Julio Bécquer to provide some power and a rotation anchored by Mike Fornieles, who had already pitched five seasons in the Majors with the Washington Senators and White Sox; and future Hall of Famer Jim Bunning, who was just starting out his Major League career with the Detroit Tigers. "Mike Fornieles was a tremendous pitcher," recalled Marianao reliever Rodolfo Arias. "Bunning was a tremendous pitcher. He was in the Minors when we got him. But later he became very famous."[27]

Marianao came out of the gate quickly, charging to the top of the standings in the first month of the season. By December 1, the Tigers appeared to have a stranglehold on first place, leading second-place Almendares by five and a half games. Habana made a run, at one point winning twelve of seventeen games in December to climb out of the cellar and into second, five games behind Marianao on New Year's Day. Marianao's dominance in the standings, along with the prevalence of games on Cuban television and the political unrest permeating Havana, "combined to send Cuban League attendance into a nosedive," Gordon "Red" Marston wrote in *The Sporting News*.[28]

In the aftermath of Castro's invasion force landing in Oriente, the Batista regime had suspended constitutional guarantees in the provinces of Oriente, Pinar del Rio, Las Villas, and

Camagüey, four of Cuba's six provinces. Constitutional rights remained in place only in the provinces of Havana and Matanzas. What followed was a government crackdown as Cuban authorities began rounding up anti-Batista elements throughout the island. Enemies of the regime responded with a "terrorist campaign," forcing military authorities to "adopt more forceful suppression tactics," R. Hart Phillips wrote in the *New York Times*. "Bomb explosions, incendiary fires, sabotaging of waterworks, public transportation, light and communications systems occur daily. . . . In Havana and Matanzas Provinces . . . police, armed with rifles and machine-guns, guard stations and public buildings."[29]

Despite the unrest, the Cuban League rolled on without interruption, including a visit by New York Yankees slugger Mickey Mantle, who threw out the first pitch of a January 6 doubleheader. In the Sunday nightcap, Marianao beat Habana 3–1, culminating a disastrous weekend for the Lions. Habana had won nine of eleven games and beaten Marianao six times to cut into the Tigers' first-place lead. But a 13–3 loss to Cienfuegos on Saturday preceded Sunday's loss, all but denying Habana any chance of catching Marianao in the standings. The Lions would have had to win fourteen of their final seventeen games to pass the Tigers. It was not to be.

Marianao clinched the pennant with a 6–5 victory against Almendares on January 30. Miñoso batted .312 to win the batting title and was named league MVP for the second time (he had also won in 1952–53). Fornieles went 11-7 with a 2.47 ERA, and Bunning went 11-5 with a 2.10 ERA. "It was a memorable experience pitching in Cuba, to know when you came back you were ready because you had faced major league hitters," Bunning recalled in his 2011 biography. "Good major league hitters. There were four or five on each team."[30]

Marianao's championship was Reyes's first as a manager. He had played for Almendares and Cienfuegos in a Cuban League career that spanned seven seasons from 1941 to 1952. But as a manager for the Cuba team of the Liga Nacional, Marianao, and the Minor League Havana Sugar Kings, Reyes had not had much success until the 1956–57 pennant. "He was very good [as a manager], very good, very intelligent and very funny," Valdivielso said. "He was a person you could play baseball for. He was always jovial. He was never angry, and [he was] intelligent and everybody got along with him. We joked with him, and he joked with us, always with respect for him as the manager he was."[31]

More than two months after the *Granma* made landfall in Cuba, Herbert L. Matthews revealed to the world what had been widely speculated in Cuba. "Fidel Castro," Matthews declared in the February 24, 1957, editions of the *New York Times*, "is alive and fighting hard and successfully in the rugged, almost impenetrable . . . Sierra Maestra."[32] The editorial writer had arrived in Havana on February 9, posing as an American tourist. With the help of Castro collaborators, Matthews traveled the more than five hundred miles from Havana to Oriente, past army checkpoints, to a home outside the Sierra. From there, he was taken into the mountains to the rebel encampment.

Castro had a hungry, ragtag force of fewer than twenty men, but Matthews described it as "the most dangerous enemy General Batista has yet faced."[33] His conclusion was the result of well-executed stagecraft by the rebels, a handful of which repeatedly marched past the camp to give the impression of a much larger force.[34] Matthews also described Castro's personality as "overpowering," and wrote that it was easy to see why his men "adored" him and why he "has caught the imagination" of Cuba's youth. "We have been fighting for seventy-nine days now and are stronger than ever," Castro told his visitor. "Above all, we are fighting for a democratic Cuba and an end to the dictatorship."[35]

Because Batista had imposed a forty-five-day censorship decree on Cuban press, radio, and television, reading Matthews's dispatch was no simple task. Government censors literally had cut out the first and second installments of Matthews's report, leaving holes in copies of the *Times* sold in Cuba. Instead, Cubans "learned of the interview from U.S. radio broadcasts and from American tourists."[36] It was not until the censorship decree was lifted on February 26 that Cubans were able to see the third installment of Matthews's report firsthand. By then, the series had caused considerable angst in Batista's regime. U.S. ambassador Arthur Gardner, a staunch Batista supporter, was completely caught by surprise. Because he did not trust Gardner, Matthews had not consulted with the U.S. embassy before the report was published.[37]

The Batista regime responded by denouncing Matthews's report as "el capitulo de una novela fantástica" (a chapter in a fantastic novel). Dr. Santiago Verdeja, Cuba's minister of national defense, in a statement published in the February 28 editions of *Diario de la Marina*, said Matthews "has not interviewed the pro-Communist insurgent, Fidel Castro, and the information obtained came from certain opposition sources." The statement also characterized it as "strange" that Matthews did not take a photograph of himself with Castro "to provide proof of what he wrote." On the same day as the statement ran in *Diario de la Marina*, the *Times* published a story with a photo of Matthews interviewing Castro as the two smoked cigars. "The truth will always out," Matthews said in a statement issued by the *Times*, "censorship or no censorship."[38]

With the *Times* portraying Castro as a freedom fighter, the regime continued to attack the rebel leader. At a luncheon at the army headquarters at Camp Columbia on March 10 to commemorate the fifth anniversary of Batista's *golpe*, the Cuban president denounced Castro as an "agent of the Soviet Union," saying "there is no doubt that the movement headed by Castro is Communist and is aided by communism."[39] Three days later, Batista found himself under siege at the presidential palace by members of the Directorio Revolucionario (DR), an insurrectionary group founded in 1955 by University of Havana students, whose goal was deposing the Cuban president. At about 3:20 p.m., on March 13, DR members armed with rifles, machine guns, and hand grenades drove a truck up to the palace and rushed the front entrance. The attackers overwhelmed Batista's personal guards, reaching the private offices on the second floor. Batista escaped to the top floor, where palace guards managed to repel the attackers.

At the same time, José Antonio Echeverría led a smaller group of insurgents who took over the offices of Radio Reloj. Echeverría was president of the Federación Estudiantil Universitaria (FEU), a student group at the University of Havana, and had formed the Revolutionary Directorate. After taking control of the radio station, he transmitted a statement over the airwaves. "People of Cuba, the tyrant Batista has met justice in his own lair," Echeverría declared. "The FEU, in the name of the people, has come to settle accounts."[40] Seconds later, Radio Reloj's signal went dead. As Echeverría tried to escape to campus, he was gunned down by police.

Two hours after it had begun, the attack was over. At least thirty-five Revolutionary Directorate members were killed at the palace. Scores of other members were captured, tortured, and murdered. Batista charged that Prío, who was in exile in Miami Beach, Florida, had provided the arms, and described the attackers as "poor fools paid by money robbed from the people, and directed by Communists."[41] What followed was a brutal wave of retribution carried out by Esteban Ventura Novo, chief of the police's anti-subversion unit. From Miami, Prío predicted that Batista "is going to fall." The Cuban people "will try to overthrow dictator Batista again and again," Prío said. "All the advantage is with the Cuban people. They can fail and fail and lose—but Batista can lose only once and then he is done forever."[42]

Months before the start of the 1957–58 season, Cuban baseball was rocked by the deaths of two icons. In April, former player Lázaro Salazar died after suffering a cerebral hemorrhage while he was managing the Mexico City Reds during a Mexican League game. In July, Adolfo Luque died of a heart attack. Salazar had been a position player and pitcher in the Cuban League from 1930 to 1947, earning MVP honors with Santa Clara during the 1934–35 and 1937–38 seasons. He also managed Santa Clara to back-to-back league pennants in 1937–38 and 1938–39. Luque had been a pitcher in the Cuban League from 1912 to 1945, compiling a 93-64 record. As a manager, he won eleven Cuban League pennants, mostly with Almendares. With his 705 managerial victories in twenty-one Cuban League seasons, he ranks second to Miguel Ángel González (846 wins in thirty-three seasons) in league history.

On July 3, Luque was watching television with family, preparing to be discharged from a clinic the following day, when he began feeling chest pains. Luque called for a nurse, but to no avail. He died at age sixty-six. Cuban fans and players expressed profound sadness during a funeral where an Almendares banner draped over the deceased manager's coffin. But Luque's death also was felt in the United States, where he pitched twenty seasons in the Majors with the Boston Braves, Cincinnati Reds, Brooklyn Dodgers, and New York Giants. Frank Graham, of the *New York Journal-American*, expressed his shock in a *Sporting News* article that appeared under the headline "Adolfo Luque is dead?": "That's what it said in the paper," Graham wrote. "Still, it's hard to believe. Adolfo Luque was much too strong, too tough, too determined to die at age 66. The paper said he died of [a] heart attack. He did? It sounds absurd. Luque's heart failed him in the clutch? It never did before."[43]

Salazar was known in Cuba as El Principe de Belén (the Prince of Belen)—nicknamed for the Havana neighborhood from which he hailed. He began his Cuban League career with Almendares and moved in 1938 to Mexico, where he played and managed in the summer while returning to his native Cuba for winter ball. After managing four teams to seven Mexican League championships in eighteen seasons from 1939 to 1956, Salazar got his dream job, signing a two-year contract to manage Almendares for the 1957–58 season. But on April 25, Salazar collapsed in the Mexico City Reds' dugout, gasping for air and rambling incoherently. "There are two outs!" Salazar cried out. "We win!"[44] The manager was taken to a hospital but never regained consciousness and died at age forty-six.

Salazar's death left Almendares scrambling to find a new manager. The team turned to a familiar face, Bobby Bragan, who had managed the Pittsburgh Pirates to seventh-place finishes in the National League in 1956 and 1957, and recently had been hired to manage the Cleveland Indians. Bragan had managed Almendares in three other seasons, leading the Scorpions to two championships. Although terms of the contract were not released, it was reported Bragan would be the highest-paid manager in Cuban League history. "I think we have a good enough club to win the flag," Bragan said of Almendares as he and his wife received a warm reception in Havana on September 27.[45]

Bragan had reason for optimism. His rotation included Major League pitcher Dick Brodowski and future Major Leaguers Miguel "Mike" Cuellar, Orlando Peña, and Mudcat Grant. The offense included future Major League infielder Tony Taylor and Major Leaguers Rocky Nelson, Willy Miranda, Sandy Amoros, and Miguel de la Hoz. Nelson had been an Almendares stalwart since 1952, leading the league in hitting (.352) in 1953–54 and homers (13 in 69 games) and RBIs (57) in 1954–55. Nelson was back after sitting out the 1956–57 season. With defending champion Marianao losing pitcher Jim Bunning and catcher Hal Smith, Almendares was "considered the best pennant bet," Rubén Rodríguez wrote in *The Sporting News*. "The Cienfuegos Elephants, with probably the best pitching staff, are rated the No. 2 choice."[46]

But Cienfuegos was dealt a potentially serious blow to its pennant hopes before the season opened on October 8. The Washington Senators refused to allow Elephants ace Camilo Pascual to pitch that winter. Pascual's Major League club claimed he needed to rest a sore arm even though the right-hander insisted his arm was fine. Pascual was originally hurt during the Major League season, struck on his upper right arm by a line drive during a Memorial Day game, and finished with an 8-17 record.

Despite Senators president Calvin Griffith's ban, Pascual continued pitching in Cuba. Griffith took the matter to baseball commissioner Ford Frick, who ruled in favor of the Senators. Once Griffith agreed to boost the pitcher's pay for the 1958 season to make up for salary he would lose by not playing for Cienfuegos that winter, Pascual withdrew from the league having pitched just three games (1-2 with a 2.15 ERA).

Without Pascual, Cienfuegos would finish last, thirteen games out of first place. Pitching dominated the first month of the season as eight shutouts were recorded in the first twenty games. On November 23, nineteen-year-old Cienfuegos pitcher Antonio Díaz tossed the first Cuban League no-hitter since 1950 to beat Habana 2–0 and win *Bohemia* magazine's $1,000 prize for such an accomplishment. Despite Díaz's feat, Almendares topped the standings as predicted. The Scorpions held as much as a five-game advantage in early December and remained in first well into the month. But as Bragan left the team briefly for the baseball winter meetings in Colorado, Marianao began gaining ground. The surging Tigers won seven consecutive games at one point and tied Almendares for first place on December 19.

At the conclusion of games played on December 29, Marianao held a two-game lead in the standings, and Adolfo Luque was forever immortalized in the pantheon of Cuban baseball. As the Cuban League celebrated its seventy-ninth anniversary, Luque was inducted into the Cuban Baseball Hall of Fame at a ceremony during the intermission of Sunday's doubleheader. Hundreds of fans gathered at Gate 1 of El Gran Stadium as Luque's name was added to an obelisk, joining those of Cuba's most revered baseball players, including longtime friend and Habana team owner Miguel Ángel González.

Since 1939—three years after the initial induction ceremony at the National Baseball Hall of Fame in Cooperstown, New York—Cuba had honored its own ballplayers. Luque's posthumous induction was an "event of deep spiritual significance to [Cuban] baseball," Nelson Varela wrote in *Diario de la Marina*. During the ceremony, league president Arturo Bengochea described Luque as an "example of sporting honesty, of firm conviction, of unselfish love in the sport. He gave everything in each of his outings."[47]

As the season entered its final month, Habana went on a torrid streak, winning thirteen of seventeen games to pull into contention. Still in third place behind Marianao and Almendares, the Lions were one and a half games out on January 9. The tight pennant race ignited tensions. On January 18, umpire Amado Maestri ejected Napoleón Reyes after the Marianao manager got into an argument with a fan, who had berated him in "strong language." Two days later, a Maestri call—he ruled outfielder Daniel Morejón had trapped a ball instead of catching it—set off a rhubarb. Almendares players swarmed the umpire to protest the call, and catcher Russ Nixon became incensed. Nixon, who would go on to a twelve-year Major League playing career and manage the Cincinnati Reds and Atlanta Braves in the 1980s, was ejected after he began removing his catching gear one piece at a time and throwing it onto the field.[48]

Eventually, Marianao pulled away from its challengers, clinching the pennant with a 3–2 victory against Almendares on February 3. A crowd of eight thousand watched as Solly Drake hit a two-out, two-run home run in the eighth inning to rally the Tigers against Orlando Peña, who had held them to three hits through the first seven innings. The victory gave Mike Fornieles an 11-6 record and 2.09 ERA. Marianao went on to win the title by four games over Almendares. Habana was third, five games out. "The good years [Marianao had] were with Napoleón Reyes," said Tigers catcher René Friol. "He was a tremendous manager, and a tremendous person. That's why we won. He was a good manager and beside that, he was a good person. That's not easy."[49]

Marianao's Bob Shaw finished with a 14-5 record and 1.48 ERA, easily making up for the loss of Jim Bunning. But sportswriters voted Cienfuegos pitcher Pedro Ramos as the league's MVP. Ramos, who in 1956 had given up one of the most famous home runs in Major League history, a tape-measure blast by

Mickey Mantle that nearly left the confines of Yankee Stadium on the fly, went 11-8 with a 2.74 ERA in the Cuban League. He received fourteen MVP votes to Shaw's five. Ramos's Cienfuegos teammate, future Hall of Fame third baseman Brooks Robinson, hit 9 home runs in 63 games to finish in a four-way tie for the league lead with Habana's Norm Larker, Almendares's Daniel Morejón, and Cienfuegos's Francisco "Panchón" Herrera. "It was a great experience for me," Robinson said. "I was single. I had my car. I had a great time there."[50]

Robinson enjoyed his one winter in Cuba despite the escalating political unrest. "Fidel Castro's insurgents are laying waste to rice and sugar plantations, harassing transportation, and taking supplies and prisoners," the *New York Times* reported on January 15.[51] On January 25, 1958, Batista restored constitutional guarantees, which had been suspended since the start of year and much of 1957. "We had bombs going off. We knew Castro was in the mountains. Batista was there," Robinson said in a 2015 interview with the Hall of Fame, "but we would have a bomb go off in the city there, and one of them went off behind the ballpark one time, so we knew there were some things happening."[52]

5

Year of the Pitcher

n the early months of 1958, Havana was either a logical, almost perfect choice for hosting a future Major League expansion team, or else the city was so torn by political violence that the safety of American Minor League players could not be guaranteed. Which impression was correct depended largely on who was talking and when. In May, Pittsburgh Pirates chairman Branch Rickey predicted a third Major League, international in scope, was a "must." The man responsible for originating the farm system and breaking baseball's color barrier said, "Cities like Havana, Toronto, Montreal, Vancouver . . . want, and should get, big league ball."[1] Earlier, during spring training in Bradenton, Florida, Milwaukee Braves chairman Lou Perini had predicted that expanding the eight-team American and National leagues into a pair of twelve-team leagues was "entirely possible" and listed Havana as one potential site.[2]

However, at around the same time Perini was musing about expansion, rumors persisted that the Class Triple-A Havana Sugar Kings would be transferred elsewhere at some point during the 1958 International League season because of political unrest in Cuba. League president Frank Shaughnessy denied such rumors before leaving Florida to visit Havana on March 26. "Owner Bobby Maduro has assured me that everything is going ahead with plans for the season," Shaughnessy said. "I'm going to Cuba to look things over first-hand."[3] Despite those reassurances, Shaughnessy conceded the league was prepared to move the franchise in the event playing in Havana became impossible. Such concerns were valid as the 26th of

July Movement's actions had already reached into the sports world on February 23.

Cuban rebels kidnapped Argentine race car driver Juan Manuel Fangio on the eve of the Cuban Grand Prix, which the five-time world auto racing champion was favored to win. Fangio had just returned to the Lincoln Hotel after piloting his Maserati to the fastest trial run on the Malecón road course, when a pair of unmasked men entered the lobby at 8:55 p.m. One of the men, Manuel Uziel, ordered Fangio out of the hotel at gunpoint.[4] The kidnapping allegedly was intended to embarrass the Batista regime and potentially cancel the second annual Cuban Grand Prix. The race was held without Fangio, although it was suspended after a driver crashed into spectators, killing six and injuring thirty-one others. Captors released Fangio unharmed on February 25. "The revolutionists treated me well," Fangio said. "Their attitude was even friendly."[5]

Despite the turmoil, Havana had experienced a gambling boom, benefiting both the Batista regime and American mobsters. The $24 million, 630-room, 30-story Havana Hilton, one of three new hotel-casinos under construction, was set to open on March 24. Meyer Lansky, briefly barred from returning to Cuba, was back in Havana, running things at the Riviera. Tampa, Florida, crime boss Santo Trafficante Jr. was in full charge of the Sans Souci and had major interests in the Comodoro and the new Hotel Capri, where movie star George Raft was a part-owner and worked as a greeter. "At Havana's handsome hotels and glittering nightclubs," *Life* magazine wrote, "the gambling casinos were collecting American tourist dollars as fast as the roulette wheels could spin and the craps dealers could rake in the chips."[6]

The good times would not last as political tensions continued. Fidel Castro issued a manifesto on March 17, declaring "total war" on the Batista government. It set April 1 as the start of the final battle, which would include a general strike backed by armed action. "Revolutionary action," Castro declared, "must be carried out progressively from this instant until it ends in the strike that will be ordered at the proper moment."[7] Castro eventually set April 9 as the date for the strike. At a special meeting in Miami on April 6, International League officials decided the season would open on April 16 in Havana "unless conditions materially changed."[8] Clashes between rebels and government troops broke out in Havana days later, but the general strike Castro had called for never fully materialized.

Regardless, Buffalo Bisons manager Phil Cavarretta expressed the team's concerns over playing in Cuba. "I don't like the idea of going over there into an atmosphere of so much potential danger," he said. "It hurts the morale of the ball club, and it will affect their play. For us, it could mean a bad start in what promises to be a very tight race."[9] On April 11, Shaughnessy alerted Buffalo team officials of the possibility of moving the series to Tampa and called an emergency special meeting at Miami Stadium on April 13. With Buffalo abstaining, the league voted 7–0 that the Bisons would have to play in Havana or face fines: forfeiture of a $25,000 bond, $2,000 for failing to appear in an opening game, and $800 for missing each subsequent game.[10]

Despite the possibility of it costing the team more than $40,000, Bisons president John Stiglmeier declared he would "leave it up to our players." On April 15, the players met for an hour before sending a wire to Stiglmeier that read, "We will go to Havana to protect our contracts with the Buffalo Baseball Club because the International League has directed us to do so. We want it known that should any incident happen to any of our players on or off the field in Havana, our families will seek damages from the International League." The Bisons received Batista's assurance of the "fullest protection," as well as a "securing pledge" from U.S. ambassador Earl E. T. Smith.[11]

The largest crowd to see any of the International League openers was reported in Havana, where 12,143 watched the Sugar Kings beat the Bisons 6–5 at El Gran Stadium. True to his word, Batista provided plainclothes police on the Bisons' bench, behind the dugout, and as an escort to and from the Hotel Nacional. There also was a small detail of police in the lobby of the hotel. "I am sure now that the situation was greatly magnified and we didn't need any protection," Cavarretta said. "After the second day, the plainclothesmen didn't show up and we didn't ask questions. They knew that we were convinced."[12]

But it was clear to the visiting contingent of Buffalo sportswriters that the political turmoil had had an impact on Havana, which "had lost its gayety without the rich tourist trade." The *Buffalo News*' Cy Kritzer wrote that "gambling casinos were virtually deserted and losing heavily. At the Havana Hilton, there were 15 employees for every guest."[13] Tony Vaughn, the manager of the Nacional casino, hailed the Bisons' arrival "as the best shot in the arm we have received lately. I can see now the upturn for us, and we thank baseball. If the Bisons hadn't come, it would have been the worst thing that could have happened, and it would have played right into Castro's hands."[14]

While Havana casinos were starting to see declining attendance, the same was not true of the Sugar Kings. Despite continued political unrest—Batista declared yet another forty-five-day "national state of emergency" on May 31, giving him virtually unlimited powers—Sugar Kings attendance rebounded significantly after a dismal showing the previous year. The team recorded 87,497 in paid attendance by June 6—3,177 more than Havana's attendance for the entire 1957 season. The accomplishment merited a trophy presented to the club by J. G. Taylor Spink, publisher of *The Sporting News*. "We are grateful to Mr. Spink," Sugar Kings general manager Paul Miller said, "for giving us something to remember our feat."[15]

The Sugar Kings could not have known attendance at El Gran Stadium would be so good when they arranged before the start of the season to play a three-game series June 6–8 at a newly built stadium in Morón, in Camagüey Province. About 250 miles east of Havana, the venue was uncomfortably close to the fighting in Oriente. How fitting that the relocated series came against the Buffalo Bisons. Their "nightmarish" three-day adventure featured a twelve-hour journey from Miami to Morón. It included a "nerve-wracking, bone-rattling bus ride over bumpy dirt roads"; one game that started at 10:40 p.m. (more than two hours behind schedule) and was suspended with the score tied at 6–6 in the seventh inning because of a curfew; and a plane landing and taking off at "air fields which were not much more than glorified cow pastures."[16]

Bisons manager Phil Cavarretta said that in twenty-four years in baseball, "I have never seen anything like this. The players deserve medals for playing Friday night's game after what they went through."[17] Others in the International League took note, specifically the Miami Marlins. They were scheduled to play a similar series July 18–20 in Morón, but Marlins general manager Joe Ryan requested that Sugar Kings owner Bobby Maduro move the series to Havana. The series in Morón against the Bisons drew 15,482. "Of course, the Sugar Kings are not out of the woods by a long shot," Miller said. "They will have to draw approximately 240,000 fans to meet operational expenses. And it appears that they will have to fight their way into the first division and bring out the fans in greater volume if the attendance goal is to be reached."[18]

Despite promising Cuban talent—shortstop Elio Chacón, the Venezuelan-born son of Cuban Hall of Fame shortstop Pelayo Chacón, was batting .330 as of June 25; left fielder Daniel Morejón was batting .301, and first baseman Rogelio "Borrego" Álvarez had clubbed thirteen home runs and driven in forty runs through sixty-nine games—the Sugar Kings were in fifth place with a below-.500 record when manager Napoleón Reyes was fired and replaced by Tony Pacheco. The Sugar Kings finished the season with a 65-88 record, last in the International League, and showed little hint of what was to come the following season. "Our attendance in Havana will gain if we can come up with a winning team," Maduro said. "I think there will be less political unrest, and that will help."[19]

On the eve of the 1958–59 Cuban League season, *Diario de la Marina* advised fans to be "prepared for one of the greatest campaigns in the history of the sport."[20] After raising its championship banner in center field, Marianao hit the field at El Gran Stadium for the October 8 opener with essentially the same team that had won back-to-back championships. Its opponent, Almendares, returned many key players, such as second baseman Tony Taylor and pitcher Orlando Peña. The Scorpions' roster also included several new additions, such as future Washington Senators and Minnesota Twins All-Star Bob Allison, third baseman Jim Baxes, and pitchers Tom Lasorda and Art Fowler. Lasorda was back in Cuba after a five-year absence and four winter seasons in Puerto Rico.

A disappointing crowd of eight thousand fans watched as Peña outdueled Marianao starter Miguel Fornieles, limiting the Tigers to four hits. Outfielder Leo Posada, a former world-class cyclist whose nephew Jorge would become an All-Star catcher with the New York Yankees, provided the winning margin in the 4–2 victory, driving in two runs with a bases-loaded double in the fourth inning. In the opener for the other two teams in the league the following night, Habana's Vicente Amor (two hits) outdueled Cienfuegos's Pedro Ramos (three hits) for a 2–1 victory in front of an even smaller crowd. The two-night opening program drew approximately half as many fans as the twenty-five thousand that attended the 1957–58 lid-lifters. The opening games provided a sign of things to come for the season as attendance would suffer and pitching—especially by Peña—would dominate.

The opening week also included a near no-hitter on October 12 by Marianao right-hander Al Cicotte, the great-nephew of Chicago White Sox pitcher Eddie Cicotte, one of the eight members of the "Black Sox" banned from baseball for throwing the 1919 World Series. The younger Cicotte, a pitcher with the Detroit Tigers, surrendered only one hit, a single by Habana outfielder Willie Tasby in the second inning. It wasn't enough to keep Marianao from winning 2–1, but it was enough to deny

Cicotte the $1,000 prize offered by *Bohemia* magazine to any pitcher tossing a no-hitter.[21]

John Buzhardt, who went on to an eleven-year Major League career, missed his chance at the prize on October 19 when Tony Taylor's fourth-inning double was the only hit off of the Habana right-hander, who beat Almendares 1–0. Of the season's first eighteen games, seven were shutouts and three came by 1–0 scores. Lasorda tossed one of those shutouts, a 5–0 victory against Habana on October 13, before losing 5–0 to Camilo Pascual and Cienfuegos on October 18.

Lasorda, a Brooklyn Dodgers farmhand who had led the International League with 18 victories with the Montreal Royals in 1958, had last played in the Cuban League in 1951–52 for Almendares. That was the season Lasorda permanently etched his name into Cuban League folklore thanks to a brawl with Marianao first baseman Lorenzo "Chiquitín" Cabrera. "He had gotten three really cheap hits off me, three bleeders, and I told reporters that he was very lucky, and he would not get one hit off me the next time I faced him," Lasorda recounted in his 1985 autobiography. "He responded by warning me that the next time he faced me he would 'cut my legs off.' . . . When I heard that, I warned him that the next time he batted against me I was going to put him in the hospital."[22]

The next time came during a Saturday night game on January 5, 1952. It was Ladies' Night and there was a packed house at El Gran Stadium. After Lasorda retired the first two batters in the first inning, Cabrera came to the plate. The first pitch came at Cabrera's neck, knocking him to the ground. On the second pitch, Cabrera swung and let the bat slip out of his hands, sending it spinning toward Lasorda's legs. The left-hander drilled Cabrera in the ribs on the next pitch. Carrying his 38-ounce bat, the six-foot-one, 220-pound Cabrera charged Lasorda, who was all of five feet ten inches and 175 pounds. "It's amazing how quickly your mind functions in a life-threatening situation," Lasorda wrote. "Run, I thought, because this guy has a bat and he's going to try to kill you.

But before I took that first step, I thought, no way, either he kills me or I kill him."[23]

Lasorda threw his glove in Cabrera's face. As Cabrera swung his bat, Lasorda ducked, grabbed Cabrera's jersey with one hand and the inside of his leg with the other and flipped the big first baseman to the ground. The crowd roared as players from both teams pulled the combatants apart. Umpire Pat Padden tripped while running out to intervene, the fall knocking him unconscious. He had to be taken to a hospital for observation.[24] Cabrera was ejected from the game and later suspended for the remainder of the season by league president Rafael Inclán. Teammates appreciated Lasorda's fighting spirit. "Lasorda was a guy who helped a lot," recalled Orlando Peña, who played two seasons with the feisty lefty. "He was always fighting with the opposition and helping us. . . . Lasorda was tremendous. He was a tremendous guy."[25] Some opponents weren't always so complimentary. "I didn't like Tommy, never did," said Eduardo Bauta, who played for Marianao from 1958 to 1960. "He was a mean, nasty son of bitch, man. He had a bad temper."[26]

Since the start of 1958, Batista had been promising to hold "fair" elections, an objective that only grew in urgency after the United States imposed an embargo on arms shipments to the Batista regime in March. "It would be entirely contrary to our policy to intervene in [Cuban] affairs," the U.S. state department said, "and we do not intend to become involved."[27] Batista hoped an election that would allow a hand-picked successor to win would also resolve his Castro problem. Batista eventually settled on November 3 as the day Cubans would cast their ballots for a new president.

But as that date approached, Cuba bore little resemblance to a country about to participate in a peaceful transition of power. Constitutional guarantees had been suspended; newspapers, magazines, and television and radio stations operated under strict censorship; and Batista's armed forces tried to maintain order. Havana was a city wracked by acts of sabotage, armed conflicts, and sporadic bombings. So many explosions rocked Havana one night that it came to be known as the "Night of One Hundred Bombs." Rail service in Oriente was almost non-existent, and few trains operated in Camagüey and Las Villas as Castro-led rebels battled the army in hit-and-run guerilla engagements. As the election approached, rebels threatened to attack any vehicles moving on highways and trains running in the country's eastern provinces. Despite the turmoil and violence, Batista declared that "no one but God" can stop the election.[28]

Cuban voters would have four candidates from which to choose: Andrés Rivero Agüero, representing the government's four-party coalition; former president Ramón Grau San Martín of the Auténtico party; Dr. Carlos Márquez Sterling of the Free People's party; and newspaper publisher Alberto Salas Amaro, representing the Cuban Union party. Grau said he believed voters would turn out at the polls despite rebel threats, but added that the election was being held "under a hail of bullets and without guarantees."[29] The underground Civic Resistance Movement urged voters to remain in their homes and not vote as a protest against a "farcical" election.[30] Two nights before the election, nine bombs exploded in Havana. Although they caused considerable property damage, no injuries were reported, and the city remained tranquil on the eve of the election.

On Election Day, Cuba's army and navy were on alert, police guarded the polls, and military intelligence and secret agents circulated throughout the capital. The election was held in relative calm as the predicted violence failed to materialize. Not surprisingly, Rivero Agüero won the election when the army headquarters announced the vote totals. Batista's handpicked successor had 651,840 votes, easily outpacing the other three candidates: Márquez Sterling (136,664), Grau (103,208), and Salas Amaro (38,024). Rivero Agüero issued a statement praising the "demonstration of love of the republic in going to the polls." But Grau called the elections a "simulation," and said, "The people have lost the elections."[31] Rivero Agüero was scheduled to be inaugurated as Cuba's next president on February 24, 1959. He would never take office.

The Griffith family had ties to baseball in Cuba dating to 1911, when then–Cincinnati Reds manager Clark Griffith signed Cuban players Armando Marsans and Rafael Almeida. Later as owner of the Washington Senators, Griffith employed Joe Cambria to scout Cuban players beginning in the 1930s. But Griffith's nephew and adopted son Calvin became one of the Cuban League's greatest detractors after gaining control of the Senators upon his uncle's death in 1955. He bemoaned the impact the league was having on his ace Cuban pitchers Camilo Pascual and Pedro Ramos and tried to keep the pair from playing in their homeland during the winter of 1958. All it took to change his mind was one visit to Cuba.

Griffith spent five days in Havana in late October, calling the experience an "eye opener," and heaped praise on the Cuban League. "I was amazed to find the four Cuban teams playing in a modern stadium as well-groomed and well-kept as any of our big-league parks," Griffith told *The Sporting News*. "Our players were living in air-conditioned apartments and homes.... I had pictured poor playing, living and eating conditions and, frankly, I was skeptical about granting my men permission to play there." Despite the ongoing political situation, Griffith expressed little concern. "The present political tensions seem to have affected baseball very little," he said. "However, at each turnstile into Gran Stadium, there is an armed policeman or soldier standing alongside the ticket-taker. He frisks everyone who enters for possible guns or explosives. They have had no trouble, however, at the ball park."[32]

Indeed, El Gran Stadium, along with Oriental Racetrack, were among the places some Havana residents could go to escape the daily turmoil. After a one-day break in the schedule for the election, the Cuban League resumed play on November 4, and pitching continued to dominate. During a seven-day stretch from November 13 to November 19, three 1–0 shutouts were recorded, raising the total for the season to sixteen. By November 19, one in every three games was a shutout. With pitching at such a premium, it was unusual to see Cienfuegos—despite a rotation that included Pascual and Ramos—mired in last place. The pair had combined for twenty-three victories two winters earlier, but by the end of November Pascual and Ramos each had compiled 2-5 records, and Cienfuegos had lost sixteen of seventeen games.

Third-place Habana, hoping to climb into contention, traded shortstop Leo Cárdenas and outfielder Román Mejías to Cienfuegos in exchange for shortstop Humberto Fernández and power-hitting first baseman Panchón Herrera on November 24, only to see Herrera sustain a fractured right leg sliding into second base six days later. The season was shaping up as a two-team race between Almendares and Marianao—not surprising, given that the Cuban League's first pitcher- and player-of-the-month awards (the initial award, given in conjunction with Union Radio, covered October and November) went to Marianao pitcher Al Cicotte and Almendares's Tony Taylor.

Cicotte led the way for Marianao with a 7-2 record and 1.10 ERA heading into December. Taylor was the only position player in the league batting above .300. After batting .311 the previous winter, Taylor had a .331 average at the end of November. A native of Central Alava in Matanzas Province, Taylor had batted .235 in his rookie year with the Chicago Cubs in 1958. He would go on to play nineteen seasons in the Majors, mostly with the Philadelphia Phillies. He began his Cuban League career with Marianao in 1954 but was traded after one winter to Almendares for shortstop José Valdivielso. "I started with Marianao, but I always associated myself more with Almendares," Taylor recalled years later. "That's where I made myself a ballplayer, in Cuba, and I made myself a ballplayer with Almendares. I made myself a Major League ballplayer in my homeland, and with Almendares. That's where I began to develop in my baseball career."[33]

After the failure of the April 9 general strike, Batista had deployed some ten thousand soldiers into the Sierra Maestra in May in hopes of wiping out the rebels. But the guerillas held off the army for two months. "Every entrance to the Sierra Maestra is like the pass at Thermopylae," Castro told visiting journalists, recalling the ancient battle between a Spartan-led Greek army and the Persian Empire.[34] It was a turning point in the war, and in August, Castro ordered Che Guevara into the central province of Las Villas and Camilo Cienfuegos into the western province of Pinar del Rio. Part of their mission was to reassert Castro's authority over the Second Front of the Escambray, a rival rebel group that had control over the central mountain range 250 miles southeast of Havana. Guevara arrived in the hills of Las Villas in October, and Castro began his march toward Santiago de Cuba in November.[35]

With Cuban newspapers and television and radio stations under strict government censorship, residents and visitors to Havana would have had little indication of this military activity in the local media during the final month of 1958. What little reporting on the fighting appeared in Havana newspapers focused on rebel casualties. Throughout December, the English-language *Havana Post* carried sporadic headlines such as "Report 94 Rebels Die in Three New Clashes," "180 Rebel Casualties Reported in Oriente," and "21 Rebels Reported Killed in 2 Clashes." Such reports noticeably omitted information about casualties or losses among Batista's forces.

To get around government censorship, Havana residents tuned into rebel-controlled Radio Rebelde for updates on the fighting. Each night at 7 and 9 p.m. on the twenty-meter band and at 8 and 10 p.m. on the forty-meter band, the announcer on 7RR began the reports by shouting, "¡Aquí, Radio Rebelde, transmitiendo desde el territorio libre de Cuba!" (This is Rebel Radio, transmitting from the free territory of Cuba!).[36] Those nightly reports informed Cubans across the country of repeated victories by rebels, who numbered some seven thousand men and were outnumbered by Batista's army at least ten to one.[37] Despite those odds, it was becoming clear to the U.S. state department that Batista would not last.

The death knell came on December 17, when U.S. ambassador Earl E. T. Smith met with Batista at his Kuquine country house. Three days earlier, the ambassador had received instructions from the State Department to inform the Cuban president he had to leave Cuba if peace was to be restored in the country. Smith had urged Washington to support Batista and Rivero Agüero, including with arms shipments. "The danger," Smith wrote in a telegram to Washington, "is that any action taken on our part to weaken Batista without setting up a strong replacement backed by the U.S. would automatically strengthen Castro and thereby benefit the Communists."[38] But U.S. president Dwight Eisenhower's administration refused to back a president-elect who did not have mass appeal among Cubans.

Smith delivered the news to an expressionless Batista: Washington viewed Batista's presence in Cuba as the primary hindrance to peace. The two-and-a-half-hour meeting convinced Batista to consider Smith's suggestion to leave the country. On December 22, Batista met with Brigadier General Silito Tabernilla, his military liaison and the son of Cuba's armed forces chief, at Camp Columbia. Batista dictated a detailed list of hundreds of names of those who should be notified in the event of an emergency. Tabernilla wrote the names on three pieces of paper, one for each plane that would be used to escape. "Keep the list in your pocket," Batista told Tabernilla. "Never separate yourself from it." Tabernilla asked where Batista would be going. "I'll decide that in the air."[39]

The ads began appearing in Havana magazine's such as *Bohemia* and newspapers such as *Diario de la Marina* in the weeks and days leading up to the Christmas holidays. The white letters on a black background repeated the same question: "¿Qué es 03C? ¿Qué es 03C?" (What is 03C? What is 03C?). The campaign was the brainchild of Emilio Guede, propaganda chief for the Civic Resistance Movement. Amid the anxiety permeating Havana, residents had cut back on Christmas spending. The Civic Resistance hoped to extend that frugality into a full-fledged spending boycott to put economic pressure on the regime. "Everybody thought it was an ad for a rum or a whiskey or something, a drink," Ralph Ávila said. "That came out of my office [at Bacardi]. That check came out of my office to pay *Bohemia*."[40]

The influential magazine for years had railed against Batista and been a staunch supporter of Castro, publishing his Sierra Maestra Manifesto on July 26. So *Bohemia* owner Miguel Ángel Quevedo Pérez would have had no issues running the ad. Other publications might not have been so bold. To avoid the scrutiny of censors, newspaper ad salesmen were told the ads were a teaser for a campaign for hair tonic and that 03c meant *cero calvicie* (zero baldness), *cero caspa* (zero dandruff), and *cero canas* (zero gray hair). In fact, it stood for *cero cinema* (zero movies), *cero compra* (zero purchases), *cero cabaret* (zero cabaret). That became obvious when Radio Rebelde started explaining the ads when they began appearing.

> **First announcer:** What is 03c? What is 03c? Now Radio Rebelde brings you the answer. Pay attention! Because 03c is a matter of life or death for you!
>
> **Second announcer:** What is 03c?
>
> **Third announcer:** What is 03c?
>
> **Fourth announcer:** 03c?
>
> **Fifth announcer:** It is the watchword for public shame! Zero cinema. Zero consumer purchases. Zero cabaret. Movement of the Civic Resistance.
>
> **Chorus:** If all of Cuba is at war; don't you go to the cabaret.[41]

Despite Radio Rebelde making the mistake of revealing the campaign's purpose before all the ads had run, censors failed to pull any of the ads.

Cleveland Indians general manager Frank Lane was becoming something of a regular visitor to Havana in the winter of 1958.

And he spent his latest visit reassuring the Cuban press. It was believed Lane opposed Latino players participating in Caribbean leagues. Lane called that perception "a big mistake" when he addressed the Havana Sports Writers' Association at a luncheon in his honor on December 16. "It doesn't disturb me in the least if Minnie Miñoso, my favorite player, plays in Havana during the winter," Lane said. "It would be a crime if Cuban players, for instance, wouldn't be allowed to play in this country." Lane also said he backed Cuban League president Arturo Bengochea's plan to allow all Latino Major Leaguers to continue playing in winter ball. "I give you my word," he said, "that when the majors get together next February I'll be the first to defend the cause of Latin-American winter ball."[42]

Satisfied by Lane's assurances, the writers could once again focus on the Cuban League race, which had tightened by mid-December. Trailing Marianao by a half game coming into the month, Almendares had overtaken the Tigers and opened a four-game lead by December 10. Marianao started chipping away at that lead, but could get no closer than a game and a half of the league-leading Scorpions in December, at least in part because of Orlando Peña. The Almendares right-hander owned Marianao. Beginning on November 29, Peña recorded four consecutive victories against the Tigers, the last of which came on December 20. Peña's 2–1 win was his ninth of the season and sixth against Marianao. "He was a very intelligent pitcher, apart from that he used spit," Cuban League broadcaster Felo Ramírez said. "He was a lion with that."[43]

Peña's dominance of Marianao was indicative of the overall mastery of pitching in the Cuban League as the circuit approached its eightieth anniversary on December 29. The Sunday before the actual milestone date, Lázaro Salazar, who had died the previous year, and José Acosta, one of the league's early stars, were inducted into the Cuban Baseball Hall of Fame. The ceremony, held between games of a doubleheader at the Gate 1 entrance to El Gran Stadium, also included the unveiling of a bust of Cuban baseball icon Adolfo Luque, who had been inducted the previous year. December 28 also saw Habana's John Buzhardt shut out Cienfuegos 2–0 to eclipse the previous league record of 30 shutouts in a season, set in 1947–48. The new standard didn't last. Pedro Ramos shut out Marianao 6–0 on Monday, and Almendares's John Romonosky shut out Cienfuegos 2–0 on Tuesday.

In a span of eight days from December 23 to December 30, there were six shutouts among the nine games played. By the end of the month, Marianao's Al Cicotte was leading the league with five shutouts, while teammate Mike Fornieles, Peña, and Buzhardt each had four. Pascual and Almendares's Art Fowler each had three. Fornieles brought the year to a close by beating Habana 5–3 on New Year's Eve. The pitcher helped his own cause with a home run in the third inning. Marianao trailed Almendares by three and a half games. When players left El Gran Stadium to celebrate the New Year, none of them could have imagined the seismic events that would take place in the early morning hours of January 1.

6

New Year's Revolution

In the closing days of 1958, *bolas*—a slang term for rumors—became an essential information source for Havana residents. The heavily censored newspaper, television, and radio reports could not be relied upon, and *bolas* about a possible coup and Batista's imminent downfall were rampant. Residents looked for any sign that might indicate when the end might come. With the same mood that had squelched Christmas spending still permeating the city, many in Havana opted for small private gatherings on New Year's Eve.

That's how Almendares infielder Miguel de la Hoz planned to ring in the new year. The Scorpions did not have a game scheduled for December 31, and De la Hoz was going to spend the night with his family. "I lived in Havana at the house of one of my aunts, where I stayed when I was playing baseball," De la Hoz recalled years later. "My parents came from about forty kilometers outside Havana to spend New Year's Eve at my aunt's house. The situation in Cuba wasn't good. They were setting off bombs. Things were very ugly."[1]

On the morning of December 31, Batista awoke in the private quarters of the presidential palace shortly before 11 a.m. He directed his aide-de-camp to invite government leaders to a low-key midnight buffet at his home at Camp Columbia. Later in the afternoon, the Cuban president was driven to his country house at Kuquine, where he called Silito Tabernilla. "I want you to come to Kuquine," Batista told his military liaison. "Bring my passport. And the list."[2] Tabernilla arrived at Kuquine to find ashen-faced officials before joining Batista in his office. "Tonight we go," Batista said. "About one o'clock." With that, Tabernilla had two tasks: Make sure everyone on the list would attend the buffet and that Batista's personal plane and two from the Aerovías Q airlines were prepped and ready to fly.[3]

The atmosphere at Batista's Camp Columbia home was somber by the time the president's motorcade arrived at 11:50 p.m. When the clock struck twelve, Batista toasted the New Year with a cup of coffee spiked with brandy. Not long after wishing the group *felicidades*, Batista gathered his military leaders in his downstairs office. Without explanation, he read from a two-page, handwritten speech:

> That in the early morning of this day came to his residence the high military chiefs who have charge of the highest military commands, advising him of the impossibility of establishing order in the republic, considering that the situation is grave and, appealing to the patriotism of all those present and to the president's love for his people, saying that he should resign his office. . . . That taking into consideration the loss of life and material goods, and the obvious injury to the national life and to the economy of the republic . . . he resigns his powers of the presidency of the republic, surrendering them to his constitutional successor.[4]

There was stunned silence as Batista initialed the document and passed it around the room for all gathered to sign it. At around 2 a.m., Anselmo Alliergo, president of the Cuban Senate, burst out of the office and announced to the guests, "Batista's resigning!" It was at that moment President-elect Rivero Agüero realized for the first time he would never take office. "Grab your wives," Batista told his nervous guests. "Get in your cars. Don't tell your chauffeurs or bodyguards anything. Get in the planes. The engines are running."[5]

When the door to Batista's house opened, politicians, military leaders, and their respective wives scrambled to their waiting limousines and made a mad dash for Camp Columbia's airfield. The military men were able to drag valuables from homes in the camp to the planes in hastily packed suitcases. The others had no such benefit. "The scene was like a bizarre dream, lit by the stark brilliance of the floodlights atop the headquarters," authors John Dorschner and Roberto Fabricio wrote in their 1980 book, *The Winds of December.* "Women in evening gowns were tugging at their children. Husbands' faces were contorted in fear. All were hurrying toward two Aerovías Q planes."[6] At 2:40 a.m., the DC-4 carrying the former Cuban president took off from Runway 9. The Batista era was over.

In his autobiography, Tom Lasorda describes a scene from that night that may be apocryphal. Despite the mood in Havana, he and Almendares teammates Art Fowler and Bob Allison had decided to take their wives out on the town for New Year's Eve. The three couples were leaving a party on the beach in the early morning hours of January 1 when they noticed an unusual sight. "Three large planes flew low overhead," Lasorda wrote. "I wondered who would be flying that late at night. It turned out to have been Batista and his cabinet fleeing the country."[7]

The Cuban New Year's Eve tradition of eating twelve grapes at midnight had long passed when most Havana residents started learning about Batista's departure. "I remember that I was in my house and my mom called me," Marianao shortstop José Valdivielso recalled. "I was sleeping. My mom said, 'Listen, Fulgencio Batista left the country.' That's all I remember about that *epopeya* (epic), like us Cubans used to say."[8] Almendares infielder Miguel de la Hoz was still at his aunt's house when he found out. "I don't know if somebody called the house or something," he said, "but my aunt's husband, his name was Ramón, said, 'Batista just left.' It was about one in the morning or something like that, around the time that we found out. And everything was calm because it was the middle of the night, at least in the area where I lived. The next day was when there were things happening."[9]

It was a chaotic scene at Havana's Rancho-Boyeros Airport at 8 a.m. People were still dressed in tuxedoes and evening gowns from the night's festivities as they desperately tried to board flights to leave the country. Early flights had managed to leave on time. But members of the 26th of July Movement—having heard that Batista had fled the country—shut down the airport. The last plane to leave was the 9:19 a.m. Cubana Airways flight bound for New York, its pilot forced to take off at gunpoint.[10]

It was shortly after 8 a.m. in Oriente when Fidel Castro was informed that Batista had left Cuba. Castro flew into a rage and began barking orders. Fearing that Batista's departure might allow forces other than his Movement to take control of the government, Castro recorded a message that was then broadcast by Radio Rebelde. "Whatever the news from the capital may be, our troops should not stop fighting at any time," Castro implored. "The dictatorship has collapsed as a consequence of the crushing defeats suffered in the last weeks, but that does not mean the revolution already has triumphed. ¡Revolución, sí! ¡Golpe militar, no! [Revolution, yes! Military coup, no!]."[11] Castro ordered Camilo Cienfuegos to advance his column immediately to Havana and take control of Camp Columbia. Che Guevara was ordered to lead his column to Havana's La Cabaña fortress.

A doubleheader was scheduled for January 1, pitting Marianao's Bob Shaw against Cienfuegos's Tony Díaz in the opener and Almendares's Art Fowler against Habana's John Buzhardt in the nightcap. Cienfuegos third baseman Johnny Goryl was unaware anything had happened while he slept. But something clearly wasn't right when Goryl, teammate Bob Will, and two other players drove to El Gran Stadium for their afternoon game. "As we were driving, everything was boarded up," Goryl recalled. "All the windows, they had these hurricane shutters on them. They had them all pulled and there was not a lot of traffic on the roads. I kind of happened to make the comment that, 'Man, these people really celebrated New Year's Eve last night. There's nothing [open] in this whole city.'"[12]

That was true even as the players approached downtown and the stadium. When Goryl walked into the team's clubhouse at the stadium, he found Cienfuegos's Cuban players, including Camilo Pascual and Pedro Ramos, gathered in a corner of the room talking excitedly. Goryl called Pascual aside and asked his teammate what was happening.

Pascual: It looks like Batista fled the country, and Castro might be coming into power here in Cuba, but we don't know that to be true. We're waiting to get word on that.

Goryl: What about the ballgame?

Pascual: If he [Batista] has left, chances are we're not going to play.

Pascual turned out to be right. "About an hour or so later, that's what happened," Goryl said. "He had fled, and then all hell broke loose. As quiet as it was coming into the ballpark, it was just as noisy leaving the ballpark. There was looting in the streets. People were knocking over these parking meters and grabbing all the money out of the parking meters."[13]

People in Havana had taken to the streets, at first to celebrate. But celebrations quickly turned to demonstrations, which evolved into rioting and looting. Parking meters, used to line Batista regime coffers, were targeted by angry rioters. Police and military units, once a ubiquitous presence on the streets, were almost nowhere to be found. Casinos, another symbol of Batista's corrupt regime, also became a prime target after the rebels had vowed for months to shut down legalized gambling in Cuba. Angry mobs ransacked casinos at the Capri, Plaza, Sevilla Biltmore, St. John's, and Deauville hotels, dragging slot machines and gaming tables into the streets, beating them with sledgehammers and setting them ablaze.[14]

Members of the Movement commandeered the CMQ television studios to proclaim a prohibition on alcohol sales, call for a general strike, and plead with rebel sympathizers to stop the destruction. Castro's speech was rebroadcast. All commercial businesses closed. The Cuban League suspended play. "It was scary because it was so uncertain. . . . We didn't know what was going to happen," recalled Tom Lasorda's wife, Jo. "Until all that happened it was wonderful. It was beautiful. It was like going to Miami or Newport Beach or anything like that. We had a wonderful time until that all happened."[15]

Castro's fears of a military coup or U.S. intervention short-circuiting the revolution proved to be unfounded. With much of its leadership abandoning the island, the Cuban military essentially collapsed. Soldiers at cartels across the country began surrendering to rebel forces. After securing the loyalty of the army at the Moncada Barracks on January 1, Castro led a two-mile caravan of trucks and jeeps through the streets of Santiago to cheers of "¡Viva Fidel! ¡Viva la revolución!" He addressed an adoring crowd of ten thousand people at the city's Céspedes Park at 2:15 a.m. the next morning and declared, "The revolution is now beginning." After a few hours' sleep, Castro would lead a caravan on what became a six-day trek along Cuba's Central Highway toward Havana.

Back in the capital, Camilo Cienfuegos and the five hundred men of Column 2 entered Camp Columbia at 6:30 p.m. on January 2, and Cienfuegos took command without incident. Before dawn the next day, Guevara and his three hundred men were approaching Havana. Ralph Ávila had been sent out from Havana to meet the caravan and guide Guevara into the city and to La Cabaña. "I found them in Matanzas; from there, I was the guide," Ávila said. "I was in a provided jeep. Che was in a Sherman tank on top of a trailer truck. And behind him, when they left Santa Clara, they had fifty to sixty cars. When we entered Havana on January 3, we brought more than two hundred cars behind us. That was incredible because in every town we kept adding and adding and adding."[16]

Guevara arrived at La Cabaña at 10:30 in the morning, and the commander of the fortress relinquished command. "They were waiting for us with open arms," Ávila said. "Batista's soldiers said, 'Why did it take you so long to get there?' They prepared breakfast for us, tin jugs with *café con leche* and bread.

They [the rebels] had gone four of five days without eating, and Ché said, 'No, no, no. Wait, wait.' He grabbed a few of Batista's guards and said, 'You guys drink that *café con leche* first and eat the bread to see if it's poisoned.'" In retelling the story, Ávila allowed himself a laugh and added an aside about Guevara: "*Ese era el diablo* [He was the devil]. And after they [the soldiers] tried it [the food], then we ate."[17]

Ávila continued to help the Revolution at La Cabaña, where he got to know Guevara all too well. "The most piggish pig in the world with the most unpleasant smell," Ávila said. "The way that man sweated was disgusting." According to Ávila, Guevara, while fighting in the Sierra Maestra, impregnated several women. "I remember they would come to La Cabaña, and he would attend to them and ordered that they be given money for the kids he had scattered all over the place," Ávila said. "But I knew him and had to stand next to him. I thought, 'How can women get close to a guy who is such a pig and so disgusting?'"[18]

Given the turmoil in Havana, baseball commissioner Ford Frick notified each of the sixteen Major League clubs that they were "free to order their players out of Cuba if they felt so inclined regardless of the players' contractual obligations with Cuban teams." That option had been in place just before the New Year because of the "imminent revolutionary situation." But Frick insisted that organized baseball would not "compel American players to return to the United States or stop playing baseball in Cuba if they do not wish to do so."[19] Not that the players had much choice. "We couldn't leave here if we wanted to," Almendares pitcher Art Fowler told the *Spokane Chronicle*. "There just aren't any planes."[20]

Washington Senators president Calvin Griffith considered withdrawing his four American players—pitchers Jim Constable and John Romonosky and outfielders Albie Pearson and Bob Allison—but decided against it after consulting with the U.S. state department. "I . . . was told none of the ballplayers should be in danger unless they took an active part in the rebellion," Griffith said. "The American players are quartered about 20 blocks from the center of Havana and should be in no immediate danger."[21]

In the immediate days after the fall of Batista, most Havana residents were staying indoors to avoid trouble. That was the case for Fowler, who was staying on the beach at the Chateau Miramar. "Our hotel was guarded by rebel forces, and we couldn't leave at night or approach the business district in the daytime," said Fowler, who would play nine seasons in the Majors and gain fame as a pitching coach with the New York Yankees in the 1970s and 1980s. "However, I am convinced the rebel army was only trying to protect the innocent citizenry by placing restrictions on activity."[22]

The major concern was food as the general strike held and businesses remained closed. "My son was a baby at the time, and it was awful because they had closed the American store," Jo Lasorda said. "This one Cuban gentleman walked miles to get me baby food."[23] When stores finally opened, Fowler "stood in line for two hours to buy provisions."[24] He had it easy compared to what Goryl experienced when he ventured out for supplies. "When we were standing in line waiting to get into that supermarket," Goryl said, "up drives this military convoy vehicle. A whole bunch of soldiers come pouring out of the back of these trucks with rifles and they were trained on the crowd. They thought we were looting. Fortunately, nothing happened. They dispersed [the crowd] and told us to get on our way. We did and got the hell out of there."[25]

By January 5, tensions had reached the point that Camilo Cienfuegos declared martial law even as Castro's handpicked candidate to be Cuba's next president arrived in Havana. Manuel Urrutia, an obscure anti-Batista judge, had been designated as "President in Arms." After his c-47 arrived at Rancho-Boyeros Airport at 4 p.m., Urrutia held a news conference at the presidential palace at 7 p.m. He restored the civil rights granted by the 1940 constitution and called off the general strike. The next day, Urrutia dissolved the Cuban Congress and announced

Cuba would be ruled by decree for at least eighteen months until elections could be held. He also declared his opposition to all forms of gambling. Slowly Havana started to return to normal as buses resumed operating, sanitation workers collected garbage off the streets, and movie theaters and night-clubs reopened. "We believe," a *Diario de la Marina* editorial proclaimed, "in the rebirth of the country."[26]

Normalcy also meant the resumption of the Cuban League. A festive mood permeated El Gran Stadium as teams returned to the field with a doubleheader on January 6. Marianao beat Cienfuegos 5–1 in the first game, giving Al Cicotte his tenth victory of the season. Almendares and Habana played to a twelve-inning 1–1 tie in the nightcap. All members of the rebel army were admitted into the ballpark for free, and bearded soldiers hobnobbed with native and American players before the game. "Most observers," *The Sporting News* concluded, "are agreed that sports will have a brilliant future here under the new regime."[27]

As Castro rode from town to town along the Central Highway, more and more people joined the convoy. Peasants lined the route to get a glimpse of Cuba's latest revolutionary hero. And at each stop, Castro would speak to pleading crowds for two to three hours. Jules Dubois of the *Chicago Tribune* and Carlos Castañeda of *Bohemia* magazine caught up with Castro in Holguín. "You can be sure that we will be friendly to the United States," Castro told the journalists, "as long as the United States is friendly to us." Castro also addressed the persistent rumor that the 26th of July Movement was a Communist revolution. "That," Castro said, "is a lie held up by Batista."[28]

The United States extended formal diplomatic recognition to Cuba's new revolutionary government on January 7, and the next day Castro's caravan finally arrived at El Cotorro on the outskirts of Havana. By then, the ranks of the victory column had swelled to between five thousand to six thousand people, making it nearly impossible to navigate through the streets. "I lived in El Cotorro," recalled Habana relief pitcher Evelio

Hernández. "When the *barbudos*, Fidel Castro and the rest of them, came from Oriente toward Havana, I lived on a street that ran exactly like the Central Highway, but my street didn't have an exit. They came cutting a path through the whole roadway. But my street didn't have an exit, and they had to go back. There was Fidel and all the bigshots, they came in that jeep. I shot film. Unfortunately, when I left Cuba, I left it behind."[29]

Eventually, Castro made his way to the presidential palace, where he and Urrutia appeared together on the balcony to address the crowd. Almendares pitcher Gonzalo "Cholly" Naranjo, who had pitched with the Pittsburgh Pirates in 1956, lived just off the Central Highway. He and his brother had gone to the entrance of their neighborhood to watch Castro from the roof of a school as the caravan entered the city. "Later, my cousin and I, we got on the trucks that followed the caravan to the presidential palace, because all the girls were going on the trucks," Naranjo recalled. "I went with them to the presidential palace. I stayed on El Malecón watching when he [Castro] spoke on the northern terrace of the presidential palace."[30]

Castro invited the gathered crowd to follow him to Camp Columbia, because it "belongs to the people now."[31] It was 9 p.m. when he entered the camp and addressed the crowd there. As Castro spoke, two white doves landed on the podium and a third on his shoulder. Whether it was an amazing coincidence or the result of superb stagecraft, *Diario de la Marina* declared it "a sign from the Lord who is sending us the universal symbol of the peace which we all desire." During the speech, Castro insisted, "We cannot ever become dictators. . . . We will never turn away from our principles."[32]

Cholly Naranjo didn't follow Castro to Camp Columbia, because his Almendares club had a game that night. The Scorpions beat Habana 5–3, giving Tom Lasorda his seventh victory of the season. Afterward, he was given permission to return briefly to the States. "We had to leave because Tommy's father was sick and my son was sick too," Jo Lasorda said. "There were still guns everywhere, even when we left to get on the plane to come home."[33] Tom Lasorda returned to Cuba in time for the January 14 All-Star Game that pitted the best Cuban players against the best players from North America. The Cuban team won 4–3 as Julio Bécquer and Albie Pearson each hit home runs. On January 18, Habana third baseman Héctor Rodríguez collected the thousandth hit of his prestigious Cuban League career. Rodríguez had played in the Cuban League since 1942, mostly with Almendares, and he became the first and only player to reach that milestone with a hit against Camilo Pascual as Cienfuegos won 2–1.

Since the league resumed play, Almendares managed to extend its lead despite losing its manager. Oscar Rodríguez had suffered a heart attack on January 1, and assistant coach Clemente "Sungo" Carreras had to take over the team. With Carreras at the helm, the Scorpions won 15 of 18 games and clinched the pennant on January 28, almost two weeks before the end of the season. It was Almendares's first title since the 1954–55 season. "Sungo took the reins," Naranjo said. "He was a coach, a trusted guy with the Almendares owners, and Sungo won the championship."[34]

Romonosky beat Cienfuegos 4–1 in the title-clinching game. As had been the case before the season was interrupted, pitching dominated. Almendares second baseman Tony Taylor (.303) was the only player to bat over .300. Nine pitchers had earned-run averages under 2.00, and hurlers combined for a league-record-shattering 44 shutouts. Marianao had the best team ERA at 1.89, led by Al Cicotte, whose 1.38 mark led the league as he won 13 games. But no one dominated like Almendares's Orlando Peña, who went 15-5 with a 1.58 ERA. He beat Marianao twelve times as the Scorpions finished the season 8 games ahead of the second-place Tigers. Peña was named the league's Most Valuable Player. "He was an extremely valiant guy with great control," Naranjo said. "He was a remarkable person. He came from some corner of the republic and practically without any instruction—he had never been outside those distant little towns on the island—but had a sense for the game and an intelligence that was admirable."[35]

Most members of the Havana Mob fled Cuba in the days immediately following Batista's departure. After spending several days tending to his Hotel Riviera, which was spared from any damage during the rioting, Meyer Lansky left for Miami on January 7, only to be subpoenaed by a U.S. Senate select committee investigating improper labor activities the next day as Castro arrived in Havana. Despite Urrutia's initial pronouncements about gambling, Castro on January 10 announced that foreign tourists would be allowed to continue gambling in Cuba, and casinos would eventually reopen in February as the country once again rolled out the welcome mat for foreign visitors.

But all was not well. The adoring crowds that greeted Castro's arrival in Havana had barely dispersed before the executions started. They began in Santiago de Cuba in Oriente Province and spread to Las Villas and Camagüey provinces as officers in Batista's armed forces faced military tribunals for "war crimes." Those convicted by the summary courts-martial of torture and murder were put to death by firing squads. "If there is one blot on its record thus far," a *New York Times* editorial admonished in its January 9 editions, "it is the summary executions of former opponents and the proposed 'war crimes' trial of hundreds more."[36]

Eventually, the tribunals moved to Havana. Despite concerns raised in the United States, Castro insisted the revolutionary courts would continue "until all criminals of the Batista regime are tried. While the revolutionists have profound human feelings, they would not retreat before any pressure."[37] By mid-January, around two hundred executions had been carried out, and some six hundred people were imprisoned at La Cabaña, awaiting trials. From his exile in the Dominican Republic, Batista—whose own regime was accused of persecuting thousands of citizens—decried the revolutionary trials, saying Castro was causing a "river of blood." Batista denounced the executions as "a symptom of barbarism."[38] With the first Havana courts-martial for some thousand "war criminals" set to begin, the Cuban League cancelled games on January 21 because of a mass rally called by Castro to whip up public support for the tribunals.

The first courts-martial began on January 22 in the Sports City Stadium in front of approximately eighteen thousand frenzied spectators. "It hurts to say this, but there were Cuban married couples who would come to watch the executions," former anti-Batista activist René Brioso recalled. "Not only would they come, but they would bring their children to watch. Even if they didn't know the person who was being executed or anything. They only went there to watch and cheer and laugh. That's all they did."[39]

7

Caribbean Spice

After the triumph of the revolution, gun-toting rebel soldiers became a common sight at El Gran Stadium. They watched Cuban League games from the stands, hung out in the teams' dugouts, and posed for photographs with players, such as Tom Lasorda, Charlie Lau, and Rocky Nelson, who mugged for the cameras while holding the rebels' firearms. In a game in which Almendares catcher Dick Brown hit a home run, a pair of soldiers—rifles slung over their shoulders—ran out onto the field to greet Brown and escort him back to the dugout, where they remained during the game.

The two became almost like mascots for the team. As it appeared Almendares would indeed win the Cuban League title, the Scorpions asked Felipe Guerra Matos, Cuba's new director of sports, for permission to bring the soldiers to Caracas, Venezuela, for the eleventh annual Caribbean Series so they could carry the Cuban flag in the opening ceremonies. "They were two of the guys who had fought in Oriente, and these two always went to games, big fans of Almendares," said infielder Miguel de la Hoz. "When we won the championship, Monchy de Arcos, who was president of Almendares, invited them to fly on the plane with us for free and to stay with us there [in Caracas], and the team paid their costs."[1]

As was the case when they had attended games at El Gran Stadium, the soldiers were well armed, carrying their ever-present guns, when they boarded the Cubana Aviación flight to Caracas. Clearly the players were used to being in the presence of armed soldiers. The same was not true for airport officials in Caracas.

"When we arrived at the airport, the Venezuelan government wouldn't let any of the soldiers disembark," Orlando Peña said. "There was a problem at the airport until they agreed to leave the arms [on the plane], and then they let them disembark."[2]

There was another passenger on that flight who normally would not have been part of Almendares's traveling team— Cienfuegos pitcher Camilo Pascual. With only seven U.S. players on its roster, Almendares was permitted to add one player as a reinforcement, and the Scorpions had decided on Pascual before the final week of the Cuban League season. It had not been a typical winter for Pascual. He had been one of the league's dominant pitchers, going 12-5 with a league-leading 1.91 ERA in the winter of 1955–56. Pascual followed that up with a league-best 15-5 record and 2.04 ERA in 1956–57.

After sitting out almost the entire 1957–58 winter season, Pascual, who went on to have a breakout season with the Senators in 1959 (17-10 record with a 2.64 ERA) tossed back-to-back shutouts to open the 1958–59 Cuban League season. But Pascual lost six consecutive games through November 29 despite a 2.89 ERA. He turned things around, going 7-3 the rest of the season to finish 9-9 with a league-leading 108 strikeouts and a 2.11 ERA. "Camilo Pascual . . . was a tremendous pitcher," De la Hoz said. "He had one of the best curves that I've seen in baseball."[3] Almendares outfielder Leo Posada agreed: "Camilo, to me, was the pitcher who had the best control and best curveball that I've ever seen in my life."[4]

The Humboldt Hotel still sits high amid El Ávila National Park, a lush, 210,000-acre mountain range along the Caribbean coast of Venezuela. The white, fifteen-story, cylindrical edifice was the brainchild of Venezuela's then-dictator General Marcos Pérez Jiménez and the end results of six frantic months of construction in 1956. The hotel included a heated Olympic-sized pool, a discotheque with a rotating dance floor, an English pub, a German beer hall, an Italian café, a Japanese restaurant, and a Louis XVI–style French salon. Perched some 7,400 feet above sea level, the Humboldt offered spectacular views of the Caribbean Sea to the north and the city of Caracas to the south.

When it opened in 1957, the Humboldt became Venezuela's hottest attraction. In its heyday, it drew guests such as Argentine president Juan Perón, Dominican Republic dictator Rafael Trujillo, and even Fidel Castro. Stars such as Cuban singer Celia Cruz and New York-born musician Tito Puente served as the hotel's entertainment. In February 1959, the Humboldt played host to Almendares, which was representing Cuba in the eleventh annual Caribbean Series. At that time of year and at that altitude, the climate took some getting used to for the contingent from Cuba. "Un frio del coño de su madre," Orlando Peña recalled, describing the frigid temperatures he experienced by using a Cuban colloquialism, which translates literally as a vulgar phrase to describe a part of a woman's anatomy but which Cubans commonly use to indicate something extreme.[5]

Named for Alexander von Humboldt, a German scientist who travelled extensively in Venezuela in the early 1800s, the Humboldt stood at such an extreme elevation that the hotel was above the clouds. "I remember Carlos Paula used to say, 'We're living in the top of the clouds here,'" said Miguel de la Hoz, who roomed with Leo Posada and Cholly Naranjo at the Humboldt. "The clouds were below us. That's how big this mountain was."[6] To access the facility, guests would travel to and from Caracas via a gondola lift. "From Caracas, we took a cable car," Posada said. "No lights. We were hanging in the middle of the cable like that, and we were looking at each other. We used to go down in the morning, eat in Caracas, stay in Caracas, play in Caracas, then come back at night to go to sleep. We didn't want to go up and down anymore. . . . One night we got up and the window was open, and we see the clouds going through the window into the room [of the gondola]. That's how high we were."[7]

Teams from Cuba had won five of the first ten Caribbean Series and three consecutive titles. But Almendares had not won a Caribbean championship since the inaugural tournament in

1949. Having taken the reins of the Scorpions in January when manager Oscar Rodríguez suffered a heart attack, Clemente "Sungo" Carreras felt a responsibility to both end Almendares's drought and continue his country's winning streak. "I hope to return with the sixth Caribbean championship," he said before the team left for Venezuela. "I have a moral obligation to see that Oscar's team wins the title."[8]

Heading into the tournament, Puerto Rico, which had won the series four times, including three in a row from 1953 to 1955, was considered the favorite. Represented by Puerto Rican League champion Santurce, Puerto Rico's roster boasted Sandy Alomar, a future All-Star who would go on to play fifteen Major League seasons; Vic Power, an All-Star with the Kansas City Athletics and Cleveland Indians; and future Hall of Famer Orlando Cepeda, who had just completed an All-Star season with the San Francisco Giants. The pitching staff was anchored by Major League pitcher Rubén Gómez, only the second Latino to appear in a World Series (1954 with the New York Giants. Adolfo Luque was the first in 1919).

Host Venezuela, represented by league champion Oriente, was still looking for its first Caribbean title. The team included Chicago White Sox first baseman Norm Cash, who would go on to be a five-time All-Star with the Detroit Tigers. Venezuela also tried to add native son Luis Aparicio. The All-Star shortstop, who was demanding a $30,000 salary from the Chicago White Sox, asked to be paid $1,800 to play in the series, but Oriente ownership deemed the price too steep. Panama, winners of the 1950 Caribbean Series, was the final team in the tournament. Represented by Cocle, the team included infielder Pumpsie Green, who would become the first African American to play for the Boston Red Sox when he made his Major League debut on July 21, 1959.

The three visiting clubs arrived in Caracas on Monday, February 9, amid the closing days of Carnival season and just two weeks after a popular uprising had toppled dictator Pérez Jiménez. The series began the next day with Cuba facing Puerto Rico in the opening game of a doubleheader, which pitted Venezuela against Panama in the nightcap. Some thirty-five thousand fans filled Caracas's University City Stadium for the opening-day twin bill. Captain Manuel Rodríguez Olivares, a member of the junta government that had replaced Pérez Jiménez, threw out the ceremonial first pitch.

The opening game was a pitchers' duel between Almendares's Orlando Peña and Puerto Rico's Rubén Gómez. Dick Brown singled in the fifth inning and scored from first base when Jim Baxes doubled, giving Almendares a 1–0 lead. The Scorpions' advantage held up until the ninth inning. Peña had allowed only two runners until Sandy Alomar singled with two outs in the ninth. Jackie Brandt, an outfielder with the San Francisco Giants, followed by hitting a triple down the right field line. "Bob Allison tries to make the play, but what happens?" Peña recalled. "The University Stadium was made of cement. The ball hit [the wall] and got away from Allison for a triple. Out came Sungo Carreras."[9]

With the score tied at 1-all, the Almendares manager ordered Peña to intentionally walk Orlando Cepeda and Vic Power to load the bases, bringing the left-hand-hitting Bob Lennon to the plate. "Peña, be careful," Carreras admonished his starting pitcher. But Lennon hit a chopper over Peña's head to drive in Brandt with the deciding run in Puerto Rico's 2–1 victory. "That was awful. We were so sad," Peña said. "Sungo tells me, 'Listen. You're going to rest [two days]. Do you think you can pitch?' At that age, you don't think twice. He told me, 'You're going to pitch against Puerto Rico [on Friday].'"[10]

But first, Cuba needed to bounce back from the narrow loss. That chance came Wednesday against Panama, 3–2 losers to Venezuela in the second game of Tuesday's doubleheader. Enter Camilo Pascual. Added to the roster as a reinforcement player, Pascual paid immediate dividends. He scattered six hits, struck out seven batters, and surrendered only two walks as Almendares won 4–1. Scorpions shortstop Willy Miranda went three for four, including a sixth-inning triple that drove in two runs and broke the game open. The same day, Venezuela beat Puerto Rico 6–5, setting up a key game between Cuba and

Venezuela on Thursday. A loss would have left Cuba with a 1-2 record and given an undefeated Venezuela team a commanding 3-0 record in the tournament.

Fans formed long lines to buy tickets hours before the scheduled start time on Thursday. After the gates opened, "not one more soul could fit in the grandstands," wrote *Diario de la Marina* columnist Eladio Secades, "while there were thousands of heartbroken fans who could not get in."[11] Those lucky enough to gain entry watched Cuba's starting pitcher, Art Fowler, hold Oriente to one run "by flaunting respectable speed, magnificent control, and resources that sometimes raised murmurs of admiration in the stand."[12] After a slow start, Cuba flexed its offensive muscles, scoring four runs in the sixth, four in the eighth, and three in the ninth for an 11–1 victory. Ángel Scull went three for six and drove in two runs. Tony Taylor went two for five, including a 420-foot home run in the sixth inning, and drove in three runs. Rocky Nelson and Carlos Paula each contributed a pair of Almendares's twelve hits.

With Puerto Rico beating Panama 9–3 in the other game on Thursday, it was a red-hot series as Cuba, Venezuela, and Puerto Rico stood tied with identical 2-1 records. Friday's schedule brought a rematch of the opening game between Almendares and Puerto Rico. True to Carreras's word, Peña started on two days' rest. Rocky Nelson staked Cuba to a 1–0 lead, knocking in Ángel Scull from third base on a hit to left with two outs in the first inning. Puerto Rico starting pitcher Lloyd Merritt, who had pitched for Habana in 1957–58, settled down after the initial frame and the game remained a pitchers' duel. Peña allowed the tying run to reach second base in the fifth, seventh, and eighth innings—Puerto Rico was aided by a Cuba error in the seventh and eighth—but he worked his way out of each jam.

A situation in the ninth inning prompted Carreras to visit the mound. "Sungo comes running out because there was a man on second base and up comes Lennon," Peña said. "When Sungo came out, Willy Miranda was talking with him, and I told them, 'Stop talking. This bastard already beat me one game. Sungo, this one's ours. Stay calm. Go back to the dugout.'"[13] Peña made good on this promise, and Cuba's 1–0 victory—coupled with a 14–5 win by Venezuela against Panama—left Cuba and Venezuela tied for first with 3-1 records.

Both clubs remained tied after Saturday's games as Cuba beat winless Panama 5–2 and Venezuela beat Puerto Rico 5–3. But Cuba's victory was not without some drama. Almendares trailed 2–1 in the fourth inning and needed four pitchers to get through the game. The Scorpions also were without their leading home run hitter. Angry about dropping a fly ball in the seventh inning on Friday, Carlos Paula had come off the field after the inning and hurt his hand by slamming it against something in the dugout. But Bob Allison, his replacement in the lineup on Saturday, came through with two hits, including an RBI-single in the bottom of the fourth that tied the game at 2-all. Cuba took the lead in the sixth on a sacrifice fly by Carlos "Patato" Pascual, Camilo's brother, and added two runs in the eighth to seal the victory and set up the series-deciding match on Sunday night.

Venezuela never had a chance. Cuba starter Camilo Pascual retired fifteen consecutive batters after giving up two hits in the second inning. He allowed only four hits and struck out nine batters. Venezuela didn't get on the scoreboard until the Oriente club managed to put up two runs in the eighth inning. By then, Cuba had already scored two runs in the first inning, two in the sixth, and three more in the seventh. Almendares added a final run in the bottom of the eighth, collecting ten hits, including three by Rocky Nelson, who drove in three runs. "Almendares won. Why?" Peña asked. "Because we had a reinforcement pitcher who was named Camilo Pascual."[14]

With two outs in the ninth inning, frustration boiled over among the partisan crowd of twenty-nine thousand. Some fans started throwing objects at Cuban pitchers warming up in the bullpen. Peña and Miguel Cuéllar responded by throwing fistfuls of dirt into the stands. The situation escalated when some fans stormed the field to attack the players. As some thirty security guards and nightstick-wielding police officers rushed to intervene, at least one UPI photographer was run over, and umpires Rubén Sánchez and Roberto Oliva were struck with clubs during the melee.

Once order was restored, Almendares finished off the 8–2 victory, giving Cuba its fourth consecutive Caribbean Series title. It also marked Cuba's sixth championship in eleven tournaments. "The Cuban League has gained a reputation in Caribbean Series competition," M. J. Gorman Jr. declared in *The Sporting News*, "comparable to that of the New York Yankees."[15]

As Almendares returned victoriously from the Caribbean Series, Fidel Castro was taking his first public steps toward consolidating power. On Monday, February 16, Castro became prime minister of Cuba following the resignation three days earlier of José Miró Cardona and the entire cabinet. Prior to that point, Castro held the title of commander-in-chief, the same title he held while leading the guerilla war in the Sierra Maestra. But while Manuel Urrutia was nominally Cuba's president, Castro was presiding over a shadow government that began meeting clandestinely within days of his triumphant arrival in Havana on January 8. His hidden government included his brother Raúl, Che Guevara, Camilo Cienfuegos, and others who would meet secretly to determine policies and strategies intended to convert Cuba into a Marxist-Leninist state.[16]

Throughout the fighting in Oriente, Castro's movement had been dogged by accusations and suspicions of having Communist ties, which Castro repeatedly denied. Even Guevara, who was a known Communist, denied those connections in the days before Castro arrived in Havana. "I have never been a Communist," Guevara told the *New York Times*. "Dictators always say their enemies are Communists, and it gave me a pain to be called an international Communist all the time. When a thing is said often enough people begin to doubt and believe, as I think your State Department did."[17]

Cuba's "old" Communists had refused to support Castro's revolution until victory was a foregone conclusion. When Urrutia selected his cabinet, Castro insisted it be as "homogenous as possible," representing the liberal and moderate elements of the 26th of July Movement. This meant excluding groups, such as the "old" Communists and the Student Revolutionary Directorate, to maintain favorable public opinion for the provisional government at home and abroad. To preserve the charade, known Communists within the Movement, such as Raúl Castro and Guevara, remained in the background, Raúl serving as military commander in Santiago and Guevara serving as chief at La Cabaña fortress. But at the same time, both "were instrumental in placing Communist-oriented personnel in strategic middle-level positions throughout the country."[18]

On February 3, Castro, speaking to reporters in the foothills of the Sierra Maestra, outlined changes that were coming for Cuba, including agrarian land reform that he said would redistribute land, benefit some two hundred thousand families, and transform the country within five years. Four days later during a speech at the Shell Oil refinery in Havana, he appealed to workers to refrain from striking. On February 10, a law was changed to reduce the required age for Cuban presidents from thirty-five to thirty, clearing a path to the presidency for the then-thirty-two-year-old Castro. And as a reward for fighting in the revolution, Argentinian Guevara was granted "native-born" status, allowing him to hold political office in Cuba.

When Miró Cardona and the cabinet resigned, the *New York Times* in its February 14 editions attributed the sudden move to a conflict over whether to reopen casinos in Havana's big tourist hotels. But it was about Castro establishing his political power. When the 1940 constitution was reinstated on February 7, Castro had already obtained a change that vested the power to direct policy in the office of prime minister. "Revolutionary power at that moment resided outside the government—in the rebel army headed by Fidel Castro," Communist Party leader Carlos Rafael Rodríguez wrote years later. "His designation as prime minister served to fuse together revolutionary power and the government."[19]

The casinos indeed reopened on February 16 with Castro reiterating the interests of tourism and the thousands of workers who depended on tourism for their livelihoods. Among the sixteen permitted to reopen with provisional three-month permits, nine were in Havana: at the hotels Havana Hilton, Havana Riviera, Capri, and Nacional; at the Tropicana, Sans Souci, and Montmartre night clubs; and at the Jockey Club and Jai Alai. Havana gaming rooms at the hotels Sevilla Biltmore, Plaza, Deauville, St. John, and Comodoro were among the twenty-seven that remained permanently closed throughout the country.

Although the casinos opened in what the *New York Times* described as "a gay atmosphere," the newspaper also noted mounting concerns over the arrests of hundreds on "charges of collaboration with the Batista Government and participation in its corruption," that had jails on the island "overflowing."[20] And on February 18, Jesús Sosa Blanco, a major in Batista's army and a convicted "war criminal," was executed at the ancient moat at La Cabaña.

On February 22, Major Camilo Cienfuegos, commander of Castro's Army in Havana, led a delegation of nine bearded, fatigue-clad revolutionaries on a goodwill visit to New York. "This is not a political trip," Cienfuegos said upon their arrival at New York International Airport in Idlewild, Queens. "It is just to show our friendship." Some fifteen hundred enthusiastic supporters greeted the revolutionaries like rock stars. "The visitors were mobbed by the friendly crowd after they passed through customs," Robert Alden wrote in the *New York Times*. "Girls pressed kisses and flowers on them. Men waved banners excitedly. The police struggled to maintain order."[21]

Castro agreed on March 3 to make his own visit to the United States, accepting an invitation from the American Society of Newspaper Editors to speak at its annual convention in Washington on April 16. Three days earlier, he had announced that general elections would take place in Cuba in two years instead of the eighteen months he had originally indicated. "Elections could not be held now," Castro said, "because they would not be fair. We have an overwhelming majority at present and it is in the interest of the nation that political parties become fully developed and their programs defined before elections are held."[22]

But even with elections pushed back, a series of moves intended to transform Cuba began to be implemented. On the same day as Castro's election announcement, his cabinet approved a law ordering the confiscation of property belonging to Batista, his vice president, all cabinet ministers appointed under Batista, deposed former president Carlos Prío Socarrás, all senators and representatives of both government and opposition parties who served from 1954 to 1958, and all provincial governors and municipal mayors who served under the Batista regime. On March 4, the government took control of the Cuban Telephone Company and reduced telephone rates. By March 19, the number of alleged "war criminals" executed by firing squad reached 483. Even *Revolución*, the news organ of the revolution, called for a halt to the executions, arguing that revolutionary justice had "fulfilled its basic objective."[23]

Rains had swept across Florida for four consecutive days, and inclement weather was about to wipe out yet another set of spring training games on Thursday, March 19. The St. Louis Cardinals had chartered a flight from St. Petersburg to Vero Beach for their scheduled game that day against the Los Angeles Dodgers. But before the Cardinals' bus left Al Lang Stadium Thursday morning, traveling secretary Leo Ward got a phone call from his counterpart with the Dodgers. "Don't bother coming," Lee Scott informed Ward. "It's raining." Cardinals manager Solly Hemus pleaded with Ward for a solution. "We've got to play somewhere," he said. "Phone around the state, Leo. As long as we have a plane we might as well use it. If you can find a dry field anywhere, we'll fly there and have an intra-squad game."[24]

The Cincinnati Reds had already been washed out on Thursday. Sitting in his office in the team's spring headquarters at Plant Field in Tampa, Florida, Reds general manager Gabe Paul had had enough. He picked up his phone and dialed long distance. "Get me Mr. Bavasi, at Vero Beach," Paul told the operator. Buzzie Bavasi was the general manager of the Dodgers, whose motto was "have plane, will travel."

Paul: "Buzzie, this is Gabe . . . raining over there?"

Bavasi: "Yes."

Paul: "Then let's take a trip to Havana."

Bavasi: "You've got a date."[25]

The hastily made plans called for the clubs to play the first of a three-game series that night at El Gran Stadium in Havana. "We had to do something," Bavasi said. "More rain was expected in Florida. It looked as if we would lose everything we gained the first four weeks of training."[26] The Reds hoped to fly to Miami, where they would fly Pan American to Cuba, but weather shut down the Miami airport. "Our players have just reached the point in conditioning where any further delay will move them backward," Paul said before leaving the Tampa airport.[27] Meanwhile, the Dodgers had flown out of Vero Beach aboard the team-owned Convair 440, but it was unable to land in Miami and had to be rerouted to Tampa before continuing to Havana. Dodgers president Walter O'Malley called Paul: "We'll send the plane back for you tomorrow."[28]

Although the Reds' arrival in Havana would be delayed until Friday, the Dodgers were prepared to do whatever was needed to get in some games. "If the weather in Havana isn't clear," O'Malley said, "we may go on to the Dominican Republic or San Juan, Puerto Rico, for a series."[29] That wasn't necessary. The Dodgers held an intra-squad game Thursday night in front of twenty-five hundred fans in Havana, playing to a 1–1 tie as pitcher Carl Erskine singled home Don Demeter in the ninth to gain the deadlock. Erskine was no stranger to Cuba. He had played for Cienfuegos during the 1947–48 Cuban League season, going 9-7 with a 2.94 ERA while he was still a Minor Leaguer in the Dodgers' farm system. "I was 20 years old and had just finished my first season in the minors," Erskine wrote years later.

"The Dodgers sent me to Havana to [work on his curveball]. . . .
I matured as a pitcher, and that experience did wonders for my
self-confidence."[30]

The Dodgers organization was familiar with playing in Cuba.
The team had held spring training camps in Havana in 1941,
1942, and 1947. The latter included Jackie Robinson as a member of the Montreal Royals—the Dodgers' Class Triple-A farm
team—as he prepared to break baseball's color barrier. Cuba
had a decades-long tradition of American teams—from the
Majors, Minors, and Negro leagues—coming to the island for
barnstorming and exhibition games. These expeditions became
known in Cuba as *la temporada americana* (American Season).
The first happened in 1891, when future Hall of Fame manager
John McGraw came to Havana as a young player for a series
of exhibition games against Cuban teams as a member of an
American "all-star" squad.

The Cincinnati Reds arrived in Havana on Friday. Before
checking into the Havana Hilton, players were brought to El
Gran Stadium for an afternoon workout. "This is great," Reds
pitcher Brooks Lawrence said. "You can get more accomplished
here in one hour than you can in three in Florida. . . . Ten days
would be enough [training in Havana]. After that, the intense
heat would begin sapping your strength."[31]

After the workout, the team checked into its hotel, greeted
by the sight of armed, bearded soldiers strolling through the
lobby. Soldiers were among the 7,655 fans at the stadium for
Friday night's game. "Castro had just taken over and there were
trials going on in the sports arena," Erskine recalled. "At the
ballpark that night, there were so many young guys with sub-
machine guns and belts with bullets across their chests, and
they were all on the field asking for baseballs."[32]

The game featured Dodgers right-hander Don Drysdale pitching against Reds starting pitcher Don Newcombe, who had
pitched for Marianao and Almendares in 1948–49. Drysdale
had gone 17-9 with a 2.69 ERA during the team's final season
in Brooklyn in 1957 and 12-13 in the Dodgers' first year in Los

Angeles in 1958. Newcombe had pitched for the Dodgers from 1949 to 1958, winning 20 games in 1955 and 27 in 1956. He was traded to Cincinnati midseason in 1958. Drysdale won Friday's match-up, striking out nine batters in seven innings as the Dodgers beat the Reds 3–2. Charlie Neal and former Cienfuegos player Dick Gray (1956–57) each hit solo home runs for the Dodgers.

Roberto González Echevarría was a teenager who had managed to get himself a box-seat ticket for the game. The future Cuban baseball historian and author of *Pride of Havana: A History of Cuban Baseball* was sitting just to the right of the screen behind home plate when Gray fouled a pitch off the screen. González corralled the ball amid a group of Castro's soldiers. "One of the *barbudos*, taller than I, reached for the ball, but only deflected it onto my chest," González wrote in his book. "I crossed my arms and bent over to protect my prey."[33] González returned to the stadium for Saturday's game, where one of the soldiers offered to take the ball to both dugouts to have it signed by the players. The ball was returned with autographs from Drysdale, Duke Snider, Sandy Koufax, Pee Wee Reese, and several members of the Reds.[34]

The Dodgers won Saturday's game as well, beating the Reds 4–3 in front of thirty-four hundred fans. Rookie catcher Norm Sherry paced the Los Angeles eleven-hit attack with a home run and a pair of hits. Erskine was credited with the victory after pitching two innings in relief. "That may have been the last game I won in my whole career," said Erskine, who retired three months into the 1959 Major League season. "I was battling a real bad arm and didn't win a game in 1959."[35]

The *Los Angeles Times* reported that it cost the Dodgers approximately $4,500 to bring both teams to Havana, but that the team "turned a small profit."[36] Both teams left Cuba after Saturday's games, and the Dodgers finally played the Cardinals on Sunday in St. Petersburg, Florida. No one knew it at the time, but the members of the Dodgers and Reds would be the last Major Leaguers to plant their spikes on a baseball diamond in Cuba for the next four decades.

8

"Bullets Were Falling . . . Like Hailstones"

Growing concern over the uncertain political situation in Cuba led the International League to formulate an emergency plan in December 1958. If conditions had deteriorated to the point where it became necessary to pull the Sugar Kings out of Havana, then Tampa, Florida, reportedly was one potential city in the United States to which to relocate the team. But league president Frank Shaughnessy was hesitant to divulge any details of the plan. "We will not be caught napping," he told the *Montreal Star*. "At this time we cannot make any statement that might impair the status of Roberto Maduro politically or financially. He definitely wants to play in the league."[1]

Tensions eased dramatically after the triumph of Castro's revolution. Both Maduro and league officials began expressing optimism for the 1959 season, which the Sugar Kings would open on April 14 in Havana against the Toronto Maple Leafs. "For the first time in the five-year life of our club," Maduro said, "it now appears we will be able to operate in an atmosphere of peace and security."[2] Shaughnessy was sufficiently buoyed by Batista's ouster that he wired Manuel Urrutia, the president of Cuba's provisional government, to congratulate him on restoring "liberty and freedom to the long-suffering people of Cuba."[3]

Cuba's two-year conflict not only had taken a toll on the country but also impacted attendance at El Gran Stadium. The Sugar Kings had drawn between 220,000 and 315,000 fans in each of their first three seasons in the International League. But attendance plummeted to 84,320 in 1957. And the uptick to 178,340 fans in 1958 was still well below Havana's first three-year average. But the prospect of a peaceful Cuba prompted speculation that the Sugar Kings might lead the International League in attendance in 1959. And general manager Paul Miller believed the team could secure more than $100,000 for radio and television rights because of increased enthusiasm for baseball.[4]

Only one voice outside the International League expressed concern. "If I were a club owner, I'd never send a team to Havana," American Association president Edward Doherty said. "It's too dangerous. You might get some of your players hurt."[5] Tom Lasorda, who had played three winters in Cuba, took offense. Before he left Havana to play in the Caribbean Series with Almendares, *The Sporting News* printed Lasorda's impassioned response to Doherty's comments:

> How can Mr. Doherty make such a statement as was quoted in *The Sporting News* if he has never been in Cuba? I have played in Cuba several winters and also played here last summer with Montreal. I can guarantee that the American players have never been treated better in any town of the United States or Canada. Even during the revolution, everyone went out of his way to be nice to us and neither we nor any member of our families were in any way molested. Before making the kind of statement Mr. Doherty made, one should investigate the conditions and not go by hearsay. Statements like this only serve to hamper the good relations between our countries and they certainly are against the good neighbor policy of the United States. I am grateful to the Cuban people and I am talking in the name of all the American players who have played here this winter.[6]

Ahead of a January 30 meeting of the directors of the International League, Bobby Maduro announced the hiring of Pedro "Preston" Gómez as the Sugar Kings' manager for the 1959 season. Gómez was born in the Camagüey sugar mill town of Central Preston in Oriente Province on April 20, 1923. Gómez, who had played a total of eight Major League games (just seven at bats) as an infielder with the Washington Senators in 1944, had been serving as a scout in Cuba for the Los Angeles Dodgers. He had managed the Mexico City Reds of the Mexican League in 1957 and 1958, and would go on to become the first manager of the expansion San Diego Padres in 1969, as well as manager of the Houston Astros and Chicago Cubs.

At the meeting in Montreal, Maduro informed fellow owners that Felipe Guerra Matos, Cuba's new director of sports, had assured him of the new Cuban government's cooperation. "I want no government subsidy," Maduro declared at the meeting. "My worry now is about a winning team; we'll have a fine year if we can be first-division." Maduro pointed to the government's crackdown on *bolita*, Cuba's popular underground numbers lottery. "I believe this will be a great help to baseball," he said. "The numbers racket took all the money out of [the] pockets of our fans. It was a national disease."[7]

Maduro also confirmed a report that Guerra Matos had offered him the position of coordinator of amateur sports, which Maduro turned down. "I have kept out of politics, and I intend to do so," Maduro said. "I have always worked for the good of Cuba and not for any particular government."[8] Maduro came to the meeting prepared to defend Havana's position within the league, but support was so uniform among the other owners that Shaughnessy never called for a vote on whether the team should be moved. "Bob Maduro has carried out every promise and agreement to the letter," Shaughnessy said. "We admire and respect him as a gentleman and a Cuban patriot."[9]

Buried eight paragraphs into Bob Addie's column in the March 7 editions of the *Washington Post and Times Herald* was a reference to Fidel Castro's ability as a one-time baseball player. The sports columnist quoted Senators scout Joe Cambria as having seen a younger Castro pitching for the University of Havana. "I gave him a long look," Cambria said, "but then decided he'd never get higher than Class B ball—or at best could struggle up to A ball."[10] When the same note was included in Addie's column in the March 18 editions of *The Sporting News*, he added his own conclusion to Cambria's assessment. "The history of Cuba," Addie wrote, "might have been changed had Castro turned out to be a good college pitcher."[11]

Thus appears to have begun the mythology of Castro's supposed prowess as a baseball prospect, a legend that seemed to grow with every subsequent telling. Even Cambria, when he met with Castro in April at the Cuban embassy in Washington, was more generous in his description of Castro's ability, saying he had "major league spirit. I strongly considered signing him. He had excellent control. He lacked major league stuff but he could have made the grade in the minors."[12] Cambria's slightly revised appraisal was modest compared to various embellishments that would follow in the years to come.

In one fabrication, published in the June 1964 edition of *Sport* magazine, former Major League journeyman Don Hoak recounts how he purportedly batted against Castro in a Cuban League game during the 1950–51 season. By Hoak's telling, Castro was among anti-Batista demonstrators who stormed the field, and the future revolutionary came to the mound, demanded the ball, and ordered Hoak to get in the batter's box. After tossing several wild pitches, umpire Amado Maestri finally enlisted the aid of military police to remove Castro from the field. Aside from the shear ludicrousness of such a scene actually playing out, Hoak's account was riddled with factual errors: Batista wasn't in power during the 1950–51 season. Hoak's only Cuban League season (with Cienfuegos) came in 1953–54, at which time Castro was imprisoned on the Isle of Pines.[13]

Another apocryphal tale was told in the pages of a May 1989 *Harper*'s article detailing how New York Giants owner Horace Stoneham was acutely interested in the "star pitcher for the University of Havana." The article quoted scouting reports supposedly written by Howie Haak of the Pirates, the Giants' Caribbean scout Alex Pompez, and Cambria. "The trouble here (and it is considerable trouble indeed)," wrote Cuban baseball historian Peter C. Bjarkman, "is that no other known source ever reports on such existing or once-available scouting reports."[14]

Cuban baseball historian Roberto González Echevarría noted that a box score published in the November 28, 1946, editions of *El Mundo* newspaper chronicles an intramural game between the Law and Business schools at the University of Havana. The box score lists "a certain F. Castro," which may or may not have been Fidel, as having pitched and lost 5–4. "This," González wrote, "is likely to be the only published box score in which the future dictator appears."[15]

Ralph Ávila was adamant that Castro was never a baseball prospect. "All that about Fidel being a baseball player, all that is a lie," Ávila said. "He wasn't a baseball player. He was only a basketball player. He was a good basketball player, a good cyclist, and all those things, but he was never a baseball player. As a Cuban, yes, he played baseball in parks and in the street like we all played. But Fidel was never a baseball player in the sense of going to tryouts with Cambria and all that. That was a lie. That was propaganda."[16]

But Castro certainly was a baseball fan, and he was scheduled to throw out the first pitch in the Sugar Kings' 1959 season opener. "A lot of people think it is only a publicity stunt.... That is not true at all," Maduro said during a preseason trip to Tampa to discuss personnel with general manager Gabe Paul and manager Mayo Smith of the Reds, with whom the Sugar Kings had a working agreement. "I remember the year that we trained in Mexico. Castro was there getting things lined up for the revolution. He came to our exhibition games every night."[17]

As a tune-up for the 1959 International League season, the Sugar Kings hosted the Miami Marlins for a four-game exhibition series in Morón. It was during that series Bobby Maduro confirmed the precarious state his team had been in before Castro's revolution toppled Batista. "If Batista had remained in power, baseball was finished in Havana," Maduro said in disclosing for the first time that the International League planned to shift the Sugar Kings to Jersey City, New Jersey. "I had a meeting set up for January 6 in Jersey City to sign papers that would move the team."[18] During the exhibition series, Maduro was so optimistic about baseball's future in Cuba, he expressed his belief that Havana was ready for Major League baseball, and it was merely a matter of time before an expansion team would reside in Cuba.

When the Sugar Kings opened the season on April 14 against Toronto, Cuban president Manuel Urrutia, Raúl Castro, and Camilo Cienfuegos joined Castro on the field for the pregame ceremonies at El Gran Stadium. A crowd of 14,106 welcomed the prime minister with what *Diario de la Marina*'s Eladio Secades described as "a prolonged applause and screams of indescribable enthusiasm."[19] After warming up his arm by throwing to Cienfuegos, Castro requested a moment of silence be held in honor of Commandant Felix Peña, who had died the previous day. Following the playing of the Cuban national anthem, Castro threw the ceremonial first pitch.

After the festivities concluded with the release of one hundred white doves, the game began badly for Ted Wieand. The Maple Leafs jumped on the Sugar Kings' starting pitcher for three runs in the first two innings, including a solo home run by Joe Altobelli, a one-time Cleveland Indians player who would go on to manage the San Francisco Giants, Baltimore Orioles, and Chicago Cubs between 1977 and 1991. Altobelli's home run was one of four during the game. Sugar Kings slugger Antonio "Haitiano" González hit a solo home run in the sixth to cut the Leafs' lead to 3–2, and teammate Borrego Álvarez tied the game at 4–4 with a home run in the bottom of the ninth inning.

But the eleventh inning belonged to Toronto. Joey Amalfitano, who had played for the Giants and would go on to manage the Cubs from 1979 to 1981, lined a one-out single. Cuban-born Héctor Rodríguez delivered a pinch-hit line drive that went for an inside-the-park home run as Tony González fell in center field while trying to field it on one bounce. The Leafs won 6–4. The next day, Castro would embark upon his first visit to the United States since taking power.

The Britannia turboprop *Libertad* of Cubana Airlines landed at National Airport outside Washington DC on Wednesday, April 15. The 9:02 p.m. arrival was about two hours behind schedule. A crowd of fifteen hundred supporters, mostly Cuban, welcomed Castro with a cry of "¡Viva Castro!" as the Cuban prime minister arrived for the start of his eleven-day, unofficial visit. Dr. Ernesto Dihigo, Cuba's ambassador to the United States, and several U.S. state department dignitaries greeted Castro as he exited the plane at the Military Air Transport Terminal. Dressed in his trademark green fatigue uniform, Castro waded through an exuberant crowd and made his way to a waiting microphone. "I have come here to speak to the people of the United States," he said in a soft voice. "I hope the people of the United States will understand better the people of Cuba, and I hope to understand better the people of the United States."[20]

The following day, he joined acting secretary of state Christian Herter for a luncheon at the Statler Hilton. Before the luncheon, a reporter asked Castro whether newspapers in Cuba were free to criticize his regime. "Every newspaper man in the United States is invited to come to Cuba and see for himself," Castro replied to what would be a daily series of questions regarding censorship, future elections, and communism.[21] On Friday, Castro spoke before an American Society of Newspaper Editors luncheon, where he denied charges of Communist influences in his regime. "I have said very clearly that we are not Communists," Castro said. "Our revolution is a humanistic one."[22]

Castro also insisted that his regime executed only war criminals, that Cuba would not abrogate the agreement that allowed for the U.S. naval base at Guantanamo, and that his government would not confiscate foreign private industry in Cuba. Not everyone was convinced by Castro's assurances. "It is clear that he hasn't yet learned that you can't play ball with Communists," said Democratic senator George Smathers of Florida, "for he has them peppered throughout his government."[23] During his Sunday appearance on NBC's *Meet the Press*, Castro denied that his brother Raúl and Raúl's wife, Vilma, were Communists and said elections would be held within four years, once Cuba could establish "conditions for free elections."[24]

After his national television appearance, Castro met with Richard Nixon in the U.S. vice president's Senate office for almost two and a half hours. After the meeting, Nixon said the United States was "interested in helping the Cuban people in their economic progress in an atmosphere of freedom."[25] Castro said he was "satisfied" with a meeting he described as "friendly" and "positive," and offered further assurances about elections in Cuba. "Don't worry about elections," he said. "The person most worried about this is myself. I'm not interested in being in power one minute more than necessary."[26] But Castro could not meet with President Dwight Eisenhower, who had arranged to be playing golf in Augusta, Georgia, during Castro's five days in Washington.

Speaking the next day at a National Press Club luncheon, Castro pointed to agrarian reform as the next big step for his regime, but he insisted his government would only "legally" expropriate uncultivated or badly cultivated land. He also placed a wreath at the Tomb of the Unknown Soldier in Arlington National Cemetery. Before leaving Washington by train for New York, Castro assessed his time in the U.S. capital. "I feel very happy toward the people of Washington," he said. "All the people here were very nice with me. I am going to leave Washington really with regret because in my short days in this city I have come to know many good people."[27]

Castro arrived at New York's Penn Station shortly after 11 a.m. on Tuesday, April 21, greeted by some two thousand Cuban flag-waving people. Some carried signs that read, "¡Viva la Revolución Cubana!" "¡Viva Fidel!" and "¡Viva El Liberador!" At one point the crowd broke into chants of "Fi-del! Fi-del! Fi-del!"[28] Thousands more lined Seventh Avenue as Castro's motorcade made its way to the Statler Hilton before he met with students at Columbia University. The next day, Castro spent three hours at the United Nations and reiterated there were no Communists in his government, and defended delaying elections because the Cuban people were "unanimously" opposed to holding elections immediately because it would risk a return of "oligarchy and tyranny."[29]

Castro took a break from his tour of New York to meet for several hours on Thursday with Bobby Maduro, who had flown from Havana to the Big Apple. Two days earlier, a Havana radio station had reported that the Sugar Kings had lost $133,000 in recent years. The team's directors had voted to open negotiations to move the team to Jersey City, New Jersey, because the club was unable to sell TV-radio rights, which had brought in $70,000 in 1958 and $100,000 in other seasons. To break even in 1959, the Sugar Kings would need to average seven thousand in attendance, but the team had been averaging only twenty-five hundred fans during the first month of the season.[30] But Maduro's conference with Castro yielded a plan to keep the Sugar Kings "permanently" in Havana. "A plan has been evolved," Maduro announced, "whereby Havana will be able to not only maintain its International League franchise but also will proceed with plans for possible participation in major league baseball if a third league comes into being."[31]

Although Maduro did not disclose specifics of the plan, the Sugar Kings owner said an administrative council would be formed in Havana to ensure the team had enough revenue— presumably with aid from the Castro regime—to continue operating. Such a plan might have been scuttled the following night if not for the actions of New York's Finest. As Castro addressed a cheering crowd of thirty thousand Friday night on the Mall in Central Park, police arrested a man carrying a homemade bomb behind the band shell stage where Castro was speaking. According to police, the twenty-three-year-old New York resident planned to detonate the bomb at the rally "for kicks." Unaware of the threat, Castro, addressing the crowd in Spanish, said that "although our languages are different, our sentiments are the same. The rich nation to the north has understood our just cause, and that understanding of our desires constitutes the real triumph."[32]

Castro's tour of the United States would conclude in Boston, but before he left New York by train on Saturday morning, he gave a final brief interview to reporters before descending to the platforms at Penn Station. Again he vehemently denied any Communist influences in his regime. "Why are you so worried about Communists?" Castro asked. "There are no Communists in my government. You should worry about our success as a nation. We are a democracy."[33]

Even before Castro left New York, concerns about Communists within his regime were on the rise in Cuba. As executions by firing squads continued, a growing number of crimes previously considered civil offenses—drug trafficking, illegal gambling, misappropriation of public funds—were suddenly deemed counterrevolutionary activities and punishable by death. "For this reason," R. Hart Phillips of the *New York Times* concluded, "some see in this the familiar pattern of elimination of enemies."[34] By early July, some six hundred prisoners would be tried by military tribunals and executed by firing squads. Ralph Ávila barely escaped such a fate.

In May 1959, Ávila was among twenty-one members of the 26th of July Movement called to a meeting at La Cabaña, only to find themselves accused of being counterrevolutionaries. "I was condemned to death," Ávila recalled. "They took us prisoner and held us there, and they held a revolutionary trial. And by about ten-something at night, we had already been condemned to death because the attorney said that we were traitors, an offense punishable by penalty of death. . . . Fidel arrived after ten like he always did, and he acted like he didn't know what was happening there. He said, 'No, I know these people. They were revolutionaries. They're good. Let's give them a chance.'" Ávila and the others were told they could leave one at a time. "One of us who was a commandant stood up and he said, 'No, Fidel, if we leave one by one none of us will ever show up again. Either all twenty-one of us leave or none of us leave.' [Fidel] was bothered and began cursing like he always did and he said, 'Well, then go to hell.' And we left."[35]

Unsettling moves continued throughout the spring and summer of 1959. On May 17, Cuban president Manuel Urrutia signed the Agrarian Reform Act, which called for the expropriation of 1,666,000 acres of land from United States sugar companies within one year of it going into effect in June. The law also called for the breakup of large farms owned by Cubans. On May 23, the government took over the Cuban airline industry, seizing control of Cubana Airlines, the José Martí International Airport Operating Company, Aerovias Q, Aereo Postal, and the Inter-American Express Company. Urrutia and his cabinet adopted the resolution authorizing the takeover, claiming the companies were operated by officials of the Batista regime or "collaborators."[36]

Further accusations against the Castro regime came when Major Pedro Luis Díaz Lanz, chief of Cuba's air force, cited growing Communist infiltration in Cuba's government in a letter of resignation dated June 30 before fleeing the island with his wife aboard a small private boat. Branded a traitor by Castro, Díaz Lanz was granted asylum by the United States. He testified July 13–14 before the Senate Internal Security subcommittee, which investigated domestic and international Communist activity. Asked whether Raúl Castro was the "strongest Communist in the Castro government," Díaz Lanz responded, "I think it is Fidel himself. I am completely sure he is a Communist. . . . He said we were going to bring back the Constitution, have democracy, have freedom, have elections. What have we got now? Most of us are not Communists, but he has given the Communists control of the country."[37]

At around the same time, Cuban president Manuel Urrutia had become a hindrance to the revolution. Limited since February to signing laws prepared by Castro, Urrutia had started delaying his signing of those laws. And on July 13, Urrutia declared on television that "the Communists are inflicting a terrible harm on Cuba."[38] Castro responded by orchestrating a series of moves to consolidate his power. On July 17, Castro accused Urrutia of "near treason" during a national radio and television broadcast and offered to resign as prime minister (but not as commander-in-chief of the military). Castro declared Urrutia was involved in "an elaborate plan of defamation against the government similar to Pedro Díaz Lanz."[39]

Upon hearing Castro's accusations, Urrutia resigned as president just before midnight. The council of ministers, meeting at the presidential palace, immediately appointed Dr. Osvaldo Dorticós, who had been minister of revolutionary law, as Cuba's new president. On July 18, the Cabinet pleaded with Castro to resume his role as prime minister. It was not until July 26, the sixth anniversary of the Moncada Barracks attack that spawned the revolution, that Castro officially rejoined the government. "As president of the Republic I can announce to you that in the face of the demand of the public Dr. Fidel Castro has agreed to return to the position of premier,"[40] Dorticós told the cheering throng of hundreds of thousands who packed the Plaza de la Revolución.

Castro also credited "the will of the people" for his return to office. "I have returned because the people are with us in the revolution," he said during a lengthy speech that night, "and are willing to die with us in the defense of the revolution." Castro also declared that he wanted "the best understanding and best relations between the people of the United States and Cuba."[41]

On the same night Castro was orchestrating his gambit, Maduro sat at El Gran Stadium, lamenting the state of Minor League baseball in Havana during an interview with *Miami Herald* sportswriter Luther Evans. With the island riveted to Castro's nationwide address, only five hundred fans came to see the Sugar Kings play the Miami Marlins. "I will try to sell the franchise if I lose money," Maduro told Evans. "But we will finish out the season in Havana."[42] Maduro sounded far different from the optimistic team owner who less than three months earlier had declared the Sugar Kings would stay in Havana permanently.

At that time, Castro had pledged to keep the team in Havana, and others rallied to the cause. The Cuban Tourist Commission provided some funds. Camilo Cienfuegos, the chief of the army, bought $10,000 worth of tickets for soldiers, and the Sugar Institute bought radio time to promote the team. But that money was almost gone. "I've lost money ever since we've been in the International League," Maduro said. "I simply no longer can afford to operate under such conditions. Castro has said the government shouldn't subsidize a team directly. I think he is right. But he can help through indirect means."[43]

Castro remained supportive of keeping the team in Havana, declaring that the "Sugar Kings are a part of the Cuban people. It is important for us to have a connection with Triple-A ball."[44] Maduro insisted he would not move the team himself. "My home is in Cuba," he said. "I wouldn't leave here. I'd want to sell the franchise and get out of baseball. But I'm not going to give it away." Maduro also seemed to have abandoned the team's motto, "Un paso más y llegamos" (One more step and we're there) and the idea of bringing a Major League team to Havana. "This talk of a third major league is silly," he said. "How are you going to have major league teams in Miami and Havana and Montreal when these cities won't even support Triple-A baseball decently?"[45]

Maduro did get an attendance boost on July 24 thanks to a two-inning exhibition game, starring none other than Fidel Castro. Part of the weekend celebration to mark the 26th of July Movement, the exhibition was played before the Sugar Kings hosted the Rochester Red Wings to open a three-game series on Friday night. With proceeds from the game earmarked to help fund Cuba's agrarian reform program, the exhibition pitted a team of revolutionary soldiers, the Barbudos (Bearded Ones), against a team from the military police.

The largest crowd of the International League season—26,532 fans—came to see Castro pitch and then stuck around for the regularly scheduled IL contest. Castro pitched to battery mate Camilo Cienfuegos in the second inning, striking out two—

home plate umpire Amado Maestri called one batter out on a high inside pitch. Castro grounded out to short in his one at bat. "His presence on the field," wrote Luis Úbeda in the *Diario de la Marina*, "provoked a noisy ovation that continued for a lengthy time as the flashbulbs of the photographers and the lights of the cameramen illuminated the entire field."[46]

With the exhibition contest completed, Cuban president Osvaldo Dorticós threw out the first pitch for the Sugar Kings–Red Wings game. The Sugar Kings scored three runs with two outs in the fifth inning on hits by Leo Cárdenas, Raúl Sánchez, Venezuelan-born Pompeyo "Yo-Yo" Davalillo, Elio Chacón, and Daniel Morejón. Havana beat Rochester 4–2, giving Sánchez the victory and a 6-3 record on the season. The Sugar Kings ran their record to 52-53, good for fourth place in the International League. Only 2,372 fans showed up for Saturday night's game. But whichever of them were still in the stands once the game rolled past midnight witnessed a much bigger spectacle than anything seen in Friday night's game.

In 1959, Frank Verdi and Leo Cárdenas were as different as two ballplayers could be. At age thirty-three, Verdi was a career Minor Leaguer, having played a single game in the Majors in 1953 with the New York Yankees. The Brooklyn-born infielder was playing out the string with Rochester, his eleventh Minor League team since 1946. Meanwhile, Cárdenas was a twenty-year-old prospect just beginning his professional baseball career. The native of Matanzas, Cuba, was playing his first season in Class Triple-A and about to embark upon a sixteen-year Major League career, mostly with the Cincinnati Reds. But Verdi and Cárdenas would forever be linked by events in the Sugar Kings–Red Wings game on July 25.

The day began with the completion of a game suspended on June 7 with the score tied at 0–0 in the seventh inning. Davalillo gave the Sugar Kings a 1–0 victory by driving home Cárdenas with a double in the eighth inning. The Red Wings appeared to be on their way to winning the regularly scheduled game until Borrego Álvarez hit a two-run home run—his nineteenth of the season—in the ninth to tie the score at 3-all and force extra innings. Billy Harrell homered in the top of the eleventh inning to put Rochester ahead briefly. But the real action started before Havana tied the game again in the bottom of the inning.

When the clock struck midnight, fireworks signaled the start of the 26th of July celebration. Fans stood to sing as the Cuban national anthem played, and soldiers inside and outside El Gran Stadium began firing their weapons in the air. The umpires conferred and debated calling the game with the Red Wings leading 4–3 after ten and a half innings, but they didn't want to risk angering the armed fans. Sporadic shooting continued and the game had to be paused several times.

George Beahon, a sportswriter covering the game for the *Rochester Democrat and Chronicle*, estimated that fifty to seventy-five men discharged some type of weapon inside the park. One soldier sitting next to Red Wings general manager George Sisler Jr., in front-row box seats, emptied his .45-caliber automatic gun into the turf near the team's dugout. According to Beahon, the number of rounds fired inside and outside the stadium was estimated at more than one thousand. "Hell," Verdi recalled years later, "bullets were falling out of the sky like hailstones that night."[47] The repercussions of that much gunfire were felt as the twelfth inning began about thirty minutes after midnight.

With Red Wings manager Cot Deal ejected minutes earlier for arguing with first base umpire Frank Guzzetta, Verdi took over the team as acting manager. Verdi stood in the third base coaching box when he was struck by a stray bullet. He clutched his head and was staggered by the impact. Some witnesses said a soldier fired his pistol in the air, and the slug ricocheted off the roof of the stadium and grazed Verdi, who said it felt like "a gong went off, like I was hit by a pitched ball right on the head."[48] Fortunately for Verdi, he was wearing a plastic liner with his ballcap. "If that bullet had been two inches to the left," Verdi said, "the boys on the ball club would have had to chip in $5 apiece for flowers."[49]

The bullets were not done falling as players and umpires immediately rushed to Verdi's aid. "I was standing near Verdi and walking forward," third base umpire Ed Vargo said. "Then I felt one bullet burn past my nose, and two more thudded into the ground just in front of me."[50] Across the diamond, Cárdenas was in position at shortstop when he was grazed by a bullet as well. "Our manager Preston Gómez told us to come back to the dugout and wait for those guys to finish shooting, but I was hit," Cárdenas wrote in his 2015 autobiography. "The bullet put a hole in my uniform above my right shoulder. It tore my skin and I was bleeding. They had to put a bandage on it. I could have continued playing."[51]

But umpires had seen enough and suspended the game with the score tied 4-all in the twelfth inning. Deal had left the dugout after being ejected and was in the Red Wings' clubhouse when Verdi and Cárdenas were shot. He walked out of the shower as his ashen-faced players returned and informed him of what had happened. "Imagine my reaction. In a few seconds, though, Frank came in," Deal recalled years later. "Frank always wore a plastic liner in his cap. I never did. If I had been in the exact place at the exact time he was . . ."[52] Verdi was taken to the Anglo-American Hospital, where he was treated and released.

The suspended game was scheduled to be completed Sunday as part of a doubleheader, but Deal said he would not force his players to take the field. Guzzetta was even more emphatic, saying he would "not umpire here on Sunday even if it costs me my job."[53] Upon returning to the team hotel, Sisler called league president Frank Shaughnessy. "He told me he'd back whatever I wanted to do," Sisler said. "I didn't want that. I wanted somebody to give me the order to get out."[54] Sisler then reached Red Wings president Frank Horton, who told the GM to bring the team home.

When it became clear the Red Wings intended to leave Cuba on Sunday, representatives of Cuba's military visited Sisler and Deal to persuade them to finish the series. "It was a tough situation," Sisler said. "The only way we could get out of it was to say we had orders to leave. We felt it was touch-and-go at the time. We just wanted out."[55] Said Deal: "They started out very polite. They tried to convince us there was no danger. They told us the importance of playing for national relations. Then they changed and got adamant. Finally, they got abusive. They called us Yellow Yankees."[56]

The Red Wings eventually managed to leave on Sunday night, departing on a pair of flights to Miami. "It was the most traumatic, harrowing experience I've ever had," Deal said. "We didn't go into Cuba apprehensively, but we left that way."[57] Despite leaving with Shaughnessy's blessing, Sugar Kings management was upset, calling the Red Wings' failure to play "absurd" and insisting there was "no justifiable reason" to cancel Sunday's games. "An atmosphere of peace, tranquility, and happiness reigned in the city when Rochester refused to play due to an incident of no importance," read a statement released by the Sugar Kings. "A large crowd had gathered at the stadium for the double bill and had to be turned away."[58]

Around the International League, officials voiced their support for the Red Wings. "I doubt if we could get our ball club down there right now," said Marlins manager Pepper Martin, whose team was scheduled to start a three-game series in Havana on August 24. "I don't blame them," Richmond Virginians manager Steve Souchock said. There was even a report that players from the Toronto Maple Leafs had signed a petition against playing in Havana. Ironically the Leafs manager was Dixie Walker, who in 1947 had been involved in a petition among Brooklyn Dodgers players designed to block Jackie Robinson from breaking baseball's color barrier. Walker announced there was no petition and no threat of refusing to return to Havana.[59]

Regardless, Maduro said he would not permit the Sugar Kings to make up the suspended and cancelled games in Rochester later in the season. Felipe Guerra Matos, Cuba's national sports director, called the Red Wings on July 27 to personally apologize about the shooting incident. He also pledged to secure the safety of all league teams playing in Cuba the rest of the season. After a few days, Shaughnessy ruled the league would complete its schedule in Havana. "I have no official protests from any of our clubs and I am not planning to call a special meeting of the board of directors," Shaughnessy said, "because no one has asked for one."[60]

Indeed, the schedule concluded without further incident. The Buffalo Bisons finished the regular season in first place with an 89-64 record. The Columbus Jets finished second at 5½ games back. Havana was 9 games off the pace at 80-73. Richmond finished fourth to round out the four playoff-qualifying teams. For the Sugar Kings, it was the first time they had reached the playoffs in their six-year existence. And it would be memorable.

1. Aerial view of El Gran Stadium of Havana. Author's collection.

2. *From left*: Oscar and Joseito Rodríguez, Joe Cambria, Roberto Ortiz, and Sandalio Consuegra of the Havana Cubans of the Florida International League. Author's collection.

3. Sugar Kings and Cienfuegos owner Bobby Maduro (right) with pitcher Jim Davis. RFM Fotos.

4. Don Zimmer (*left*) with Cienfuegos teammate Pedro Ballester. RFM Fotos.

5. Napoleón Reyes, playing with Cienfuegos, went on to manage the Havana Sugar Kings and Jersey City Jerseys. RFM Fotos.

6. Marianao teammates (*left to right*) Claro Duany, Quincy Trouppe, and Minnie Miñoso. Courtesy of the National Pastime Museum.

7. Gene Mauch, playing with Cienfuegos, went on to manage the Minneapolis Millers. Author's collection.

8. Almendares first baseman Rocky Nelson led the Cuban League in home runs and RBIs in 1954–55. Courtesy of the National Pastime Museum.

9. Minnie Miñoso dives back into first base during a Cuban League game. Courtesy of the National Pastime Museum.

10. Almendares pitcher Tom Lasorda went 8-3 with a 1.89 ERA during the 1958–59 Cuban League season. RFM Fotos.

11. Joe Cambria (*left*) with Cuban-born members of the Washington Senators. Courtesy of the National Pastime Museum.

12. Almendares infielder Tony Taylor led the Cuban League in batting in 1958–59. Bohemia archives.

13. Cienfuegos shortstop Leo Cárdenas was struck with a stray bullet during a game when he played for the Sugar Kings. Bohemia archives.

14. (*opposite top*) Almendares teammates
(*left to right*) Mike Cuéllar, Tony Taylor, Ángel
Scull, Mudcat Grant, and Orlando Peña. Author's
collection.

15. (*opposite bottome*) Almendares pitcher Orlando
Peña was the Cuban League MVP in 1958–59.
Author's collection.

16. (*above*) Tom Lasorda (*arms raised*) celebrates
Almendares' 1958–59 Cuban League title with his
teammates and club officials. Author's collection.

17. Fidel Castro warms up for an exhibition game with Los Barbudos, a team of rebel soldiers. Courtesy of the National Pastime Museum.

18. Fidel Castro and Che Guevara in the stands at El Gran Stadium. Courtesy of the National Pastime Museum.

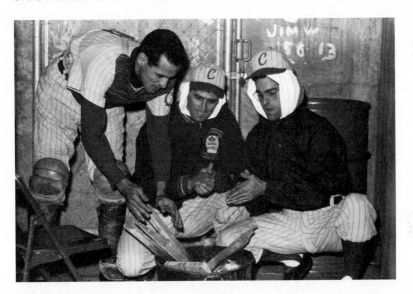

19. Sugar Kings players (*left to right*) Enrique Izquierdo, Raúl Sánchez, and Cookie Rojas try to keep warm in the dugout at Metropolitan Stadium during the 1959 Junior World Series against the Minneapolis Millers. Courtesy of the Minnesota Historical Society.

20. Fidel Castro celebrates the Sugar Kings' victory in the Junior World Series. Courtesy of the National Pastime Museum.

21. Fidel Castro congratulates pitcher Luis Arroyo after the Sugar Kings won the Junior World Series. Courtesy of the National Pastime Museum.

22. Fidel Castro with Minnie Miñoso at El Gran Stadium. Courtesy of the National Pastime Museum.

23. Cienfuegos ace Camilo Pascual was one of the most decorated pitchers in the Cuban League. Prensa Latina Servicio Fotografico.

24. Cienfuegos pitcher Pedro Ramos was the Cuban League MVP for the 1960–61 season. Courtesy of the National Pastime Museum.

25. Luis Tiant was named Cuban League Rookie of the Year for the 1960–61 season. RFM Fotos.

9

Title Town

For months, the Sugar Kings' prospects of remaining in Havana had been a rollercoaster of emotion, with Bobby Maduro alternating between optimism about the team's long-term viability and resignation about its imminent demise. The second half of the season had once again generated positive feelings. After July 4, the Sugar Kings closed out the season with a 44-28 record to secure a third-place finish in the International League and the team's first playoff berth. "Havana is set for 1960 in our league," Frank Shaughnessy declared. "If the economy was strong in Cuba, Havana would be one of the great cities of professional baseball. The enthusiasm is there. The Cuban fans know their baseball, and they cheer the good plays by the visitors as they do their own."[1]

The Sugar Kings reached the playoffs on the strength of their pitching. Ted Wieand led the team in victories (16-11 with a 3.19 ERA). Walt Craddock, who had played three seasons with the Kansas City Athletics, was 12-9 with a team-leading 2.61 ERA. Raúl Sánchez was 11-5 with a 3.10 ERA, and Miguel Cuéllar went 10-11 with a 2.80 ERA. Emilio Cueche and Vicente Amor each won nine games, and reliever Luis Arroyo, who had pitched three seasons with the Pittsburgh Pirates, had 8 victories and a 1.15 ERA in 41 appearances. On offense, outfielder Carlos Paula, formerly of the Washington Senators, led the Sugar Kings with a .312 batting average. Outfielder Tony González batted .300 with 20 home runs and a team-leading 81 RBIs. Despite batting just .196, first baseman Borrego Álvarez hit a team-leading 22 home runs. But Havana had to bring up Ray Shearer from Class Double-A Nashville to replace Paula, who was suspended from the playoffs for disciplinary reasons.

Paula's absence didn't matter as Havana cruised through the International League playoffs, sweeping the second-seeded Columbus Jets in four games in the first round. In the championship round, the Sugar Kings needed five games to beat the fourth-seeded Richmond Virginians, who had beaten the top-seeded Buffalo Bisons. The Sugar Kings easily outdrew their International League counterparts with 43,492 fans attending Havana's four playoff games at El Gran Stadium. The other eleven playoff games at Buffalo, Richmond, and Columbus averaged approximately five thousand fans.

When the Sugar Kings beat Richmond 1–0 in the league championship–clinching game on September 22, "pandemonium" broke out as 13,023 fans celebrated by throwing seat cushions and storming the field. Havana would represent the International League in the Junior World Series against the American Association champion Minneapolis Millers. "This," a beaming Fidel Castro said in the Sugar Kings' clubhouse after the game, "is a happy day for Cuba."[2] Even Ray Shearer, who was upset about moving from Nashville to Havana, had to admit things worked out for the best. "Boy, I was really teed off about it," he said. "In the first place, my wife was not well and it meant discomfort for her. But I reported [to the Sugar Kings] and now, of course, can figure it was a lucky break."[3]

Losing outfielder Lee Howell to military service in the middle of the playoffs allowed the Millers to bring up one of the top players in the Boston Red Sox's organization. And the team didn't want to waste any time. The first round of the American Association playoffs series against the Omaha Cardinals was tied at two games apiece heading into Game 5 on Tuesday, September 15. A team representative greeted Carl Yastrzemski at the Minneapolis airport at around 4 o'clock in the afternoon and drove the nineteen-year-old directly to the game.

The Southampton, New York, native had been signed by Boston on November 29, 1958, as an amateur free agent. Yastrzemski had excelled in his first professional season at Raleigh in the Class B Carolina League, batting .377 with 15 home runs and 100 RBIS in 120 games. When Yastrzemski arrived in Gene Mauch's office at Metropolitan Stadium, the Millers manager immediately asked, "Can you play tonight?"[4] Of course, Yastrzemski was ready. The future All-Star and Hall of Famer started at second base and went one for three. His lone hit came in the tenth inning as consecutive singles by Yastrzemski, Joe Macko, and Stu Locklin gave the Millers a 4–3 victory. Umpire Tom Bartos called Yastrzemski safe on a close play at home for the winning run.

Unfortunately for the Millers, the result would not stand. The other American Association teams had voted that Yastrzemski would not be certified as eligible until September 18, the day Howell was set to leave for military service. Omaha general manager Bill Bergesch protested the game on the basis that Yastrzemski was ineligible. League president Ed Doherty upheld the protest and ordered the game be replayed as part of a doubleheader on September 16. With Yastrzemski on the bench, the Millers swept both games, beating Omaha 5–3 in the first game and 3–2 in the nightcap to take the first-round series four games to two.

The Millers needed seven games to dispense with the Fort Worth Cats in the championship round. After the Millers won the first two games, Fort Worth won three in a row to put Minneapolis on the brink of elimination. But the Millers won the final two games of the series. In the clinching game, lefty Ted Borland held the Cats to five hits and struck out seven as the Millers won 4–2. "I had the best stuff I've had in two years," Borland said. "Never won a ball game I enjoyed more."[5]

Third baseman Johnny Goryl, playing out of position at shortstop, played brilliant defense, including an eighth-inning play that may have saved the game. With two runners on base, Goryl snared a "nasty skidder" to his right and threw out Ray Bellino. Goryl also drove in the winning run on a dribbler that got stuck in the mud. "This is my fifth wedding anniversary," Goryl said. "Pretty good present, huh?"[6] Goryl had played the previous winter for Cienfuegos and was in Havana as Castro came to power. He would get the chance to return to Cuba as the Millers made their second consecutive appearance in the Junior World Series. "This year's team gave me a little more satisfaction in winning the playoffs than last year's," said Mauch, who went on to win 1,902 Major League games in twenty-six seasons as a manager with the Philadelphia Phillies, Montreal Expos, Minnesota Twins, and California Angels. "We had our backs to the wall when we came back and won this one."[7]

Doherty commended the Millers for the perseverance they showed in winning the league. "These Millers are great competitors," he said. "They did a fine job coming from behind to win the last games and the series. They came back just like they did after I had to take that victory away from them against Omaha."[8] But more than that, Doherty relished the idea of the American Association champs beating the winners of the International League for a sixth consecutive year. Given his dislike of playing in Cuba, the prospect of achieving that goal against the Sugar Kings no doubt was even more enjoyable: "The greatest kick I get is beating Shag Shaughnessy. There's nothing I want more right now than beating him [for] the sixth straight time in the series. I'm counting on the Millers."[9]

Rain fell in Minneapolis on Sunday, September 27, delaying the 1:30 p.m. start time for the first game of the Junior World Series by a half hour. Before the game, someone quipped about wishing the series had started in Havana. "Started? Should have played all seven games there," Bobby Maduro shot back. "We can get over 30,000 into our stadium. We'd have shown you some crowds."[10] Only 2,486 fans braved the inclement weather in Minneapolis. Yet despite the cold, damp conditions, the Sugar Kings were backed by a vocal rooting section, waving Cuban flags and shaking maracas in the box seats behind the Havana dugout on the third base side. The Cuban fans would have plenty to cheer about in a game played partly in a steady drizzle.

Starter Ted Wieand limited the Millers to four hits as the Sugar Kings turned three double plays after an erratic first inning. "Wieand has pitched very fine ball for us," Sugar Kings manager Preston Gómez said. "All season our pitching is exceptional."[11] Havana used a four-run third inning to chase Minneapolis starter Ted Bowsfield, who hadn't allowed a hit until two outs in the third. But Bowsfield surrendered back-to-back singles to Yo-Yo Davalillo and Elio Chacón and consecutive walks to Tony González, Daniel Morejón, and Ray Shearer as the Sugar Kings scored two runs. A bloop single by Borrego Álvarez off of reliever Billy Muffett drove in two more runs. The Sugar Kings scored another run in the fifth on an RBI-single by Enrique Izquierdo.

Despite losing the first game 5–2, the Millers remained confident they could bounce back as they had throughout the postseason. "You might say I'm impressed but not frightened," Mauch said of the Sugar Kings. "Our pitching failed. When it's right, and it should be, we can beat them. They gave us 'five outs' in the first inning, and we couldn't do anything about it. We beat ourselves this time, and we don't figure to do that very often."[12] Havana's Game 1 performance gave Frank Shaughnessy reason for optimism despite the International League having lost the Junior World Series for five consecutive years. "Maybe we can take it this time. I've got a better team going for me than usual," Shaughnessy said after the game, crossing his fingers. "We've still got to win three games."[13]

The weather deteriorated the following day, and only 1,062 fans turned out Monday night for Game 2. "After the first game, the weather was so bad," Goryl recalled years later. "The temperatures were in the twenties and low thirties. It was snowing and everything else."[14] Conditions were such that several Sugar Kings players, including Izquierdo, Raúl Sánchez, and Octavio "Cookie" Rojas, sat in the dugout, huddled around a makeshift fire built in a wastebasket. "With that kind of cold we tried to stay at least a little bit warmer," Rojas recalled. "You can imagine with that kind of cold that we weren't accustomed to . . . it was more of an advantage for the team from Minnesota. . . . They were more accustomed to the cold."[15]

The frigid temperatures, however, didn't impede the Sugar Kings in the early innings. Havana starter Miguel Cuéllar limited the Millers to five hits through seven innings as the Sugar Kings held a 5–2 lead. Minneapolis's two runs had come on a second-inning, two-run home run by Roy Smalley, who had played eleven seasons in the Majors with the Cincinnati Reds, Milwaukee Braves, and Philadelphia Phillies and whose son Roy Smalley III would go on to play eleven Major League seasons in the 1970s and 1980s. Smalley could tell Cuéllar was tiring as the game dragged on. "He wasn't throwing nearly as hard after about the fifth inning," said Smalley, whose assessment of Cuéllar proved to be correct.[16]

Home runs by Lu Clinton and Red Robbins tied the score in the eighth inning. Clinton's two-run homer chased Cuéllar before Robbins homered off reliever Luis Arroyo. Ed Sadowski homered off Arroyo in the bottom of the ninth inning to give the Millers a 6–5 victory and tie the series at 1–1. Arroyo had shown an effective screwball but surrendered both home runs on fastballs. Sadowski's home run came on a 2-2 count. "I shouldn't have risked the fastball so much," Arroyo said, "with the wind blowing like that to left."[17]

With more rain and colder temperatures in the forecast for Tuesday night, the Minor League commission postponed Game 3 in Minneapolis and moved the remainder of the series to Havana. "So much snow fell," Rojas said, "that we couldn't continue the series there."[18] Minor League president George Trautman cited "fairness to the players" in announcing the commission's unanimous agreement. "It is simply too cold here to play ball or watch it and since they share in the gates of only the first four games, they are entitled to a break," Trautman said. "There is great enthusiasm in Havana, and we are certain of good baseball weather there."[19]

Both teams would fly to Havana on Wednesday, with the series set to resume Thursday night at El Gran Stadium. Despite the

Sugar Kings having home-field advantage in their more spacious ballpark for the rest of the series, the Millers remained confident. "We are all right," Mauch said. "I don't think home-park edge for just one more game was vital. The boys have an increased financial incentive now, and that could be important. As far as the Havana park is concerned, at least three home runs we hit Monday night would have been out of Gran Stadium when I played there, and the fences have been shortened since then."[20] But Maduro seemed to savor the premature change in venue. "We didn't have the power to match some teams in the smaller parks," Maduro said. "But it's hard to hit the ball out of our stadium."[21]

The Cubana de Aviación flight carrying the Sugar Kings arrived at José Martí International Airport at 5:08 p.m. on Wednesday, September 30. A deafening ovation rose from the waiting crowd the moment the first Sugar Kings players exited the door of the airplane and began descending the stairs onto the tarmac. The plane carrying the Millers had arrived a short time earlier. And once both teams had disembarked, a huge caravan of cars transported all the players, team executives, and dignitaries of both leagues from the airport. "People were lined up on the sides of the streets welcoming us into Havana," Goryl recalled. "That was quite an interesting experience to say the least."[22]

The caravan delivered the teams to an amphitheater in nearby Marianao, where they were introduced during a ceremony that included speeches and bands playing both national anthems. Marianao commissioner Efrén González presented Raúl Sánchez with a certificate naming Havana's Game 3 starter an honorary "favorite son" of the city. Despite the fanfare, at least one member of the Millers didn't fully enjoy the experience in Cuba. "You had to be there to understand what it was like," Carl Yastrzemski wrote in his 1990 autobiography. "Sheer chaos and anarchy. People marched in the streets, parading with guns and signs. Worse for us, they did the same thing at the ballpark."[23]

Before the Millers were driven to the Havana Hilton later

that night, Bobby Maduro addressed the significance of the series. "This is a national event," he said. "No Cuban team ever has played in the Junior World Series before, and it is important to the people."[24] The magnitude of the series was evident the next day when Fidel Castro threw out the ceremonial first pitch before Game 3. The presence of the Cuban prime minister had taken on superstitious significance since he showed up unexpectedly during the decisive game of the International League playoff. Richmond had two runners on base with one out, but Sánchez struck two batters to end the inning after Castro arrived at the ballpark. The Sugar Kings went on to win 1–0.

Havana's good luck charm was back at El Gran Stadium for the Junior World Series, and Cuban fans were grateful. "Castro came through the center field fence, walking with his entourage," Goryl said. "With everyone having a handkerchief out, waving it back and forth as fast as you can and shouting 'Viva, Fidel,' you could actually—over their chant—you could hear the handkerchiefs going back and forth and making a flapping noise. It was pretty damned impressive."[25]

Castro, along with his brother Raúl, walked to home plate amid the thunderous ovation and addressed the pleading crowd of 24,938. "I came here to see our team beat Minneapolis, not as premier but as a baseball fan," he said. "I want to see our club win the Little World Series. After the triumph of the revolution, we should also win the Little World Series."[26] Castro then welcomed Mauch and the Millers players before greeting Preston Gómez and the Sugar Kings players one by one. After throwing out the first pitch, Castro watched the game from behind home plate.

Castro's presence in the box seats was far from the only evidence of Cuba's revolution as nearly three thousand soldiers, armed with rifles and bayonets, attended the game. Many lined the field, while others stationed themselves in the dugouts. "It was wall-to-wall military people, on the field, in foul territory," Goryl said. "We were lucky to be able to get the game [played] because there were so many soldiers from Castro's army that were there, for crowd control and just to watch the game."[27]

Many of the soldiers were teenagers. "Young people not more than fourteen or fifteen years old were in the dugout with us, waving their guns around like toys," Millers pitcher Ted Bowsfield recalled. "Every once in a while, we could hear shots being fired outside the stadium, and we never knew what was going on."[28] Mauch recalled one soldier making a slicing motion across his throat as center fielder Tom Umphlett entered the dugout after making a catch to end an inning. "Our players were truly fearful of what might happen if we won," Mauch said. "But we still tried our hardest, figuring we'd take our chances if we did win."[29]

Despite their unease with the situation, the Millers led 2–0 after Ed Sadowski doubled home Red Robbins with a run in the second inning, and Yastrzemski clubbed a 400-foot home run into the left-center-field bleachers in the sixth. Minneapolis starter Tom Borland held Havana to four hits through seven innings, but the Sugar Kings tied it in the eighth. Tony González singled home Yo-Yo Davalillo to make the score 2–1. Then Ray Shearer singled home Daniel Morejón to tie the game.

The Millers had chances to win in the bottom of the ninth and tenth innings. Havana shortstop Leo Cárdenas robbed Umphlett of a hit with the winning run on second base in the ninth. And Minneapolis failed to score in the tenth despite hitting three consecutive singles. Shearer threw out Yastrzemski at third base, and Stu Locklin was thrown out trying to scramble back to first base on his hit. Shearer then gave Havana a 3–2 victory with his RBI-single in the bottom of the tenth inning. "No doubt about it. That was one of the best ball games I ever saw, and I've seen a couple," Shaughnessy said. "The World Series didn't have plays this one had or half the color."[30]

Even away from El Gran Stadium, Yastrzemski never felt comfortable in Havana. Armed soldiers were an ever-present reminder on the streets around the Havana Hilton, where the Millers were staying. "We had been warned not to leave the hotel between games," Yastrzemski wrote. "It was like a revolution in the streets, even though it wasn't violent. But with the guns and the noise it was just scary. In the daytime, though, we'd go shopping, making sure at least six of us went together."[31]

In the lobby of the Hilton, Yastrzemski met American businessmen who shared his anxiety. "They were scared and wanted to get out, but there was no way out," he said. "People in the lobby would tell me they had been sitting around for two weeks, waiting for a flight. Some of them had tried to take their money out of Cuba and discovered that they couldn't."[32]

Castro adjourned a cabinet meeting so he could attend Game 4 on Friday night. Sitting in box seats behind home plate, Fidel was among the 14,115 fans—about 10,000 fewer than had attended Thursday night—watching as Havana beat Minneapolis 4–3 in 11 innings to take a three-games-to-one series lead. Ted Bowsfield allowed only a pair of unearned runs—an error led to Havana scoring on sacrifice flies by Morejón and Shearer in the third inning—before the Millers starter tired in the Havana heat and left in the seventh inning with a 3–2 lead. But as they had the previous game, the Sugar Kings rallied late.

In the ninth, Minneapolis reliever Murray Wall surrendered consecutive singles to Chacón, González, and Morejón as Havana tied the game at 3-all, before reliever Vito Valentinetti got the Millers out of the inning. But Valentinetti came unglued in the eleventh inning, giving up three walks and uncorking two wild pitches before Morejón singled in the winning run. Thousands of fans threw themselves onto the field to celebrate, while those who remained in the stands threw seat cushions. *Diario de la Marina* columnist Eladio Secades delighted in the return to El Gran Stadium of "large, deafening crowds" and "crazy enthusiasm that had been absent for some years."[33]

Facing elimination, the Millers responded the next day by beating Havana 4–2 on a hot Saturday night. With Castro seated in the bleachers among the 21,175 noisy fans, Ted Wills scattered six hits and struck out twelve Sugar Kings. Havana could not capitalize on its first home run of the series—a two-run shot by Morejón that tied the score at 2-all in the sixth—as the Millers once again made a loser out of Arroyo. After relieving Emilio Cueche, the southpaw surrendered three consecutive hits, allowing the Millers to go ahead 3–2. Minneapolis added another run on Goryl's triple.

On Sunday night, the Millers once again staved off elimination, beating the Sugar Kings 5–3. The loss sent a hopeful crowd of 15,042 home disappointed and sent Fidel Castro to Bobby Maduro's office at the stadium. Maduro's twelve-year-old son, Jorge, was with his father after the game when a worried Castro showed up to discuss the series. "My father gets to his office, and Fidel Castro was there," recalled Jorge Maduro, who had spent the series either working as a batboy or roaming from seat to seat during the games rather than sitting in the owner's box seats. "And he tells him, 'Bobby, who is the best player? Who is the best pinch-hitter? Because tomorrow we have to beat these Americans. My problem isn't with the city but with the American government.' And then my father says, 'Look Fidel, stay calm. Let me talk with my manager, please. Get out of the office. I need to meet with my manager.' All that I was able to experience."[34]

In the Millers' clubhouse, Mauch was heaping praise on second baseman Roy Smalley, who had saved the victory with his glove. "I never saw anyone have a better night at second than Roy did," Mauch said of his brother-in-law (Smalley was married to Mauch's sister Jolene). "He had four plays of the kind that you do or you don't. If [future Hall of Famer] Red Schoendienst in his best days had blown any of them, it would have been excusable. Roy made all four." Despite his stellar play in the field, Smalley was more irked by missed opportunities at the plate. "I should have hit that ball 500 feet that went for a sacrifice fly in the sixth," he said. "And I should have hit that double play ball in the seventh out of the park, too. But it was a good win."[35]

Pitching on just one day's rest, Bowsfield tossed four and one-third innings in relief of starter Tracy Stallard to pick up his first postseason victory. "There was a lot of satisfaction in that one," Bowsfield said. "I threw nothing but fastballs, and they were working. I'll be ready if they need me in the last one."[36] Bowsfield's victory tied the series at three games apiece and forced a decisive Game 7. "The odds are now even," Mauch said with what the *Minneapolis Star* described as a "glint in his eye."[37]

If the Millers were to complete an epic comeback from being down three games to one, they would have to wait another day. The rain that started mid-afternoon on Monday had left the field at El Gran Stadium in such bad shape that the Minor League commission decided at 6:30 p.m. to postpone the game. Instead Game 7 would be played Tuesday night. "I'd just as soon have played it and got this thing over with," Mauch said. "The postponement might help us a bit though. The extra day should have Ted Wills ready for relief if he's needed. Tom Borland still is going to be the starter."[38]

Despite Monday's postponement, Bobby Maduro predicted Tuesday's rescheduled game would draw at least as many as the almost 25,000 fans who attended the first game of the series in Havana. Even before Game 7, the series was virtually assured of drawing the second-highest number of fans in Junior World Series history. Already 78,858 had watched the series (75,310 during games in Havana). The record was set in 1944, when 129,618 watched the Baltimore-Louisville series. And gate receipts were already at $101,000, second to the record $108,757.97 set for the Kansas City–Rochester series in 1952.[39]

With the weather clear on Tuesday, October 6, a crowd of 24,990 attended El Gran Stadium for the series finale. Castro would be back in his box seats behind home plate for this contest. The previous two games, he had sat in the bleachers and in the Sugar Kings' dugout, respectively. Among superstitious Cuban fans—so the theory went—Havana had lost those games because Castro was not sitting behind home plate, as he had when the Sugar Kings won the first two games played in Havana. But before settling into his box seats on Tuesday night, Castro purportedly stopped by the Millers' bullpen, where pitcher Stu Locklin was warming up. According to Locklin, Castro paused, looked at the players in the bullpen, patted the gun on his hip, and said in Spanish, "Tonight we win."[40]

Before the game, the partisan crowd sang the Cuban national anthem with "a chorus as we have never heard before," Luis Úbeda wrote in the *Diario de la Marina*, "such was the fervor with which all the fans yearned for the triumph of the Cubans."[41] The desire for a Sugar Kings victory was such that it drove some fans to invoke talismans of Santeria, an African-based religion that combines the worship of traditional Yoruban deities with the worship of Roman Catholic saints. At one point, a fan threw a black hen on the field. In one of the boxes behind home plate, one woman stood with a lit candle. "Her religious faith," Úbeda wrote, "led her to that end."[42]

Once the game began, Borland and Sugar Kings starter Ted Wieand each cruised through the first six batters they faced, and each pitched out of jams in the third inning without surrendering a run. Weiand held the Millers to four hits in seven innings but two were home runs. Lu Clinton put Minneapolis on the board first, leading off the fourth inning with a line drive home run over the left-field fence. Joe Macko gave the Millers a 2–0 lead when he homered in the seventh.

The Sugar Kings rallied to tie the score in the bottom of the eighth inning. Elio Chacón started the rally with a single through the box. Morejón then sliced a ball that clipped the right-field foul line and bounced into the overflow crowd on the field in foul territory for a ground-rule double. That was it for Borland, who was pulled in favor of reliever Murray Wall. As Wall warmed up, two soldiers brought a note from Castro's box to Shearer, who was standing in the on-deck circle behind home plate. The newspaper account didn't reveal the contents of the note, but after Shearer stepped into the batter's box for his at bat, the Sugar Kings right fielder promptly struck out against Wall, looking at a called third strike.

Larry Novak then pinch-hit for first baseman Borrego Álvarez. With a two-strike, no-balls count, Mauch came to the mound to talk to Murray. "Look, we've got an open base," Mauch told Murray, according to Goryl, who had come over from his shortstop position to join the mound conference. "You can attack with your slider or your breaking ball, but don't give in to him. If you walk him, that's fine because then we'll set up the double play or whatever to get out of the jam."[43]

Murray nodded, saying okay to the Millers manager, who left the mound. "Gene goes back to the dugout, and as he turns around, Murray goes into his delivery, first pitch, throws a fastball and [Novak] doesn't miss it. He goes up the middle," Goryl said. "Gene goes ballistic. [Murray] was trying to just kind of throw it out of the zone, and he didn't. He couldn't get it out of the zone, and it ended up costing us the ballgame."[44] Novak's single to center drove in Chacón and Morejón with the tying runs. "He hit the same pitch he missed before," Wall said. "I thought I had him. I know I made the right pitch."[45]

Billy Muffett relieved Wall and got out of the inning, but the damage was done and the stage was set for a dramatic bottom of the ninth. Sugar Kings relief pitcher Raúl Sánchez, who had replaced Weiand in the eighth inning, walked to lead off the ninth. After Davalillo sacrificed Sánchez to second base, Muffett intentionally walked slugger Tony González, who was batting .364 (eight for twenty-two), to face Morejón. The Sugar Kings left fielder had had a stellar series, batting a series-leading .391 (nine for twenty-three) with a home run and six RBI. Morejón did not disappoint, whacking the first pitch he faced to right field for a single. Sánchez, who had been on second, raced around third and slid head-first across home plate ahead of the throw to give Havana a 3–2 victory and the Junior World Series title.

As teammates mobbed Sánchez at home plate, thousands of fans stormed the field. "Indescribable was the scene of jubilation that was produced last night," Úbeda wrote, "when Daniel Morejón hit a bullet to right field to drive home . . . the third run of the Cubans, which served to proclaim them world champions of the minor leagues."[46] Leonardo Agüero was a twenty-seven-year-old fan in the crowd, who joined the revelers on the field. "I was behind third base, right there above the dugout in the first row," he recalled years later. "I jumped on the field and I was trampled by fans. I went to look for something, a base, a glove, a player's cap, but I couldn't get anything."[47]

Jorge Maduro was in the crowd as well. "Everybody rushed the field, the players running to the dugout, the clubhouse, and I was in the middle of all those people," Jorge recalled. "My father was looking for me because it was a mass of people on the field. And then I get to the clubhouse, my father is there. [There is] a photograph with Preston Gómez, and [Sugar Kings coach Reinaldo] Cordero with his arm around me, my father, and [Sugar Kings GM] Paul Miller. . . . It was a tremendous celebration. Fidel Castro was in the clubhouse."[48]

Before heading into the clubhouse to congratulate the Sugar Kings, Castro addressed the fans from the field. "I knew we couldn't lose," the emotional prime minister said. "I hoped everyone would behave as they did."[49] Castro also consoled the Millers, telling Mauch, "If there's anything, I can do, give me a call."[50] The Millers, who had managed to come from behind throughout the postseason, finally couldn't rally to victory. "I never thought we'd lose this one," Mauch said. "Even when we were down three games to one, I was sure we could win—but we didn't. This club fought back a long way this season. It was a shame it couldn't go all the way."[51]

Despite losing, Yastrzemski, for one, was glad to be done with the series. "We were so overjoyed at going home that we went crazy that night at the team party in the hotel," Yastrzemski wrote. "One of the players threw a chair into the pool; someone else threw a table. The fun was broken up when what looked like a platoon of soldiers suddenly appeared. They wanted to arrest us all."[52] According to Yastrzemski, Mauch, recalling Castro's offer, called the Cuban prime minister, who showed up shouting orders. Castro provided an armed escort to the airport the next morning. "It was still a little hairy," Yastrzemski wrote. "They searched every piece of luggage. A lot of guys were smuggling jewelry out, or had a lot of cash. They stuffed it in their shoes, or in their underwear. When that plane—a two-engine job—finally took off we cheered as if we had won the Junior World Series."[53]

In the living room of his apartment in Jersey City, New Jersey, fourteen-year-old Al López-Chávez listened on the radio as the Sugar Kings won the Junior World Series. The same radio that had captured broadcast signals during the revolution from Ejército Rebelde, Castro's rebel forces, also managed to pull in Cuban stations that brought Cuban League and Sugar Kings games into his home at 59 Garrison Avenue. "I remember listening to that broadcast in that living room in that apartment in Jersey City," recalled López-Chávez, whose family had left Cuba for the United States in 1957.[54]

What he remembered most about listening to those games against the Millers was a specific sound. "The siren, 'Rrraaaaah-hhh,'" López-Chávez said. "In the games between Habana and Almendares and Cienfuegos and Marianao, if you went to a game at the Stadium del Cerro, it was always a very lively crowd with lively entertainment. There was a band. . . . The same thing would happen during the Sugar Kings games, and during a rally, I guess, to celebrate a score 'Rrraaaaahhhh.' It was deafening. You would hear the drums in the background. It was by far livelier than going to a game here [in the United States], that's for sure."[55]

Before his family left Cuba, López-Chávez had been an avid Almendares fan, attending games at El Gran Stadium for years. Future Cuban Baseball Hall of Fame pitcher Jorge Comellas was a family friend and neighbor in the Lawton section of Havana. And as a seven-year-old, López-Chávez got to wear an Almendares uniform as an honorary "mascot," joining star outfielder Roberto Ortiz on the field at El Gran Stadium. Listening in New Jersey as Havana won the Junior World Series, López-Chávez could not have imagined that within a year and a half he would be reunited in the United States with one of the teams from his homeland.

10

Regarding Cienfuegos

The Cuban League was about to get a wider audience, one that would stretch beyond the island. Prior to the start of the 1959–60 season, the league reached an agreement to televise twenty-six games in nine major U.S. cities on a tape-delayed basis. The Cuban-American Television Production Company had arranged to have games carried by WOR (New York), WBKB (Chicago), KTTC (Los Angeles), KRON (San Francisco), KDKA (Pittsburgh), WISN (Milwaukee), KHOU (Houston), KLOR (Salt Lake City, Utah), and WRVA (Richmond, Virginia). To broadcast games to American audiences, five cameras, including two with "Zoomar lenses," would record the action at El Gran Stadium. Games would be beamed to a studio via microwave and then put on video tape.

The plan was to distribute one game per week with the game footage edited down to a ninety-minute tape. "We're editing out the unnecessary movements on the field, but won't cut any of the main action," the head of the production company, Max Cooper, said in explaining the broadcasts. "For example, when a pitcher is coming in to the mound in relief, we cut that. Also the pitcher's warm-ups and the unimportant things a player does before taking his position in the batter's box."[1]

As part of the deal, Cooper's production company would pay $1,000 to each player who hit a grand slam and $10,000 to any pitcher who tossed a no-hitter. Panchón Herrera, fresh off winning the International League Triple Crown (.327 average, 37 home runs, and 129 RBIs) with the Buffalo Bisons, captured the first $1,000 prize. The Habana first baseman slugged a grand slam on October 13. The home run came in the bottom of the ninth inning to propel the Lions to a 5–2 victory against Cienfuegos.

Marianao pitcher Miguel Fornieles nearly earned the first no-hitter bonus on opening night. In front of eleven thousand fans on October 8, the Boston Red Sox reliever held Almendares hitless through the first seven innings before Granny Hamner, who had played with the Philadelphia Phillies from 1944 to 1959, laced a line drive to left field that glanced off the glove of Orestes Miñoso for a double. Fornieles surrendered one more hit before locking down the 2–0 victory. Orlando Peña, who had beaten Marianao twelve times the previous season en route to being named the league's MVP, took the loss, giving up home runs to Julio Bécquer and Steve Demeter.

The following night, rain kept the crowd down to just 3,060 fans as Cienfuegos opened its season against Havana. The 1959–60 Elephants, regarded as one of the greatest teams in Cuban League history, took the field with a team stout with pitching and loaded on offense. Cienfuegos was talented enough to potentially give owner Bobby Maduro a Cuban League title on the heels of his Sugar Kings delivering International League and Junior World Series championships. On this night, Habana would win, beating Cienfuegos 2–1 as Camilo Pascual struck out seven batters in the first seven innings before surrendering a pair of runs in the eighth. Even in defeat, Pascual, coming off a season in which he went 17-10 with 2.64 ERA for the Washington Senators, served notice of what to expect during the winter.

Havana was barely done basking in the glow of the Sugar Kings' Junior World Series title and the opening of the Cuban League season before political events began to take a sinister turn in Cuba as Castro and the Communists in his regime consolidated power. During a September 30 television-radio interview, Castro lashed out at Cuba's leading newspapers—*Diario de la Marina* and *Avance*—for their "campaign against the rev-

olution." Castro said *Diario de la Marina* was working to benefit "foreign interests, war criminals of the Batista regime, and
other enemies of the revolution," and described the attitude of
Avance as "highly suspicious."[2]

To deal with increased counterrevolutionary threats, Castro
on October 16 promoted his brother Raúl to the cabinet-level
position of minister of the armed forces, placing his younger
sibling in direct control of Cuba's military. But the shocking
development came days later, when Huber Matos, the military chief of Camagüey Province, sent Castro a letter of resignation on October 19. Matos cited the increasing penetration
of Communists into Castro's regime as his reason for resigning. In response, Castro and Major Camilo Cienfuegos, the
chief of Cuba's revolutionary army, flew three hundred miles
to Camagüey on October 21 to arrest Matos.

Stoked by government radio broadcasts denouncing Matos,
thousands of Camagüey residents flooded the streets surround-
ing the Agramonte provincial military headquarters. Upon
arriving, Cienfuegos strode into the headquarters unopposed
and arrested Matos for treason. "Matos is more than a traitor," Castro told the gathered crowd minutes after the arrest
in a speech that was broadcast back to Havana. "First he is an
ingrate because he was disloyal to the people of Camagüey who
always supported him. . . . Matos conducted his own secret
campaign and tried to create a Trojan horse in the very inside
of the Cuban revolution."[3]

Back in Havana, airplanes identified as a B-26 combat plane
and a C-47 transport dropped anti-Castro leaflets on the city. The
leaflets contained an open letter to the people of Cuba signed
by Pedro Díaz Lanz. The former chief of the Cuban Air Force
had resigned his post and fled to the United States, where he
accused the Castro government of being infiltrated by Communists. Volleys of anti-aircraft artillery failed to bring down the
planes. At around the same time, explosions erupted in parts
of Havana. Two people died and forty-five were wounded in
what news accounts described as a terrorist attack that included

"bombings." But it's possible the casualties resulted from the anti-aircraft shells.

Regardless, Castro seized the opportunity to unleash a torrent of accusations during a four-hour television and radio interview that ended at 3 a.m. Castro, who had returned from Camagüey and was at the Hotel Nacional when the leaflets were dropped, accused the United States of bombing the Cuban capital. "Our reply to these air attacks," Castro railed, "must be the training and arming of the peasants and workers, the professionals and even the women."[4] Philip Bonsal had been U.S. ambassador to Cuba since February. He believed the leaflet drop had come at an opportune time for Castro. "The 'bombing' came as a providential diversion from the potentially very serious Matos affair," Bonsal wrote in his 1972 book. "It enabled him to electrify his mobs with what was then the completely fraudulent issue of an external aggression designed to crush their Revolution."[5]

In the days that followed, the government began rounding up anti-Castro elements throughout the island. About forty-four people were arrested in Havana. The army announced the arrest of thirty-eight officers, who had served under Matos in Camagüey. On Monday, October 26, the thirteenth anniversary of the opening of El Gran Stadium, the scheduled Cuban League game was postponed because Castro held a rally at the presidential palace. "Every day our enemies are more insolent and audacious," Castro told the gathered crowd of three to four hundred thousand during his three-and-a-half-hour speech. "The world must know that the Cubans will die fighting against any internal or foreign enemies."[6] Bonsal described Castro's speech in ominous terms. "He shook his fist, roared defiance at the northern sky, foamed at the mouth, and in every way comported himself in a manner reminiscent of Hitler at his most hysterical and most odious."[7]

On Friday, October 30, the Cuban Cabinet suspended the right of habeas corpus, permitting government authorities to detain persons without charges or a hearing. Whatever hope Bonsal may have harbored about U.S.-Cuba relations ended during those critical final two weeks in October. "Castro's performance on the 'bombing' spelled the end of my hope for rational relations between Cuba and the United States," Bonsal wrote. "It also triggered the separation from the regime of those with any previous standing in the Cuban establishment."[8] This volatile period also brought about the mysterious disappearance of one of the most popular figures in Cuba.

On the night of Wednesday, October 28, Camilo Cienfuegos, having reorganized the military command structure at Camagüey, boarded a twin-engine Cessna 310 for his return to Havana. He never arrived, his flight vanishing without a trace. In the days that followed his disappearance, Castro himself led a massive search effort that involved air force and civilian planes, navy vessels, army patrols, and even peasants. Search parties scoured the plains and hills of Las Villas and Camagüey provinces, as well as the waters off the northern coast of Cuba for the missing flight, which had been piloted by Lieutenant Luciano Farinas and included another soldier. "Let us hope," Castro said. "We are searching for a man too valuable to the revolution to resign ourselves easily to his loss."[9]

Born into a working-class family in Havana on February 6, 1932, Cienfuegos was handsome with a broad bearded smile, the picture of the romantic revolutionary with his long hair and ever-present cowboy hat. After moving to the United States in the 1950s, Cienfuegos migrated in 1956 to Mexico, where he hooked up with Castro's rebels, later distinguishing himself during the fighting in the Sierra Maestra. But while Cienfuegos was personally loyal to Castro, he was not necessary an ideologue. "I knew Camilo before he was a revolutionary," said Ralph Ávila, who knew Cienfuegos from their younger days playing baseball in the Havana neighborhood of Lawton. "Camilo wanted to be a baseball player. . . . His father was a Communist and his brother was a Communist, but not Camilo."[10]

Because of his revolutionary exploits and his good looks, Cienfuegos had become a beloved figure in Cuba by the time of his disappearance. He was the second-most popular man in Cuba, behind only Fidel Castro. Even Americans playing in the Cuban League seemed to feel his loss. "The person I met that I had a nice relationship with was Cienfuegos," said future Cleveland Indians and Minnesota Twins All-Star Jim "Mudcat" Grant, who pitched for Almendares in 1959–60. "He was a gentleman. It was too bad he was killed. We all felt real bad with the news."[11] Elephants slugger George Altman, a future All-Star with the Chicago Cubs, said he was "saddened" by Cienfuegos's disappearance. "He seemed to be a really nice fellow."[12]

The search for Camilo Cienfuegos covered an area up to two hundred miles west and northwest of Camagüey. During the search, numerous reports surfaced that Cienfuegos had been found alive but injured. The Cuban Air Force investigated one sighting of two small planes at Cayo Anguila, a key in the Atlantic about sixty miles north of Caibarién, Cuba. But it was determined they were old wrecks. On October 31, Castro flew to Cayo Francés, twenty-two miles off the north-central Cuban coast, to investigate a report of a crashed plane, which proved false as well.

One report of Cienfuegos's rescue originated from the Cuban Army and sent jubilant crowds into the Havana streets on November 4. But president Osvaldo Dorticós quickly issued a statement saying the report was unconfirmed. Disappointed demonstrators marched to the presidential palace and attacked a loudspeaker truck that delivered the president's statement. Some demonstrators even attacked two American photographers chronicling the assault. The next day, the regime linked the false report to Dominican dictator Rafael Trujillo.

At one point, the Cuban government enlisted help from the United States, which launched naval planes from Key West, Florida, and the U.S. base at Guantanamo, Cuba. Those planes searched off the Cuban coast on November 2 but did not fly over the island at the request of the Castro regime. On November 7, about thirty civil air patrol aircraft and one U.S. Air Force plane flew over the Florida Everglades—searching an area south of Sarasota—at Cuba's request because a ship's captain had reported seeing Cienfuegos's plane headed toward Florida ten days earlier.

Unsuccessful in locating Cienfuegos, the search eventually was called off. El Gran Stadium was dark once again— the games scheduled for November 13 canceled—so Castro could address Cienfuegos's disappearance. During that radio-television address, Castro declared that the only possibility was that Cienfuegos's plane had gone down over the ocean. But he blamed the American press for spreading wild rumors. "There is no doubt of the plot against the revolution," Castro said, "particularly abroad."[13]

Rumors about Cienfuegos's fate ran rampant. Was his plane mistakenly shot down by another Cuban aircraft that was dispatched to take out a light aircraft dropping incendiary devices on Cuban sugarcane fields? Did Fidel Castro orchestrate Cienfuegos's death? Maybe Cienfuegos had become too popular for Fidel's liking. Did Raúl Castro personally kill Cienfuegos because the two clashed over the Matos arrest? Was Cienfuegos an anti-Communist? Perhaps he was merely the victim of an inexperienced pilot and bad weather. "My belief," Bonsal wrote, "was that he paid the price for his recklessness in flying a plane of doubtful airworthiness with a semiskilled pilot late in the evening and under unfavorable weather conditions."[14]

Castro's heated anti-U.S. rhetoric in the wake of the leaflet drop caused the Los Angeles Dodgers enough concern that the team sent confidential letters to the organization's Americans playing in Cuba. The letter advised Don Bessent (Marianao) and Tom Lasorda and Art Fowler (Almendares) to return to the United States because of the political turmoil in Cuba. Bessent, who had been suffering from dizzy spells after being beaned on October 31, asked for and was granted his release and returned to the United States. But Lasorda and Fowler opted to stay. Both had played in Cuba during recent tumultuous winters. Lasorda had been a vocal defender of playing in Cuba. Another such advocate was Cleveland Indians general manager Frank Lane, who was surprised once word of the Dodgers' letter got out. "They probably don't know," Lane said, "what the situation is here."[15]

Also causing a stir in the early weeks of the Cuban League was the October 31 resignation of Almendares manager Oscar Rodríguez. The Scorpions skipper had to step down the previous winter after suffering a heart attack. He was replaced by Coach Sungo Carreras, who led the team to Cuban League and Caribbean Series titles. Rodríguez had sufficiently recovered to return to his managerial duties for the 1959–60 season. But barely three weeks into the season "doctors decided that the emotional strain might bring on another attack," Rubén Rodríguez wrote in *The Sporting News*.[16] So Oscar Rodríguez resigned and once again was replaced by Carreras. But in taking over a team in last place, Carreras was unable to reproduce the magic of the previous winter. "Sungo would say, 'Last year you made me big,'" Cholly Naranjo recalled. "'This year, they want to kill me.' That's life."[17]

Almendares's struggles certainly contributed to flagging attendance for Cuban League games at El Gran Stadium. So Almendares and Cienfuegos decided to experiment with playing a game outside Havana. Following the example of the Sugar Kings, the teams scheduled a game in Morón in Camagüey Province for November 26. Cienfuegos used another fine outing by Camilo Pascual and three home runs to beat Almendares 8–2 in front of a crowd of about six thousand at Morón Stadium. Another six thousand had to be turned away. The Elephants jumped on Almendares starter Orlando Peña for five first-inning runs on home runs by Tony González and Dutch Dotterer. George Altman contributed a 425-foot, three-run homer in the fifth that landed on the street.

In earning his sixth victory of the season, Pascual struck out ten batters to raise his league-leading total to 89 strikeouts in 76 innings. That put him on pace to potentially eclipse the league record of 206 strikeouts (in 179 innings) set by Wilmer "Vinegar Bend" Mizell for Habana in 1955–56. The game improved Cienfuegos's record to 16-12, one and a half games behind league-leading Marianao, and dropped last-place Almendares to 8-21, ten games off the pace.

Following the game in Morón, Almendares teammates Cholly Naranjo, Leo Posada, and Miguel de la Hoz—like Cuba's missing revolutionary Camilo Cienfuegos—almost didn't make it back to Havana on their own trip from Camagüey Province. After the game, the trio piled into Naranjo's late-model convertible Corvette for the late-night, four-and-a-half-hour drive to Havana along Cuba's Central Highway. "That Corvette is only two seats," Posada said, recounting the story during the 2016 Society for American Baseball Research convention in Miami. "I'm sitting in the middle with the stick between my legs. Mike is on my right side. [Naranjo] is driving. I said, 'Cholly, let me drive for a while.' He said, 'No, I'm fine.' Okay so here we go."[18]

After they had passed Matanzas, about sixty-five miles east of Havana, Posada turns to see Naranjo asleep at the wheel and snoring. "We go into a very large curve . . . and the car starts going outside the curve and it starts hitting the shoulder," Posada said. "I said, 'Cholly, no!' And he yanks the steering wheel and we go [spinning] zoom, zoom, zoom, three times. Now we're going backwards to Havana, facing Matanzas." After getting the car straightened out and pointed in the right direction, Posada told a suddenly alert Naranjo, "You're alright now. You can keep going. You're not going to sleep anymore." Naranjo "drove all the way back to Havana," Posada recalled, "no problem."[19]

On the day Almendares and Cienfuegos were in Morón for their game, Castro appointed Che Guevara as president of the National Bank of Cuba. Guevara, the most anti-U.S. member of the Castro regime, replaced Felipe Pazos, who was a "leading spirit of the moderates in the Castro government."[20] But Pazos was so appalled by Castro's October 26 speech that he approached President Dorticós to complain about how damaging it would be for U.S.-Cuba relations. Of course, Dorticós reported Pazos's concerns to Castro, who promptly denounced Pazos during a cabinet meeting.

As head of the central bank, Guevara would be responsible for setting Cuba's financial policies, as well as controlling imports, exports, and foreign exchange.[21] Months after Guevara's appointment, Almendares pitcher Orlando Peña and Willy Miranda—the longtime Scorpions shortstop had been traded to Habana for shortstop Humberto "Chico" Fernández in the closing days of November 1959—would have a chilling encounter with Guevara in his office at the National Bank.

The trial of Huber Matos began on Friday, December 11. Applause from a small group of civilians greeted the former Cuban Army major as he entered the army movie theater that would be the site for his military tribunal. Aside from civilians, the audience included soldiers and members of the press. Cuban representatives of foreign news organizations were permitted into the makeshift courtroom, but non-Cubans, including American correspondents, were kept out. It was the first time that foreign newsmen had been specifically barred from public hearings since Castro took power. An hour after Matos's arrival, Castro, carrying his favorite automatic rifle, entered the theater for the proceedings.

Matos, along with five captains and eleven lieutenants who had protested his arrest in October, were charged with treason, sedition, and conspiracy. The former army commander of Camagüey Province denied conspiring against the regime. "If the tribunal thinks it is good for the revolution, condemn me—even to death," Matos testified. "I am always ready to defend the revolution."[22] Matos told the military court that he resigned because of ideological differences with Fidel and Raúl Castro over Communist infiltration into the revolutionary army. "Communists are not necessary in the armed forces," Matos said. "I didn't want to become an obstacle to the revolution."[23]

Castro himself took the witness stand to loud applause on December 14. After striding onto the stage, the prime minister removed his army jacket, placed a microphone on a cord around his neck, and proceeded to deliver a seven-hour speech denouncing Matos. Turning his back on the judges and lawyers sitting on the stage, Castro addressed the prisoners, witnesses, soldiers, and newsmen in the audience, charging that Matos's resignation "was part of a prepared plot to cause a crisis in the government." Castro declared that "to destroy the plot, I had to go to Camagüey. This was a delight for reactionaries."[24]

Castro accused Matos and his officers of counterrevolutionary activities, and accused the former major of carrying out the plans of U.S. interests, big land owners in Cuba, former members of the Batista regime, and the dictatorship of the Dominican Republic. He claimed Matos's resignation "was a result of ideological differences. Matos and we don't think the same about what is a true revolution. Matos has tried to present himself as a victim of me, the revolution, and my commanders."[25]

The next night, the tribunal convicted Matos of counterrevolutionary activities against the Castro regime and sentenced him to twenty years in prison. Three captains who served under Matos were sentenced to seven years each. Thirteen others each received three-year sentences, and another five received two-year prison terms. Matos declared his trial to have been a "flagrant violation of the [United Nations] Declaration of Human Rights."[26]

Years later, after he served out his sentence and was able to leave Cuba for the United States, Matos placed the blame for Cienfuegos's death squarely on the Castro regime. "There was only one single week between my arrest and the disappearance of Camilo," Matos said. "There is no question that they killed Camilo, for my arrest put Camilo in a position of crisis. He had to discuss me with Fidel. When Fidel saw in him an attitude that wasn't one of unconditional support . . . Camilo told me that he was in a very difficult situation." [27]

The success of the November 26 Almendares-Cienfuegos game in Morón—crowds at El Gran Stadium had been averaging about two thousand—prompted Cienfuegos to schedule a return visit to Camagüey Province for December 15 against Marianao. Other such games away from Havana followed but not before the Elephants won twenty-three of thirty games to take a seven-and-a-half-game lead on January 10. Cienfuegos added to its lead on January 16 as some seven thousand fans—the best gate for a league game in weeks—watched the Elephants beat Marianao 5–2 in a jammed park in the city of Cienfuegos, two hundred miles east of Havana. Almendares and Cienfuegos played at Palma Soriano in Oriente on January 23, with the Scorpions winning 6–5. The next night, Cienfuegos beat Marianao 7–3 in Santiago de Cuba, drawing a crowd of fifteen thousand in the capital of Oriente Province.

The victory also clinched the Cuban League pennant for Cienfuegos with two weeks remaining in the season. Camilo Pascual won his league-leading fourteenth game of the season against only five losses. Pascual—named as one of Cuba's most distinguished athletes for 1959 by a vote of Cuban sportswriters—went on to record another victory and finish with a league-leading 15-5 record. He also led the league with 163 strikeouts and finished with a 2.03 ERA. Pascual led a pitching triumvirate that included Pedro Ramos and Raúl Sánchez as Cienfuegos became the first team in league history to boast three Cuban-born pitchers to record double-digit victories. Sánchez finished with a 12-4 record and league-leading 1.64 ERA to earn league MVP honors. Ramos was 12-5 with a 2.65 ERA. Cienfuegos pitchers had a combined team ERA of 2.13, to set a league record.

The Elephants were equally as dominant on offense, clubbing 72 home runs, breaking the record set by the 1956–57 Cienfuegos team by 19. George Altman hit 14, Borrego Álvarez hit 12, Leo Cárdenas hit 11, and Tony González hit 10. González led the league with a .310 batting average. With such a balanced team, Cienfuegos won 48 games, eclipsing the previous record of 47 set by the 1951–52 Almendares club. "One of the greatest [Cuban] teams of all time with the super extraordinary pitching that we had with Camilo Pascual, Pedro Ramos, Raúl Sánchez," Cienfuegos second baseman Cookie Rojas called it. "We had a team with good young players. . . . We had tremendous defense. We had a team that could beat any team in the Majors, in my opinion, because of the talent that we had. And we saw that because of the players who established themselves in Major League Baseball for many years."[28]

Normally upon completion of the Cuban League season, Willy Miranda and his family would load some of their possessions on a trailer and take the ferry to Key West and points north for the upcoming Major League season. But the end of the 1959–60 season was different "because the Castro regime was watching closely."[29] Just how closely became apparent during an encounter with Che Guevara at the National Bank of Cuba that included Miranda and Orlando Peña. "When we get there to the office, Che Guevara was sitting like this, with both legs up [on the desk]," Peña recalled. "He stood up. He looked like a bastard. He looked like a son of a bitch. 'How can I help you?'"[30]

Miranda explained he was a baseball player and wanted to know what he needed to do to bring his car—the vehicle had an American license plate—back to the United States via ferry. After Guevara pressed a button to ring a bell, a beautiful woman emerged from a long hallway. "She comes and says, 'Follow me,'" Peña said. "We get to the office, and she sits down and she talked about the boxers, the artists, and everything, and in the end, she said, 'With Che Guevara, you will not able to take the car because the ferries are going to stop running in a few days. So, if you paid $3,000 for that car to give it to your father, you have to pay $3,000 to me.' She said this to me and Willy."[31] As the players were leaving, Guevara addressed Miranda:

> **Guevara:** I don't understand baseball. What I understand is soccer.
>
> **Miranda:** Okay, that's fine, Mr. Guevara, but let me tell you, you're Argentine. But for Cubans it's baseball.
>
> **Guevara:** No, no, for Cubans it's not baseball. None of that. That's a tale.
>
> **Miranda:** Well, then go to hell.

Guevara: Remember, Mr. Miranda, that you have a pistol that was given to you by a family member. Roberto Fernández Miranda, who was a general in the [Batista] military, gave you a pistol. You have to turn that in to be able to leave the country.[32]

The players were stunned by what Guevara knew. "Willy was like, '*Coño*, who was the son of a bitch who sold me out?'" Peña said. "Roberto Fernández Miranda was the brother of Marta Fernández Batista, Batista's [second] wife. They were family. He had the pistol because it was a gift. Willy never even brought it out. Willy went and threw away the pistol in the building where he lived next to the stadium. He threw it the hell away so he could leave. He would say, 'Who could have been the Cuban that sold me out?' Somebody sold him out. Because how would Che Guevara know that he had a pistol that was given to him by Roberto Fernández Miranda? He could not have guessed that."[33]

The encounter may have been what finally convinced Miranda to leave Cuba for good after the 1959–60 season. It had been his worst season in the Cuban League, as well as his only season not spent entirely with Almendares. "He planned leaving without even telling my mother," Willy Miranda Jr. said years later. "We got out easily because we took out the same things we always did. . . . My father would come out later. He got on a Pan Am flight by himself under another name, thanks to friends."[34]

11

The Last Series

As Major League Baseball's 1959 trade deadline loomed, Gabe Paul approached Calvin Griffith with a stunning proposal during the Minor League meetings in St. Petersburg, Florida. The Reds general manager offered the Senators president $1 million for third baseman Harmon Killebrew and pitcher Camilo Pascual. In fact, Paul had first approached Griffith with an offer of $500,000 for Killebrew—the 1959 American League home run co-champion (tied with Cleveland's Rocky Colavito with 42 homers)—back in August. Paul suggested the trade would not take place until the off-season interleague trading period between November 17 and December 15. Griffith rejected that overture "right away," but promised to think it over as a favor to Paul.

When the two met again in Florida, Griffith told Paul he "couldn't possibly sell Killebrew." Paul's second attempt, however, also included a $500,000 offer for Pascual. "Calvin gave me a more emphatic 'no'—or maybe I thought it was more emphatic," Paul said. "Anyway, I felt that I could have offered a million for Pascual and Washington would have turned it down."[1] Griffith confirmed as much when he was asked about the offer. "We were flattered by the tremendous offer for both ballplayers but money don't do you a bit of good if you're trying to get a team together," Griffith said. "Pascual is the best pitcher in the majors, barring none. The money was tempting but it wouldn't make up for players like Killebrew and Pascual."[2]

Griffith even conceded that "Pascual would be more valuable to us" than Killebrew, who would go on to hit 573 home runs and be inducted into the National Baseball Hall of Fame in 1984. Such was the esteem Griffith held for Pascual—and for good reason. Pascual had just completed his first All-Star season, compiling a 17-10 record with a 2.64 ERA and 185 strikeouts with the Senators. He continued to show All-Star form in the winter, finishing with a Cuban League–leading 15-5 record. He also led the league with 163 strikeouts and finished with a 2.03 ERA. And after Pascual led Cienfuegos to the league championship, the Elephants were counting on him to perform similarly in the Caribbean Series.

The 1960 Caribbean Series returned to Panama, the site of Cienfuegos's previous tournament title in 1956, when Pascual and Pedro Ramos each won a pair of games. Cienfuegos was favored to win its second title as the twelfth edition of the Caribbean Series opened on Wednesday, February 10, with Cienfuegos playing Venezuela's Rapiños team. The other series-opening game pitted Puerto Rico's Caguas team against Marlboro from Panama. Aside from the formidable pitching rotation of Pascual, Sánchez, and Ramos, Cienfuegos added Almendares hurler Orlando Peña to replace Ted Wieand and shore up the bullpen. Peña had followed up his stellar 1958–59 Cuban League season by going 10-9 with 3.26 ERA in the just-concluded winter season.

Cuba wasn't the only team in the Caribbean Series stocked with Major League talent. First baseman Victor Pellot, known in the United States as Vic Power (Cleveland Indians) managed Caguas, which also had future Major League All-Star Tommy Davis (Los Angeles Dodgers). The Puerto Rican team counted future Hall of Famer Orlando Cepeda (San Francisco Giants) among its reinforcements. Marlboro's roster was reinforced with New York Yankees third baseman Héctor López. Rapiños was led by future Hall of Fame shortstop Luis Aparicio (Chicago White Sox), but was without Norm Cash, who had led the team in home runs and RBIs. The future Detroit Tigers All-Star was forced to return to the United States to fulfill a military obligation. But future Major League All-Star Willie Davis (Dodgers) was added to the roster.

Rapiños represented Venezuela by winning the Occidental League playoff but didn't have to play against the Venezuelan Association playoff winner to determine which team would advance to the Caribbean Series. The Venezuelan Association had suspended play on December 23 because of a strike by native players. The announcement came four days before the scheduled end of the regular season and despite potentially the circuit's most dramatic finish. Only one and a half games separated the four clubs. The strike was in response to the league's refusal to lift a two-year suspension of Alejandro Carrasquel, the former Pampero manager. Carrasquel, who was fired in November, had punched club official Eddy Moncada—breaking his jaw—during an argument. It was the first time a Latin winter league had suspended play since the Caribbean Confederation joined Organized Baseball in 1949.

As the Caribbean Series was about to begin in Panama, Cuba was hosting a state visit from Anastas Mikoyan. The first deputy premier of the USSR had arrived in Havana on February 4 at Fidel Castro's invitation. Until that visit, Cuba and the Soviet Union did not have diplomatic relations (Batista had broken off relations after taking power in 1952). Mikoyan's visit—arranged officially to open a Soviet exhibition on science, technology, and culture—came at a time when U.S.-Cuba relations were under considerable strain with Castro ratcheting up anti-U.S. rhetoric.

When the Russian turbo-prop plane carrying a party of forty rolled to a stop at José Martí Airport, an army band played the Cuban and Soviet anthems. Castro strolled onto the airfield to personally greet Mikoyan. Raúl Castro, Che Guevara, and known Cuban Communist leaders also were among the welcoming committee. Later that evening, Cuban president Osvaldo Dorticós received Mikoyan at the presidential palace.

On February 6, Mikoyan met with Raúl Castro in Matanzas. Dorticós hosted a reception for Mikoyan at the presidential palace on February 8. The next day, Mikoyan praised Cuba's agrarian reform program while visiting the National Agrarian Reform Institute, which oversaw the country's expropriation and redistribution of land. "The big landowners of Cuba have nothing to complain about," Mikoyan said. "The Cuban government will pay for the expropriated land in twenty-year bonds with 4.5 percent interest."[3]

A crowd of 12,880 packed Olympic Stadium in Panama City for the start of the Caribbean Series. Opening ceremonies included a parade of pretty women dressed in traditional Panamanian garb, Panama president Ernesto de la Guardia throwing out the first pitch, and Felipe Guerra Matos, Cuba's director of sports, leading the Cuban delegation as it marched onto the field. After Cuba and Venezuela took the field, Pascual and Rapiños starter Billy Muffett breezed through the first three innings before both clubs got on the scoreboard in the fourth inning.

Cuba scored twice in the top of the inning before Muffett could record a single out. After Tony González doubled, Román Mejías followed with a hit and George Altman singled to drive in both runners. Muffett then struck out Borrego Álvarez, Leo Cárdenas, and Dutch Dotterer to end the inning. Venezuela responded with three runs in the bottom of the inning as Luis "Camaleón" García doubled home a pair of runs and Les Peden singled in another. But Cuba took control of the game, scoring three runs each in the fifth and seventh innings.

The three-run outburst in the fifth came on hits by Ozzie Álvarez, Pascual, and Don Eaddy and a double by Mejías. Cuba chased Muffett in the seventh as González opened the frame with a walk, Mejías picked up his third hit of the game, and Altman bunted for a hit. Borrego Álvarez drove in two runs off of reliever Marcelino Sánchez. A hit by Dotterer drove in Altman with the third run. Venezuela knocked Pascual out of the game with a pair of runs in the eighth, but Orlando Peña closed out the game in relief—foreshadowing his importance for the remainder of the series—as Cuba won 8–5. Puerto Rico beat host Panama 4–3 in the second game of the night.

The next night, Cuba beat Puerto Rico 4–2 despite managing only two hits against Caguas starter Earl Wilson. Cuba scored two runs in the second inning on a walk, error, line drive double by Cárdenas and a sacrifice fly by Dotterer. Cuba's only other hit came in the eighth, a two-run home run by Dotterer. Cienfuegos starter Raúl Sánchez handcuffed Puerto Rico batters, allowing just four hits until the ninth. Tommy Davis spoiled the shutout bid with a two-out, two-run home run. But Pedro Ramos came in to get the final out of the game.

Cuba completed a trifecta on Friday, February 12, sweeping its first game against each of the other three teams in the tournament by beating host Panama 6–4. But the victory did not come easily. After Marlboro starter Ken Rowe surrendered three walks and a hit to allow Cuba a first-inning run, Leonardo Martínez Ferguson entered the game in relief and blanked Cienfuegos until the seventh, when Dan Dobbek homered. But Panama had jumped on Cuba starter Orlando Peña for a 3–1 lead and was up 4–2 after Dobbek's home run. To the crowd of about ten thousand partisan fans, it appeared Panama would hand Cuba its first loss of the tournament. But Cuba rallied for four runs in the bottom of the ninth inning for the victory.

Don Eaddy led off the frame with a hit, and Dobbek followed with a walk off of reliever Bob Walz. After Walz struck out Mejías, Panama manager Bobby Shantz, a former Major League All-Star, brought in lefty Bill Kirk to face the left-handed-hitting Altman, who drove in Eaddy with a single. Kirk was replaced on the mound by Humberto Robinson, but Borrego Álvarez crushed Robinson's second pitch out of Olympic Stadium for a three-run, game-winning homer. Cuba was two victories away from clinching the Caribbean Series with three games to play.

While Cuba was inching closer to securing a Caribbean Series title, Fidel Castro was inching closer to reestablishing diplomatic relations with the Soviet Union. Mikoyan was on the ninth day of his visit to Cuba, when Castro, in Mikoyan's presence, declared that ties with the USSR would be restored "very soon."

The promise came during a reception given by a group of Cuban industrialists and manufacturers. Mikoyan was more noncommittal, saying he had not discussed reestablishing of diplomatic relations, but he said the Soviet government was willing to sell military planes to Cuba if Castro's regime requested them.

Before Mikoyan left Cuba the next day, he and Castro signed a commercial agreement through which the Soviet Union agreed to buy five million tons of sugar from Cuba over a five-year period and give the island a $100 million line of credit. The agreement made the Soviet Union the second-largest buyer of Cuban sugar behind the United States. The statement released by Cuba's Ministry of Foreign Relations declared that Cuba and the Soviet Union "consider that the consolidation of world peace depends in a notable measure on the development of the most ample and effective international collaboration, on the basis of full mutual respect and of the inalienable rights of each nation to freely decide its own political, economic, and social path."[4]

Aside from a two-run home run by Borrego Álvarez in the second inning, Cienfuegos hitters had few answers for Al Grunwald, Venezuela's starting pitcher in Cuba's game on Saturday, February 13. The Kansas City Athletics lefty struck out twelve batters through eight innings as he and Cuba's Pedro Ramos combined for a classic pitching duel. Grunwald's Rapiños teammates began cutting into Cuba's 2–0 lead in the fourth inning as Willie Davis hit a solo home run off of Ramos. Venezuela tied the score in the eighth when Ramos ran into trouble, forcing Peña to enter the game in relief. Peña struck out Luis Aparicio, the first batter he faced, but surrendered a game-tying single to Davis before getting out of the inning.

In the top of the ninth inning, Venezuela took a 3–2 lead as Peña gave up a pair of singles, a wild pitch, and a sacrifice fly by pinch-hitter Billy Muffett. But Grunwald couldn't hold the lead. Dotterer walked to open the bottom of the ninth, and after a hit batsman, Eaddy singled home Dotterer with the tying run. Grunwald fanned Dobbek for his thirteenth strikeout but a fielder's choice loaded the bases. Altman walked to give Cuba a 4–3 victory to improve to 4-0 in the series. Only host Panama, at 2-2 after beating Puerto Rico 8–7 in the night's other contest, had any chance of catching the Cubans.

Camilo Pascual took the mound on Sunday with the chance to clinch the tournament title for Cienfuegos, and he turned in a masterful performance as Cuba beat Puerto Rico 4–0. The only hit Pascual surrendered came when Puerto Rico shortstop Felix Torres led off the fourth inning with a clean single to shallow center. Pascual struck out seven and walked only one batter. He needed just eighty-eight pitches—throwing sixty-five for strikes—and faced twenty-eight batters, one over the minimum (a double play erased Torres after his fourth-inning single). The near no-hitter gave Pascual his second victory of the tournament and a 6-0 career record in the Caribbean Series. "Camilo was on fire that day," Peña recalled years later. "He came over to me, and I asked him, 'Camilo, how do you feel?' He said, '*Estoy entero*' (I'm whole). Camilo was a very serious kid, very serious."[5]

Pascual's clinching victory completed an extraordinary ten-month period for the twenty-six-year-old right-hander. Including his 17-10 mark with the Senators and 15-5 record in the Cuban League, Pascual compiled a 34-15 record between the start of the 1959 Major League season and the conclusion of the Caribbean Series. While Pascual was dominating Puerto Rico in his final Caribbean Series start, his teammates were racking up twelve hits against Caguas pitcher José Santiago, who had pitched for the Cleveland Indians and Kansas City Athletics in the mid-1950s. Yet the game remained scoreless until the fourth inning, when George Altman scored on the front end of a double steal, and Dutch Dotterer drove in another run with a single. That was all the run support Pascual would need, but Cuba scored twice more. Tony González, who went four for five, scored a run in the eighth, and doubled in another run in the ninth.

The following night, Cuba wrapped up a six-game sweep by beating Panama 10–7. Pedro Ramos picked up the victory with relief help from Peña, his third relief appearance of the series. Cuba's fifth consecutive Caribbean Series championship was its seventh overall title in twelve tournaments. Attendance for the series totaled 53,458, with $75,621 in gross receipts. Cuba divided a winning team share of $4,882. "It was a tremendous series," Peña said. "That series was something else. The stadium in Panama wasn't very big, but it was full. There were even fans on the roof."[6] Unfortunately, it would be the last Caribbean Series played for ten years.

Long before Mikoyan's visit to Cuba, the United States began viewing Castro warily. The "honeymoon period" had effectively ended in April of 1959, and by June the United States decided "it was not possible to achieve our objectives with Castro in power."[7] On October 31, 1959, the State Department recommended to President Dwight Eisenhower a plan authorizing the CIA "to support elements in Cuba opposed to the Castro Government while making Castro's downfall seem to be the result of his own mistakes."[8] At a meeting of the National Security Council on January 14, 1960, Livingston Merchant, the State Department's undersecretary for political affairs, described Cuba as "the most difficult in all the history of our relations with Latin America."[9]

The following day, CIA director Allen Dulles asked the Special Group, a secret subcommittee of the National Security Council that reviewed covert operations, for authorization to begin plotting against Castro, whom Eisenhower referred to as a "madman."[10] At a Special Group meeting on February 17, 1960, Dulles proposed having the CIA sabotage Cuban sugar mills, but Eisenhower directed him to formulate a bolder plan. The president "felt that any program should be much more ambitious, and it was probably now the time to move against Castro in a positive and aggressive way which went beyond pure harassment."[11]

While his administration was covertly trying to undermine the Castro regime, Eisenhower publicly insisted the United States had no intention of intervening in Cuba. The president used a tour of Latin America—with visits to Puerto Rico, Brazil, Uruguay, Chile, and Argentina between February 22 and March 4—to drive home that point. The United States' history of intervening in Cuba's affairs dated to the turn of the twentieth century, but the president assuaged concerns during the tour by not trying to rally anti-Castro or anti-Communist sentiments. "We subscribe to the policy of non-intervention," Eisenhower said. "We repudiate dictatorship in any form, Right or Left."[12]

But as Eisenhower wrapped up his trip with a second stop in Puerto Rico on March 4, a French freighter loaded with ammunition and explosives for the Cuban Army exploded in Havana harbor, killing one hundred persons and injuring three hundred more. The 4,310-ton *La Coubre* entered the harbor at 9 a.m. As the cargo from Antwerp, Belgium, was being unloaded, the first blast rocked the vessel at 3 p.m. Other explosions followed. Cuban president Osvaldo Dorticós took to the airwaves after a cabinet meeting that night and denounced the "barbarous and cowardly act against the people of Cuba."[13]

Speaking the following night at the Colón Cemetery as twenty-seven dock workers killed in the explosions were buried in a mass funeral, Castro suggested the United States, which had tried to prevent Cuba from purchasing arms from Europe, was responsible. "We have the right to believe that those who did not wish us to receive arms and tried to prevent that by diplomatic means are among those guilty of this sabotage," Castro said. "We have no proof, but we have the right to believe that these are the guilty ones."[14] Castro also referenced the 1898 sinking of the *Maine* in Havana's harbor. "The United States concluded it was a mine that caused the explosion and went to the transcendent act of declaring war on Spain," he said. "We didn't need to abuse our intelligence so much to reach conclusions about this. We can conclude who the international forces are that encourage our enemies."[15]

Although the United States did not deny attempting to persuade Belgian authorities to block arms shipments to Cuba, the State Department "categorically and emphatically denied"

Castro's insinuation of responsibility for the explosions. "It is regrettable that under the strain resulting from this disaster, the prime minister would seek to attribute to our government responsibility for a disaster which we deplore and for which we have expressed our grief," U.S. State Department spokesman Francis Tully said. "This government will promptly express through diplomatic channels its vigorous protest to this unfounded and irresponsible accusation."[16]

In response, U.S. secretary of state Christian Herter summoned Cuban diplomat Enrique Patterson to express his displeasure and warn that Castro's statements could only further deteriorate U.S.-Cuba relations. In Congress, some members demanded reprisals: reducing the amount of sugar the United States bought from Cuba. Amid this mood, Dulles presented his expanded plan to a combined meeting of the Special Group and the National Security Council on March 17. Titled "A Program of Covert Action against the Castro Regime," the proposal outlined multiple operations "to bring about the replacement of the Castro regime with one more devoted to the true interests of the Cuban people and more acceptable to the U.S. in such a manner as to avoid any appearance of U.S. intervention."[17]

The program called for four major courses of action: formation of a unified Cuban opposition to the Castro regime located outside Cuba, initiation of an anti-Castro propaganda offensive, creation of a covert intelligence and action organization within Cuba, and development of a paramilitary force outside Cuba. Eisenhower approved the plan, making the overthrow of Castro a U.S. priority. But he insisted on one condition: U.S involvement must never be revealed. "The great problem is leakage and breach of security," Eisenhower said. "Everyone must be prepared to swear he has not heard of it."[18]

12

International Tensions

Jorge Zayas apparently left Cuba just in time. The editor and publisher of *Avance*, fearing his imminent arrest because of the newspaper's vocal anti-Castro editorial stance, fled the country on Wednesday, January 20, 1960. Two days later, the Castro regime confiscated the influential afternoon daily. From the safety of the United States, Zayas penned an editorial in the *Miami Herald* denouncing Castro. "I helped Fidel Castro get into power because I thought he was good for Cuba," Zayas wrote. "I was wrong. Now I must speak out in hopes of helping my country rid itself of him."[1]

As Castro continued his crackdown on counterrevolutionary activities, tensions between Cuba and the United States continued to escalate. The month of January had seen rhetoric between the two countries intensify. U.S. vice president Richard Nixon had warned that foreign investments in Cuba might cease if the Castro regime continued to make outside investors feel unwelcome. Castro responded by calling Nixon's statement an "insolent declaration."[2] Nixon and others again brought up the prospect of reducing the amount of Cuban sugar bought by the United States. And Castro accused the United States of supporting counterrevolutionary activities, including bombings in Havana and the burning of sugarcane fields.

State-run media outlets in Cuba launched particularly scathing verbal attacks on Eisenhower and other U.S. officials. The *Revolución* newspaper criticized the U.S. president for having "embraced the butcher [dictator Francisco] Franco" during a visit to Spain.[3] Radio Mambi in Havana referred to U.S. secretary of state Christian Herter's "conspiratorial plans" and described him as "a robust wolf of the imperialist den." The station also called the late former secretary of state John Foster Dulles a "concoctor of world tragedy," and described Eisenhower as "the little old golf player who misrules the United States."[4]

Despite the political atmosphere in Cuba, Sugar Kings general manager Paul Miller tried to put a positive spin on the team's situation when International League officials gathered in Buffalo, New York, for the league's annual midwinter meeting. "Our baseball fans have more money in their pockets than ever before," Miller said. "Everything is fine in Havana, baseballwise. Laborers have received substantial salary increases, rents have been lowered, and utility rates have been cut 30 percent. We are negotiating a $100,000 radio-television contract as compared to the $20,000 contract last year for radio only. We'll televise twice weekly."[5]

Miller's rosy outlook notwithstanding, Frank Horton, the president of the Rochester Red Wings, submitted a "disaster plan," giving league president Frank Shaughnessy the authority to call for a telephone vote to quickly relocate the Sugar Kings from Havana in the event of trouble in Cuba. The league adopted Horton's proposal in an amendment to the league's constitution by a 6–2 vote on January 29. The two no votes were cast by Miller and Toronto Maple Leafs general manager Danny Menendez.

Ford Frick's concerns mirrored those of the International League owners when he arrived at the Belleaire Biltmore in Clearwater, Florida, in February. The commissioner remained in close touch with Herter as he moved into his base of operations for spring training. The U.S. state department had advised Frick to "adopt a policy of watchful waiting" on Cuba. "I would say that unless conditions worsen, there will be no action by me, or by Frank Shaughnessy," Frick said. "However, Bob Maduro is on notice that if the position of the United States, and American baseball players, is placed in a more critical stage something will have to be done. I'm being guided not only by the State Department, but by my own sources of information in Cuba."[6]

Asked what would be done if any player requested to skip playing in Cuba, Frick said any player making such an appeal would not be forced to play "if conditions warranted." But he also warned that he "would not tolerate an effort by any player to use Cuban conditions to get him off the Havana [Sugar Kings] roster or any club. I would not give the player his free agency, in any circumstances. Maduro believes that everything will be straightened out. I hope so, and so does Washington. Havana has been an important part of O.B."[7] Regarding an exhibition series in Havana between the Cincinnati Reds and Baltimore Orioles, Frick acknowledged the possibility the series could be canceled. "Contracts have a cancelation clause," he said. "Nobody wants our players to compete in an area of unpleasant or troublesome association. However, we shall see."[8]

Two days before the three-game series was scheduled to start on March 28, Orioles president and general manager Lee MacPhail canceled the series. "We simply did what we believed best for the Baltimore club," MacPhail said. "We had ten or twelve players who didn't want to make the trip, but we could have gotten together a squad without any trouble if we had wanted to make the trip. If there was one chance in a thousand that anything might happen, what right have we to expose our ball club to the chance of an incident, however slim?"[9]

The decision was MacPhail's alone, and he did not consult with Frick or the U.S. state department. "We would have no objection to the Orioles playing in Havana," a State Department spokesman said. "In fact, the department probably would look with some favor on our boys playing there. After all, half of the [Washington] Senators are Cubans."[10] The Reds wanted to play in Havana. Gabe Paul had spent two days in Miami trying to convince MacPhail not to cancel the series. "Three games would have drawn 40,000 fans in Havana," Paul said. "I wish we could have helped [El Gran Stadium owner] Maduro."[11]

After he was informed of MacPhail's decision, Maduro fired off an angry telegram to the Orioles' president:

> You have taken a most unwise decision at a most inopportune time. Were not the game scheduled, it would have been highly commendable that two major league teams come to play as best possible means of easing tensions between our governments and as another contribution from baseball to the welfare of the people. How absurd it is to have the American ballet theatre group, American automobile show, hell drivers and American players on our squad treated royally here while Baltimore players are scared to come. Your disregard for Cuban baseball and your irresponsibility in overlooking the material damage that you are inflicting upon our club have no justification.[12]

At first, MacPhail reacted to Maduro's telegram with a "no comment," before continuing: "There's not much we could do, could we, if anything happened to our players down there?"[13]

Revolución, the semiofficial newspaper of the Castro regime, labeled MacPhail "Public Enemy No. 1 of Cuban baseball," and writer Fausto Miranda, the brother of former Orioles shortstop Willy Miranda, wrote that, "Sports writers in Cuba find it difficult to understand how any big-league club could have as a [general] manager a man whose capabilities are so negative. Your decision against bringing Baltimore here to play is an attack on our baseball that we censure forcefully."[14]

To counter the impression that Havana had become an unsafe place for Americans to play baseball, the Cuban government invited all the writers covering the International League to take a three-day tour of Cuba. Maduro cabled Shaughnessy on March 28 to extend the invitation on behalf of the Cuban Tourist Commission and to urge the league commissioner not to follow MacPhail's example. Maduro reminded Shaughnessy that an American ballet company was performing throughout Cuba without incident. "We trust teams in the International League," Maduro wrote, "will not be influenced by the action of Baltimore."[15]

Seven writers, one broadcaster, one photographer, and an International League club official toured Cuba on April 5–7. The delegation included Lloyd McGowan (*Montreal Star*), Shelley Rolfe (*Richmond Times Dispatch*), Andy McCutcheon (*Richmond News Leader*), Neil MacCarl (*Toronto Star*), Don Hunt (*Toronto Telegram*), Al Nickelson (*Toronto Globe-Mail*), Tom Keys (*Columbus Citizen*), Buffalo Bisons team secretary Eugene McMahon, Columbus Jets broadcaster Joe Hill, and Jets team photographer Joe West. The delegation was treated to a cocktail party, toured the new North Coast Highway, and enjoyed a night at the Tropicana cabaret. "Fighting to protect his franchise, Maduro finds himself beset by problems no other club ever has had to face there," Rolfe wrote after the tour. "He has had to assure everybody the athletes would be safe from gunfire. Not everybody has been assured."[16]

As the defending Junior World Series champion Sugar Kings held training camp in Morón, the team's roster began to take shape for the 1960 International League season. The big loss came on April 8, when the Reds bought Tony González's contract from Havana, its Minor League affiliate. González had been the Sugar Kings' best hitter in 1959, leading the club in batting average (.300), runs (86), hits (169), doubles (31), and RBIS (81) while hitting a league-leading 16 triples. His performance earned him the chance to train with the big league club in Tampa, Florida. "All of the scouts, including those with other clubs," said Reds general manager Gabe Paul, "tell me he's ready for the big leagues."[17]

But on April 12, the Sugar Kings learned of the return of two other players: shortstop Leo Cárdenas, a key player from the 1959 season; and Orlando Peña, who had pitched for the team in 1957 and 1958. After hitting 13 home runs with Havana in 1959, Cárdenas was being given a chance to earn a spot with the Reds before being sent down to the Minor League camp in Cuba. But Peña was being demoted after spending 1959 in Cincinnati. With its roster finalized, the Sugar Kings broke camp in Morón on Saturday, April 16, and played an exhibition doubleheader in Holguín on Sunday. The team left for Havana at 8 a.m. on Monday, with a practice scheduled at El Gran Stadium that night.

The weekend had seen a whirlwind of news regarding the Sugar Kings' future in Havana. In the April 17 editions of the *Rochester Democrat & Chronicle*, George Beahon reported that the team would be relocated to Jersey City, New Jersey, within thirty days, following the first 13 scheduled games in Havana. "We refuse to answer that question," Shaughnessy said when asked whether the team would finish the season in Cuba.[18] The next day, however, International League secretary Harry Simmons refuted the report of the Sugar Kings' imminent relocation, calling it "another slice of the same sausage." Simmons said the league would only abandon Havana "if the U.S. declared it insecure." He noted that U.S. secretary of state Herter had lamented the Orioles' decision to cancel their Havana exhibition games. "The best thing for U.S.-Cuba relations," Simmons said, "would be for the International League to play in Cuba."[19]

The 1960 season opened in Havana on Wednesday, April 20, as the Sugar Kings played host to the Rochester Red Wings. The opening ceremony, attended by Shaughnessy and Felipe Guerra Matos, Cuba's director of sports, included members of the Sugar Kings presenting Red Wings players with cigars. But the start of the game was delayed a half hour, awaiting Fidel Castro's arrival at El Gran Stadium. The prime minister eventually threw out the first pitch and told the 12,045 fans in attendance that he "expected a victory by the *Cubanos*."[20] It was not to be as the Red Wings beat the Sugar Kings 4–3 in ten innings.

After striking out the first two batters he faced to open the game, Havana starter Miguel Cuéllar surrendered three consecutive hits, and the Sugar Kings trailed 1–0 after the first inning. Red Wings right fielder Charlie James hit a two-run home run in the third to increase Rochester's lead to 3–0. Meanwhile, Red Wings starter Bob Keegan didn't allow a single Havana batter to reach base through the first five innings. The Sugar Kings tied the score in the sixth inning, two runs scoring on Jim Pendleton's triple. But Pendleton fell down ten feet from home plate and was tagged out as he tried to score on a wild pitch. It would prove to be a costly mistake. Had Pendleton scored, the game would not have gone into extra innings, allowing Luke Easter to hit a home run to right field and give the Red Wings the victory.

The Red Wings won again the following night. Peña—who at one point retired twelve consecutive batters—valiantly pitched into the tenth inning with the score tied 1-all only to lose the game. He surrendered three runs after recording the first two outs of the inning for the 4–1 loss in front of 1,756 fans. Rochester completed the opening-series sweep with a 7–3 victory on Friday as only 1,828 turned out for the game. It was the first time in seven seasons the Red Wings had swept a series in Cuba, where they had lost nine of eleven games in 1959. "The only reality has been that in the three defeats of the Cuban team," Luis Úbeda wrote in *Diario de la Marina*, "there has been bad luck on the one hand and mental errors on the other."[21]

The first shipment of Soviet petroleum arrived in Cuba on April 19 as the tanker *Vishinsky* docked in the south coast port of Casilda to deliver 75,000 barrels of oil. As the latest step in cementing closer ties between Cuba and the Soviet Union played out, Castro continued to rail against the United States. The day before the Soviet oil arrived, he had claimed the U.S. naval base at Guantanamo was involved in organizing counterrevolutionary activities on the island. Days after suggesting a private meeting with Eisenhower and Herter could improve U.S.-Cuba relations, Castro compared U.S. policies to those of Adolf Hitler, Benito Mussolini, and Francisco Franco. And on April 22, Castro took to the television airwaves to attack Eisenhower and Herter for participating in what he described as a "well-prepared and premeditated plan" against his regime.[22]

Castro continued to stoke anti-U.S. sentiments during a three-and-a-half-hour speech in the Plaza de la Revolución on May Day. He decried "foreign interests" that had ruled Cuba in the past and declared the Cuban revolution to be "real democracy." The crowd of 250,000 responded to Castro's invectives with shouts of "¡Cuba, sí; Yanquis, no!" (Cuba, yes; Yankees, no!) that lasted for thirteen minutes. When he indicated there would be no elections, the crowd erupted in chants of "Revolution, yes; elections, no!"[23]

May also brought the seizures of two anti-Castro newspapers. On May 11, members of two newspaper workers' unions—the Collegium of Journalists of Havana Province and the Printshop Workers' Union—seized the *Diario de la Marina*. Under the headline "¡Cubanos!" a front-page story in the paper's final editions on May 12 declared, "Today we will bury 128 years of ignominy. The *Diario de la Marina* is dead!" The article invited all Cubans to join a funeral march and symbolic burial that night "in a grand act of revolutionary reaffirmation."[24] On May 16, newspaper workers seized *Prensa Libre*, which in March had been accused of "treason to the fatherland" by the Castro regime-sponsored newspaper *Revolución*.[25]

What followed over the next two months only served to further strain the deteriorating relations between Cuba and the United States. On May 7, Cuba formally reestablished diplomatic relations with the Soviet Union. On May 17, Radio Swan began broadcasting anti-Castro propaganda from Swan Island, located south of Cuba in the Caribbean Sea, about 110 miles off the Honduran coast. The fifty-thousand-kilowatt station was established by the CIA under the cover of the Gibraltar Steamship Company. The "commercial" station sold airtime to various Cuban groups. Radio Swan's anticommunist message reached not only its target audience in Cuba, but also the entire Caribbean, in "one of the CIA's most ambitious, and notorious, psywar operations."[26]

By the end of May, five anti-Castro groups operating in exile in Miami joined under the banner of the Democratic Revolutionary Front. The front united the five disparate groups— Movement of Revolutionary Recovery, Montecristi Group, AAA, Partido Auténtico, and the Christian Democratic Movement—

under a five-man directorate to coordinate "active opposition" to the Castro regime. The most active of the groups—the Movement of Revolutionary Recovery—called for an armed uprising against Castro in its manifesto: "Fidel Castro's execution of the Marxist plan is destroying the national economy and bringing ruin and famine to the Cuban people."[27]

In June, escalating tensions centered around oil and sugar. On June 7, American and British oil refineries in Cuba—owned by Esso Standard Oil and Shell Oil in Havana and Texaco in Santiago de Cuba—refused to refine Soviet crude oil for the Castro regime. The Cuban government responded by seizing the Texaco refinery on June 29. On July 1, the Castro regime seized control of the Esso Standard and Shell refineries. Following an all-night session, the U.S. Congress passed a bill on July 3 that allowed Eisenhower to set Cuba's sugar quotas to any level until March 31, 1961. Castro responded by denouncing the U.S. action as "imperialism" and seizing all U.S.-owned sugar mills in Cuba.

On July 6, the Castro regime suffered perhaps its highest-profile defection when José Miró Cardona, Cuba's ambassador-designate to the United States, resigned and requested asylum in the Argentine Embassy in Havana. Miró Cardona had played a key role in the revolution against Batista and served as Cuba's first prime minister after the revolution, from January 7 to February 12, 1959, before Castro forced him out and assumed the role of prime minister. In a letter to Cuban president Osvaldo Dorticós, Miró Cardona wrote, "The ideological divergences between the policies of the government and my conscience are already insoluble."[28]

Dan Daniel may have written the epitaph for Organized Baseball in Havana when he wrote in the *New York World-Telegram & Sun*, "International League ball in Havana is an island of freedom in a sea of Communism, Soviet affiliation, and Castro terror." In his column, Daniel argued that having a team in Cuba "would not be compatible with our national interests" and implored commissioner Ford Frick to "bar all players in Organized Ball, even if they are natives of Cuba, from competing in the winter operations of the Cuban League, or appearing with other Caribbean teams in Havana." The columnist concluded, "The climate in Cuba no longer is healthy for our national pastime."[29] Events in Havana in late June would bear that out.

Facing financial trouble, Bobby Maduro met with International League officials in New York on June 26 to apply for a $20,000 loan. The declining value of the Cuban peso and rules requiring Maduro pay visiting teams' share of gate receipts and 60 percent of American players' salaries in dollars had taken a toll. The Sugar Kings owner said $13,000 of the loan would be used to pay guarantees to the teams, with $7,000 used for salaries. Maduro also requested that ownership of the Sugar Kings be transferred into his name from the Cuban corporation that held the team, allowing for a quick franchise relocation should conditions in Cuba warrant such a move. League directors discussed the Cuba situation the next day during the scheduled league meetings in Toronto. "We all like Bob Maduro too well to embarrass him in any way," one unnamed league official told *Buffalo News* writer Cy Kritzer. "But he is in a tough spot. I wonder if the league will finish the season in Havana."[30]

With Maduro in New York, El Gran Stadium was rocked by an explosion on the nearby waterfront before the start of a June 26 doubleheader. The explosion occurred at a Cuban Army munitions dump at Havana harbor, killing two and injuring another two hundred. The blast shattered windows within five miles and knocked out electricity, delaying the start of the Sugar Kings' game against Rochester by an hour and a half. "About five minutes before game time, there was a terrific explosion," said Red Wings general manager George Sisler Jr. "It shook the park but wasn't close enough to injure anyone in the stands. Following the explosion, a huge cloud of black smoke rose over the city. The lights went out at the park, but it didn't seem to affect the entire city."[31]

Shaughnessy had seen enough. On Thursday, July 7, he decided the Sugar Kings would be moved from Havana within the next few days. The transfer to Jersey City, New Jersey, would become official with a "home game" at Roosevelt Stadium on Friday, July 15. "We have to protect our players, and the only way to do it is get them out of there," Shaughnessy said from Montreal. "The league decided last winter that if a situation arose in which there was any danger to our personnel I was to have the authority to move the franchise. Maduro probably won't like it. But it is in his interest. We just want to make sure everyone is safe."[32]

Maduro reacted bitterly upon hearing the news in Havana. "The International League is making a big mistake," the Sugar Kings owners said. "Baseball was a strong link between the Cuban and American peoples, and it should never be broken."[33] In denouncing the transfer of his team, Maduro also explained the significant personal financial impact of the move. He said the team owed money to four banks, including $100,000 to one institution "and I am responsible for that loan."[34] Maduro said he wasn't sure whether he would plead his case during the league's board of directors' meetings the following week in New York, but he said he would not go to New Jersey to run the team if the Sugar Kings were relocated there. "If I am going to lose money," he said, "I prefer to lose it in my own country."[35]

The team was in Richmond, Virginia, in the middle of a four-city, fourteen-day road trip when players learned the Sugar Kings would never return to Havana. Manager Antonio "Tony" Castaño broke the news during a squad meeting before the start of Friday's series opener against Richmond on July 8. The news wasn't well received. Castaño said "five or six" of the Sugar Kings' eleven Cuban-born players indicated they would return to Cuba at the end of the road trip, which concluded with a four-game series in Miami, July 11–14. Castaño refused to say whether he would continue managing the team. He had made his decision but sealed it in an envelope to be opened after the Miami series. "I don't want to influence anybody," Castaño said.[36]

In Cuba, Castro reacted with his typical vitriol—which was

carried on television in Havana—calling the relocation of the Sugar Kings an "aggression" against the Cuban people. "American players when they came here got nothing but respect and admiration," Castro said. "The people treated them cordially and there is no record of attacks on players of any kind. But violating all codes of sportsmanship, they now take away our franchise. It's another aggression they've committed. We never told our players not to play in the United States in spite of attacks against us."[37]

Located on nineteen acres at Droyers Point off the Hackensack River in Jersey City, Roosevelt Stadium opened on April 22, 1937. It served as home to the Jersey City Giants, the New York Giants' Minor League affiliate in the International League, until 1950. The Brooklyn Dodgers had played fifteen "home" games at Roosevelt Stadium in 1956 and 1957 before moving to Los Angeles for the 1958 season. With the transfer of the Sugar Kings, Roosevelt Stadium once again would have International League baseball after a ten-year absence. Al López-Chávez had followed the Sugar Kings on radio since his family moved from Havana to Jersey City in 1957 when he was twelve years old. "I couldn't believe it," López-Chávez recalled, "when my father told me that this was happening."[38]

After a telephone call with Shaughnessy on Friday, July 8, Jersey City parks commissioner Bernard Berry ordered a "crash crew" to clear weeds and build up the pitcher's mound in preparation for an inspection of the twenty-five-thousand-seat ballpark the following week. "Jersey City is ready to take over," Berry said. "With only one major league team [the Yankees after the Dodgers and Giants had moved to California] in New York, I am confident the baseball fans of this area will support International League baseball. The fans are screaming for the return of a team here for years."[39]

Not all area residents shared Berry's optimism about Jersey City's new baseball team. "I don't know if the people will support the team," Union City resident Neil Craig said. "You can never tell." Some fans pointed to the memory of the Jersey City Giants as a reason to doubt the Sugar Kings' prospects for success. "Too many people remember the way the New York Giants handled the team here," Hudson County patrolman Anthony Marsella said. "One season we had a good team while New York was just getting by. In the middle of the season, New York called up every player we had and that was the end of the team. It also killed off the gate." Jersey City's Michael Priddy was more blunt. "I'll never go to a game here," he said, "as long as the Yankees are in New York."[40]

After meeting with Gabe Paul on Sunday in Richmond, Paul Miller said the Reds, who already had a working agreement with the Sugar Kings, had consented to operate Havana's revoked franchise only for the remainder of the season. "I'm not in this of my own choosing," Paul said. "The Reds have no desire to own a Triple-A team."[41] Miller would stay on as the team's general manager, but Tony Castaño would not return as the team's field manager. Rather than waiting until the end of the road trip to announce his decision, Castaño said he would return to Havana after the series in Miami. "I don't know why," he said. "It's just in my mind." Miller and Paul were surprised by Castaño's announcement but held out hope the manager would change his mind. Four of the Sugar Kings' eleven Cuban-born players—Raúl Sánchez, Orlando Peña, Borrego Álvarez, and Leo Cárdenas—were considering returning to Cuba as well. "You've got to realize these decisions might not be final," Miller said. "Some of the Cubans are under terrible emotional pressure."[42]

The transfer of the Sugar Kings was officially finalized during a two-hour meeting on Monday in Jersey City between Paul, Miller, Shaughnessy, and Berry. On Tuesday, the city commission voted 4–0 to approve the leasing of Roosevelt Stadium. Under terms of the agreement, the team would pay the city $7,500 to lease the stadium for the remainder of the season, including thirty-five home games. Jersey City also would receive 6 percent from the proceeds of every ticket sold after the first

125,000. The contract included a club option for 1961 and could be renewed for four years.

Everyone was all smiles until Paul announced the city's newly minted International League team would be called the Jersey City Reds. Berry and two other commissioners objected to the name, fearing "Reds" would have a double meaning because of the Castro regime's purported Communist influences. They preferred the name "Jerseys." Miller suggested letting fans decide. The club finally settled on Jerseys. "It doesn't really matter," Miller said. "When the team is winning people call them angels. When it's losing, you know what they call them."[43]

Napoleón Reyes was working as a scout for the Cincinnati Reds when he was tabbed to replace Castaño as manager. "They were both great baseball men," Cookie Rojas said. "Castaño, for all the years that he played—and he was a champion batter in Cuba in years past—and Napoleón Reyes, another great baseball man, was a different type of person. He was much more excitable. He brought a lot of joy to the baseball field with his personality. But he was a very intelligent man inside baseball, and he had the opportunity to direct the rest of the season in New Jersey."[44]

Reyes had ties to Jersey City, having played with the New York Giants' then–Class Double-A affiliate in 1942 and 1943, and the Triple-A team in 1950. He had played in three seasons with the New York Giants (1943–45). Reyes had a distinguished career in Cuba. He played seven seasons in the Cuban League between 1941 and 1952 with Almendares and Cienfuegos and managed Marianao for seven seasons (1954–60), winning two Cuban League championships. "The first to leave [Cuba] was Napoleón Reyes," Peña said. "Napoleón Reyes left first because he had clashed at the University of Havana with Fidel Castro. Fidel Castro and he never got along. Napoleón Reyes would say that Fidel Castro was *un hijo de puta* [a son of a bitch], just like that, in front of everybody."[45]

After word reached Cuba that Reyes had taken over as the

team's manager, *Revolución* denounced Reyes as a "traitor and an enemy of his own people." The semiofficial newspaper of the Castro regime said Reyes "behaved like a Yankee" and dubbed him the "Díaz Lanz of baseball," after Pedro Díaz Lanz, the former chief of the Cuban Air Force, who was one of the country's first major defectors. *Revolución* also accused Reyes of working "for the United States State Department and the Yankee dollar and is a traitor to the cause of Cuban baseball which in this case is the same cause as the Cuban revolution."[46]

Reyes clearly would not be welcomed back in Cuba and would not be able to continue as Mariano's manager in the 1960–61 Cuban League season. There was enough concern about *Revolución*'s denouncement of Reyes that Austin Conley, Jersey City's chief of police, assigned a pair of detectives to guard Reyes in the dugout for the opening series in Jersey City. Detectives also would guard him and his family at the Hotel Plaza, where the team would be staying. Reyes remained undaunted. "Baseball is my business and I follow orders," he said. "Will I ever go back to Cuba? Listen, I'm more nervous about this [opening] game than I would be about going back there."[47]

Borrego Álvarez, Jim Pendleton, and Cookie Rojas each blasted home runs as the newly christened Jerseys played their final game as the Havana Sugar Kings, beating the Marlins 7–3 in Miami on Thursday, July 14. The victory concluded a lengthy road trip that left the team in fourth place in the International League, sixteen and a half games behind the first-place Toronto Maple Leafs. Despite speculation of mass defections by the team's Cuban players, none decided to quit and return to Cuba. But Raúl Sánchez and Andrés Ayón were given permission to travel to Havana to retrieve their families. The rest of the team boarded a late flight from Miami to New York International Airport in Idlewild, Queens, and arrived in Jersey City at 6:30 a.m. on Friday.

After just a few hours of sleep at the Hotel Plaza, the team's official welcome to Jersey City began at Journal Square at 2:30

p.m. City commissioners Bernard Berry and William McLaughlin greeted Reyes. McLaughlin, director of the city's Department of Public Safety, announced that he had assigned fifty policemen to work Friday's opening game against the Columbus Jets in the event of protests by Castro sympathizers. Although Reyes thought having bodyguards at the hotel was unnecessary, "the wives of several Cuban players, who came to Jersey City with their husbands, felt safer with a detective on duty at the hotel," Joseph O. Haff wrote in the *New York Times*.[48]

Before the scheduled 8:10 p.m. start time, a motorcade transported team members and their wives through the streets of Jersey City. The lead convertible carried Reyes, Berry, McLaughlin, players Peña and Enrique Izquierdo, and "Miss Jersey City," a green-eyed, twenty-two-year-old blonde named Delphine Lisk, who "doesn't have to remain in Jersey City to win beauty contests," Haff wrote. Cheers and welcoming shouts greeted the motorcade as it traversed what the *New York Times* writer described as "areas where Puerto Rican, Cuban, and Negro families predominate."[49]

Once at Roosevelt Stadium, the players stepped onto the field prior to the game wearing the same Sugar Kings home uniforms they had used in Havana—save for the stitched-on patch displaying "Jersey City" in red script that covered the "Cubanos" script that had adorned the team's uniforms all season. So abrupt had been the team's transfer to the United States there had not been time to produce new uniforms for the Jersey City opener. A crowd of 7,155 fans turned out for the inaugural game. All 1,250 box seats were filled, "many by teenagers or women without wedding bands," the *New York Times* reported.[50] Unfortunately, the home fans didn't get to witness a victory as the Jets beat the Jerseys 8–3. Peña and Luis Arroyo surrendered five earned runs in a combined one and a third innings.

Despite the initial loss, the Jerseys opened to rave reviews from International League officials. "Everything's wonderful," Shaughnessy gushed. "The attendance was excellent. It's amazing how they fixed the park up so fast." Jets manager Harold Cooper said, "This could be the best thing that ever happened to this league. This is close to being the Big Time. Look at this crowd. We'd be lucky to have 3,000 in Havana."[51] The following night, the Jets won 4–2 with only 1,147 in attendance. "Judging from the affection shown by the spectators at Roosevelt Stadium," Robert L. Teague wrote in the *New York Times*, "hardly anyone noticed the final score."[52] Columbus completed the sweep on Sunday, beating the Jerseys 3–1. The Jerseys remained a dark horse to reach the first division of the league for much of the season but fell short, finishing with a 76-77 record, for fifth place, twenty-three and a half games out of first and out of the playoffs.

Despite attendance struggles—the franchise drew 75,000 fans in thirty-five dates in Havana but only 47,715 fans in thirty-eight games in twenty-nine dates in Jersey City—the team managed to avoid red ink. That was thanks to a TV-radio contract with WNTA in Newark, New Jersey. The deal paid the Jerseys $35,000 for broadcast rights (despite the station dropping TV coverage after the first home stand). The club was committed to giving it another go in 1961. "Manager Nap Reyes and I plan to stay in Jersey City over the winter, meeting people, drumming up season-ticket sales, and revamping the club," said Jerseys vice president Bill Bergesch. "If we can sell 2,000 season box tickets, we'll be in good financial shape next year."[53]

For the players, it was a difficult season away from their homeland, unsure what the future would hold. "Many of us who stayed with our wives and children, we were in a hotel in New Jersey," Rojas said. "We had almost the entire floor in a hotel to be able to establish ourselves, take care of each other, because it was such a radical change that forced that movement. You can imagine the situations we dealt with, not just on the field but also in our normal lives, the adjustments we had to make. . . . We had to help each other, try to get the rest of our families out of Cuba little by little while establishing ourselves here. . . . It was a very difficult situation. But we survived."[54]

13

The Last Season

Luis Tiant's talent was obvious to anyone who watched him pitch as a youngster. "When I was 10 or 11," he wrote in his 1976 autobiography, "people kept telling me I had my father's abilities."[1] No small praise considering Luis Tiant Sr. was a star pitcher in the Cuban League and Negro leagues during the 1920s, '30s, and '40s. But the elder Tiant was forty-one by the time Jackie Robinson broke baseball's color barrier, so he never had the opportunity to pitch in the Majors. "There is absolutely no question about it. He would have been a great, great star [in the Majors]," Hall of Famer Monte Irvin said. "What a pitcher! He had a great fastball and a screwball, and no one could mix pitches any better than he did. He knew how to pitch."[2]

Tiant Jr., who was born November 23, 1940, remembers watching his father pitch at La Tropical, brought to games by an uncle when he was a young boy. "I saw him play," Tiant said. "There was a pitcher who was my father's good friend, Adrián Zabala. Every time he saw me in the stadium with my uncle, he would call over my uncle so he would take me over to the dugout to sit me in the dugout with the players. I would sit there in dugout. I watched plenty of games there. I don't remember too much, but I saw him play."[3]

Like his old man, the younger Tiant developed a lightning fastball. But Tiant Sr. didn't push his son into baseball as he was growing up in Nicanor del Campo in the Marianao district of Havana. Tiant Sr. preferred Luis concentrate on his studies, to no avail. "Someday," Tiant Jr. wrote. "I wanted to be a professional baseball player."[4] After starring for the Havana team in the juvenile league as a teenager, Tiant tried out for the Sugar Kings before the 1959 season but failed to make the team. "Your boy will never make it," one team official told Tiant's father. "He should accept that, and maybe get a job in the fruit market as a salesman."[5]

But Beto Ávila, a family friend who had played in the Cuban League, watched Tiant during a practice at La Tropical and recommended the young pitcher to the manager of the Mexico City Tigers of the Mexican League. "They signed . . . like seven or eight players, and I was in that group," Tiant said. "That's where they saw me, and they were interested in me. . . . I said yes that I would go. My father signed. That was in January. I left Cuba at the beginning of February, and I went to Mexico to begin training. And that's where I started."[6] Tiant went 5-19 with a 5.92 ERA as a rookie, but three of his victories were shutouts. After the season, he returned to Cuba and tried out with Almendares for the 1959–60 Cuban League season.

For a month, Tiant took the forty-five-minute bus ride every day from Nicanor del Campo to the Scorpions' tryout camp in Ciudad de los Deportes. As camp winded down, Tiant had no indication of his status and confronted general manager Monchy de Arcos, who in 1962 would recommend that the Cleveland Indians buy Tiant's contract from the Mexico City Tigers. "They said they were going to sign me, but when the time came I could see there wasn't anything," Tiant said. "They hadn't told me anything, so I asked what was going to happen. That's when they told me they weren't going to sign pitchers. They signed a bunch of pitchers, but they didn't want to sign me."[7]

Rebuffed in his initial attempt to join the Cuban League, Tiant returned home. But the next day, he showed up at Habana's camp, where manager Fermin Guerra found a reserve roster spot for the right-handed pitcher. It didn't last. "We went a time, a week or two that we didn't win a game," Tiant said. "I was pitching during practices and that sort of thing. They had told me they would sign me, but when they started to lose, they cut me. They said they didn't want me. . . . Fermin sent the trainer to tell me they didn't want me to keep coming to the team."[8]

Tiant went to Nicaragua to play winter ball. After the winter, he returned to Mexico City, where he compiled a league-best 17-7 record with 4.65 ERA and met his future wife, Maria del Refugio. Returning to Cuba after the 1960 Mexican League season, Tiant arrived at José Martí International Airport to find his parents and Guerra, who greeted Tiant with a contract offer for the 1960–61 Cuban League season. But Tiant wasn't interested after being cut by Habana the previous winter. "He came to find me at the airport," Tiant said. "He had talked to my father, and he came to look for me at the airport with my father. They wanted me to sign with Habana, but I didn't want to. . . . I was champion pitcher in Mexico, and there he was waiting for me. I didn't even know he was waiting for me at the airport. I told him no, I didn't want to sign with him. My father convinced me. He told me, 'Sign with them, son.' So, I signed, but I wasn't going to sign."[9]

After Cuba's Minor League franchise was revoked in July, American participation in the Cuban League also was in doubt. Relations between the United States and Cuba had deteriorated to the point where the Castro regime had seized nearly $1 billion in American property on the island as of August 1960. By September, baseball commissioner Ford Frick barred non-Cuban players from playing in the Cuban League. "The situation in Cuba has reached a point at which I no longer want to be responsible for the lives and welfare, and financial return, of American players there," Frick said. "The order barring Americans from Cuban clubs is self-explanatory."[10]

Frick's ban meant Almendares, Habana, Cienfuegos, and Marianao would field all-native rosters for the first time in decades. Cuba's government-controlled press reacted with derision toward Frick's edict. Writing in *Revolución* on September 9, Fausto Miranda praised the notion of a season devoid of U.S. players because not all Americans who had played in the

Cuban League were like "Max Lanier, Jim Bunning, or Forrest Jacobs. . . . There was a large number of drunkards and malingerers who had to be sent back home at midseason."[11] This exchange was the latest salvo in a cold war between the two countries that continued throughout the month.

On September 5, the Castro regime seized a multimillion-dollar printing plant used to publish Latin American editions of *Time* magazine and the Spanish-language *Reader's Digest*. On September 16, the Cuban government seized all three U.S. banks in Cuba—First National City Bank of New York, First National Bank of Boston, and Chase Manhattan Bank—and their estimated combined net worth of $35 million to $40 million.[12] The next day, Cuba restricted U.S ambassador Philip Bonsal's movements to an area within ten square miles of the U.S. embassy. When Castro arrived in New York on September 18, he had already been informed by the U.S. that he would be restricted to remaining in Manhattan during his stay for the United Nations General Assembly meeting.

Castro's party of eighty at first took up residence at the Hotel Shelburne in midtown Manhattan. But Castro stormed out of the hotel on September 19 in a huff over prices ($20 per day for twenty rooms, plus a $10,000 security deposit) and moved into the Hotel Theresa in Harlem. Shelburne owner Edward Spatz called Castro's departure "a prearranged propaganda move."[13] Indeed, Soviet premier Nikita Khrushchev visited Castro in Harlem the next day and then made an even bigger show of greeting and embracing Castro at the United Nations.

Addressing the General Assembly on September 26, Castro accused the United States of having "decreed the destruction" of his government and heaped praise on the Soviet Union during a four-and-a-half-hour speech.[14] Castro also declared he was "seriously considering requesting within the framework of international law that United States naval and military forces be withdrawn from the Guantanamo base" in Cuba.[15] By the end of the month, the United States announced it would close its $110 million Nicaro nickel processing plant in Oriente Province.

The move came hours after the U.S. state department advised American residents in Cuba to send home their wives and children because the United States could not "provide normal protection to U.S. citizens through regular diplomatic channels."[16]

The following month, the United States imposed an embargo on exports to Cuba, outlawing shipments of American goods, except food, medicine, and medical supplies, to the island. In announcing the sanctions on October 19, the U.S. state department stressed Castro's attacks on U.S. businesses. "The Government of Cuba has instituted a series of arbitrary, illegal, and discriminatory economic measures," a formal statement read, "which have injured thousands of American citizens."[17] The next day, the United States recalled Bonsal to Washington "for an extended period," indicating the U.S. ambassador to Cuba might not return during what remained of the Eisenhower administration. It would likely be up to the next administration—Nixon and John F. Kennedy were embroiled in a heated presidential campaign—to decide whether to send a new ambassador to Cuba.[18] In response to the embargo, on October 25 the Castro regime nationalized 166 U.S.-owned enterprises, virtually eliminating major U.S. investments in Cuba. Among the businesses were various hotels and casinos, such as the Riviera, Nacional, Capri, and Deauville, that had once been at the heart of the Mob's operations in Havana.

For the first time in seven years, the World Series was not being telecast in Cuba when the New York Yankees and Pittsburgh Pirates stepped onto the diamond at Forbes Field on October 5 for Game 1. Interest in the 1960 Series remained high in Cuba, but local telecasts became the latest casualty of the tensions between the United States and Cuba. The *El Mundo* newspaper accused the United States of practicing "baseball imperialism" by barring Americans from playing in the Cuban League.[19] And Frick took his ban a step further, ruling his order would apply to the Caribbean Series as well. The annual tournament was scheduled to be played in Havana in 1961, but Americans playing in the winter leagues in Puerto Rico, Venezuela, and Panama would not be permitted to participate unless relations between the United States and Cuba dramatically improved. On October 12, Frick called for the series to be moved out of Cuba.

As the start of the Cuban League season approached, baseball officials in the United States privately worried that Castro might reciprocate by prohibiting Cuban players from returning to the United States to play in the 1961 Major League season. Such a ban would impact some teams more than others, as *Washington Daily News* writer George Clifford noted: "All of baseball would be hurt, but no organization worse than the Senators. Besides varsity members [Pedro] Ramos, Camilo Pascual, José Valdivielso, and Julio Bécquer [Ramos, Bécquer, and Valdivielso had completed the only All-Cuban triple play in Major League history on July 23, 1960], such a move would deny the Nats the services of [Zoilo] Versalles and a host of minor leaguers."[20]

The Cuban League season opened on October 16, two hours late, while awaiting Castro's arrival. The prime minister had delivered a three-and-a-half-hour television speech before heading to El Gran Stadium to throw out the ceremonial first pitch. Castro and his cabinet remained for the game and watched as Miguel Fornieles tossed a three-hitter to give Marianao a 4–0 victory against Cienfuegos. The defending champions— hampered by Pascual's decision to sit out the winter to rest his ailing shoulder and Raúl Sánchez's sore arm—struggled early, posting a 3-3 record through October 26.

Almendares, the previous season's cellar dweller, roared out of the gate to a 4-1 record. Habana dealt the Scorpions their first loss as Tiant tossed a four-hitter and struck out eight in his league debut. "Almendares, I beat them like six times; Marianao I beat them two or three times," Tiant said of his rookie season. "Cienfeugos was the team that would beat me. Those *cabrónes* [bastards], I couldn't beat them too many times. They would hit me, and we wouldn't hit."[21]

If not for Frick's ban on U.S. players, it is possible Tiant might not have had the opportunity to play in the Cuban League that season. Prior to 1960, each of the four teams were permitted eight stateside players on their rosters. The exclusion of American players opened up thirty-two spots for native-born players. "This year, they had to fill their teams with what would pass for the Class B and C players in Cuba," Frank Lane said. "Actually, today Cuba should be a scouting paradise, although I was the only American observer there in the first week of the league season. . . . There are 24 new kids in the league this fall that our scouts know little about. And they are all up for grabs."[22]

The Indians general manager's purpose while in Cuba, aside from scouting, was to seek an audience with Castro. He was rebuffed in three attempts to meet with the Cuban prime minister. Instead, Lane met with Felipe Guerra Matos, Cuba's sports minister, who assured Lane that Cuba would not interfere with Cuban players wishing to return to the United States for the 1961 Major League season. "I was told, 'Your ambassador, Mr. Bonsal, made 15 futile attempts to see Dr. Castro, and then went home. So, you shouldn't be discouraged if you tried only three times,'" Lane said of trying to talk to Castro, "[but] Col. Matos . . . gave me the assurance I wanted, and I am sure it will be respected unless conditions grow a lot worse than they are now."[23]

During his visit, Lane also met with Bobby Maduro, unseated as Sugar Kings owner when the team was forced to relocate to Jersey City in July. Maduro was having "a difficult time of it," Lane said. "I had dinner with Bob at the Hotel Nacional, and it was like dinner in an armed camp. There are ears on every side. We talked baseball and kept away from his personal affairs. But I know he is not the wealthy man he used to be."[24] Lane also described Cuban Major Leaguers as struggling. "Under the Castro regime the middle class has been wiped out. Some of these players had some of their baseball earnings in housing, etc., which has been taken over by the government," he said. "They don't complain outwardly, especially to an American, but from some of their acquaintances I've heard of their hardships."

For two years, Washington Senators owner Calvin Griffith had threatened to move the team to Minneapolis only to be blocked by his fellow American League owners. In 1959, New York Yankees owner Dan Topping had given voice to the league's concerns: "The Yankees will never vote to leave the nation's capital without an American League team."[25] Even as Griffith's dalliances with Minnesota continued, his fellow AL owners focused on the potential of expanding into two cities. After the 1960 season, AL owners weighed applications from Dallas–Fort Worth and Minneapolis–St. Paul, among others, with the 1962 season as the target for expanding. The National League also eyed expanding in 1962 into New York and Houston.

But everything changed on October 26, 1960, with the stunning news that Griffith would move the Senators to Minneapolis. The bombshell announcement also included an expansion team to replace the Senators in Washington and a new franchise in Los Angeles for the 1961 season, beating the NL to the punch for the first expansion in the Majors. AL owners voted 6–2, with the dissenting votes coming from the Cleveland Indians and Detroit Tigers. "It was difficult to uproot our family tradition in Washington," Griffith said, "but I would like to emphasize that it was my own stipulation that Washington fans would not be without a major-league team."[26]

Had events played out very differently, it's possible one of the Major League expansion teams awarded in 1961 or 1962 could have been in Havana. "Major League Baseball had already decided that there was no choice, that it had to expand," Ralph Ávila said. "And then the first club that was going to be considered for expansion was Havana, which was the club whose games were being televised and had the quality of players that was needed, because the Sugar Kings were producing players. They were sending players throughout the Major Leagues, mostly to Cincinnati."[27] Big league baseball in Cuba had been

Maduro's vision before the aftermath of the revolution forced the relocation of Sugar Kings. "If Cuba had remained free," said Andrés Fleitas, who played thirteen seasons in the Cuban League between 1942 and 1955, mostly with Almendares, "Cuba would have had a Major League team."[28]

Despite a tight pennant race—a mere one and a half games separated Cienfuegos, Almendares, Habana, and Marianao after the games of November 9—the Cuban League was "rapidly going broke," the *New York Times* declared.[29] Average gate receipts had dropped to an estimated $2,000 on weeknights and $3,000 on weekends. To break even, one league official estimated, the league needed an average daily attendance of forty-five hundred, but attendance frequently was down to about one thousand fans per game. Various efforts were employed to offset the league's flagging attendance.

Admission prices were dropped from $1 to $0.60. Government radio began broadcasting the slogan "Be a patriot and go to the ball games." The Cuban players' union, led by Orestes Miñoso, voluntarily agreed to accept salary cuts during a November 2 meeting. United Press International reported that Miñoso, who had earned an estimated $2,500 per month the previous season, was expected to draw around $400 per month for the 1960–61 season.[30] When Cuba's National Sports Directorate rejected a request by team owners for a government subsidy of $80,000, several Cuban labor unions announced plans in November to buy up box seats for games to help prop up the league. "There were problems but not enough that affected us [players]," Marianao first baseman Julio Bécquer recalled. "We kept playing baseball and the season went on."[31]

Even a shortage of baseballs, the result of the U.S. trade embargo, hampered the league. An order of five hundred dozen baseballs from a U.S. manufacturer reached the island only because the U.S. state department made an exception because the order had been placed and was being prepared for shipment before the embargo went into effect.[32] Foul balls caught in the stands had to be returned to the field as fans shouted, "Give it back, remember the *divisas* [foreign exchange in U.S. dollars]." "Baseball, once the favorite sport in this island," R. Hart Phillips wrote in the *New York Times*, "is about to become a casualty of the Cuban revolution."[33]

What had been a contentious campaign ended on November 8 with the closest popular vote count in a U.S. presidential election in seventy-six years. Kennedy beat Nixon by a wide margin in the electoral college (303–219), but when the official final popular vote tabulations were announced on December 15, Kennedy had beaten Nixon by just 112,801 votes among the more than 68.8 million ballots cast. Officials in Cuba believed little would change because of the election. Cuban president Osvaldo Dorticós said he expected the next administration would continue to try to "strangle the economy" of Cuba. "We are not optimistic about the United States," Dorticós added. "And we have no choice."[34]

Throughout the campaign, Cuba had been a major point of disagreement between the two candidates. Kennedy blamed the Eisenhower administration—and by extension vice president Nixon—for a Cuba policy that was "the most glaring failure of American foreign policy[,] . . . a disaster that threatens the security of the Western Hemisphere."[35] Nixon described Kennedy's proposal for the United States to "support a revolution in Cuba" as a "shockingly reckless proposal" that might lead to a "world war that every American of both parties wants to avoid."[36] Castro, of course, derided both candidates during the election, calling them "cowardly hypocrites," and "two ignorant, beardless kids."[37]

In the weeks after the American election, fear and anxiety permeated life in Cuba. The Castro regime on September 28 had established the Committees for the Defense of the Revolution, neighborhood watch groups designed to weed out counterrevolutionary activities. "Life today in this once gay, cosmopolitan capital is strangely different," R. Hart Phillips wrote in the

New York Times. "The faces of the pleasure-loving Cubans wear no smiles. The flood of hate, pitting class against class, father against son, neighbor against neighbor, and church against state, has affected every Cuban. There is no middle ground."[38] A December 6 dispatch from the U.S. embassy in Havana to the State Department concluded that "popular support of the Castro regime has dropped markedly" during the previous three months, but that it was "not likely that the Castro regime will fall without considerable bloodletting and destruction of property."[39]

On December 2, Eisenhower authorized the use of $1 million to help the growing number of Cuban refugees in South Florida. Their numbers would begin to swell further as the month wound down. On December 26, a late-night flight from Havana brought five young children to Miami International Airport, where they were greeted by Father Bryan Walsh. What would become known as Operation Pedro Pan was officially under way. The operation was the brainchild of Walsh, head of the Catholic Welfare Bureau; and James Baker, headmaster of Ruston Academy, a private American school in Havana. It would eventually help Cuban parents to send more than fourteen thousand of their children to the United States, to "save them from 'Communist indoctrination.'"[40]

As children continued to be spirited out of Cuba, the Cuban government on January 2 demanded that the staffing at the U.S. embassy and consulate in Havana be reduced to eleven within forty-eight hours. The next day, the United States formally terminated diplomatic relations with Cuba. "There is a limit to what the United States in self-respect can endure. That limit has now been reached," Eisenhower said in a released statement. The Castro regime's actions, he said, "can have no other purpose than to render impossible the conduct of normal diplomatic relations with that government."[41]

Circumstances had made Havana's hosting of the thirteenth Caribbean Series untenable. Ford Frick had already barred

U.S. players from participating in the series because of diplomatic tensions with Cuba. That meant the teams participating in the annual tournament would have to find replacements for the American players on their rosters. Frick had dealt a death blow on October 22, when he was in San Juan, Puerto Rico, for the opening of the Puerto Rican League. The baseball commissioner announced that Puerto Rican players, as American citizens, would be included in his ban unless U.S.-Cuba relations improved. "It would not be wise," Frick said, for the Puerto Rican champion to play in Havana.[42]

To resolve the issue, Caribbean baseball officials gathered in Miami on January 4. The Cuban League was invited to send representatives to the meeting, but none attended. Representatives from the leagues in Puerto Rico and Panama, and from both Venezuelan leagues, unanimously agreed to hold a tournament in Caracas, Venezuela, on February 10–15, replacing the Caribbean Series scheduled for Havana on the same dates. It would not be until 1970 that the Caribbean Series would be reconstituted. The new tournament would operate under the name Inter-American Series. The champion from Venezuela's Central League would be the host team.

While Latin American baseball officials were busy setting up a replacement for the Caribbean Series, Organized Baseball executives gathered in New York on January 4. National League president Warren Giles and American League president Joe Cronin met with Frick in his Rockefeller Center headquarters to discuss the situation in Cuba. At the same time, incoming secretary of state Dean Rusk expressed his doubts that Cuban players would be allowed to return to the United States for the April 11 start of the 1961 season. "Right now, of course, there isn't anything I can say as I don't know what new turn developments will take," Frick said. "However, if Cuban players should be barred from coming here quite a few clubs would be hit rather hard and we certainly would have to make some provisions for meeting this new emergency."[43]

In the National League, the Philadelphia Phillies stood to lose

Panchón Herrera, Tony Taylor, and Tony González. In the American League, the relocated Minnesota Twins would be without the services of ace pitchers Camilo Pascual and Pedro Ramos, future All-Star and American League MVP shortstop Zoilo Versalles, and infielder José Valdivielso. Yet owner Calvin Griffith expressed confidence the situation would be resolved. "All the panic could be a bit premature," he said. "I don't see why Castro wouldn't let the ballplayers out of Cuba. He has never tried to stop them before. The Cubans love baseball. Maybe I'm being too optimistic, but I don't see the international situation affecting baseball. I feel certain we'll be able get Castro's permission, and then visas, for all our Cuban ballplayers."[44]

The developments came quickly. The Cuban government suspended issuing exit visas to Cubans and foreign residents, except Americans, on January 6. However, Cuban players were assured they would have "no trouble" traveling to the United States to join their American clubs. "We will do everything possible to solve your problems," United Press International quoted an unnamed high-ranking Cuban Foreign Ministry official as saying. "The Revolutionary Government will not interfere with your departure."[45]

Standing five feet, eleven inches tall, Julio Bécquer hardly cut the figure of the prototypical power hitter. The Marianao first baseman had never hit more than eight home runs in any Cuban winter (8 in 69 games during the 1954–55 season). But he hit three home runs in four games from December 15 to December 18, giving him a league-leading eleven homers to go along with a league-leading 35 RBIs in 37 games. He opened the new year by hitting his twelfth and thirteenth home runs. With more than a month remaining in the season, Bécquer was threatening to break the Cuban League record of 16 home runs, set by former Major Leaguer Lou Klein while playing with Habana in 1952–53.

Despite Bécquer's run production, Marianao remained last in a tight four-team race. As of games played on January 11,

Cienfuegos led second-place Almendares by a half game, while Habana was a game back. Marianao was four and a half games off the pace. Little changed heading into the final week of the season. Half a game still separated the first-place Elephants and the Scorpions. Even before the final game was played, sportswriters had voted Pedro Ramos as the league's MVP. The Cienfuegos starter had fifteen victories and a 1.94 ERA heading into his final start on February 8, the last night of the season.

After Habana had been eliminated on February 7, Cienfuegos and Almendares entered the finale with 34-31 records. More than twenty thousand fans, including Fidel Castro, attended El Gran Stadium. Ramos faced Orlando Peña, who had gotten knocked around early in the season. The Almendares ace was 3-4 before rattling off three consecutive victories without surrendering an earned run in late November and was 10-5 heading into the season finale. But Cienfuegos tagged Peña early and often. The Elephants scored three first-inning runs off of the right-hander on consecutive hits by Borrego Álvarez, Tony González, Román Mejías, and José Joaquín Azcue, along with errors by outfielder Ángel Scull and Peña.

Azcue, who went three for three, doubled in the fourth to knock out Peña, who surrendered five runs (four earned) on seven hits while lasting only three and two-thirds innings. "Ramos beat me in the last game, that *cabrón* [bastard]," Peña said. "We lost because I didn't pitch well. That game, I don't know. There was something, sadness in the players because we were going to be leaving Cuba, all those things. . . . There were certain things going on, and I couldn't concentrate. Joaquín couldn't have hit a double off me normally. I couldn't get him out. I pitched him outside, and he hit a double off me and he beat me."[46]

Despite dominating most of the game, Ramos had his own issues in the first inning and had to pitch out of a bases-loaded jam. Almendares third baseman Miguel de la Hoz, whose bloop single loaded the bases with none out, described the opening frame:

We could have won that game in the first inning. The fourth batter was [Tony Taylor], and Pedro had him at three balls and no strikes. . . . [Ramos] threw a fourth ball around his head, a terrible pitch, and he swung. Up comes Carlos Paula and [Ramos] put him at three balls and no strikes. Then he threw two strikes and then a very high pitch, which would have been ball four and a problem for him, but [Paula] swung and struck out. [The next batter] flew out to the outfield and [Ramos] got out of the inning. . . . Pedro got himself in trouble and then we got him out of trouble. . . . That would have been two runs with the bases loaded, and right there the game changes.[47]

After the first inning, Ramos dominated Almendares, scattering seven hits, striking out four, and allowing just two runs for a complete-game 8–2 victory that gave the Elephants their second consecutive league championship.

Ramos helped his own cause by going three for four, scoring a run and driving in another on a triple. He finished with a league-leading 16-7 record. But surrendering Almendares's second run in the ninth inning cost Ramos the ERA title. Julio Moreno beat him by one point, 2.03 to 2.04. Ramos pitched 216⅔ innings, compared to 75⅓ by Moreno. Ramos's MVP season gave him 66 victories in seven Cuban League seasons, surpassing the 58 wins by teammate Camilo Pascual, who sat out the 1960–61 season. That didn't matter to Ramos when assessing their careers. "The best Cuban pitcher from that time was Camilo Pascual," Ramos said. "It's possible his numbers and mine don't say the same thing, but I consider Camilo a better pitcher than me."[48]

Cienfuegos's championship produced one of the closet pennant races in Cuban League history, with four games separating the four teams. "It was one of the best seasons in Cuba," Almendares infielder Leo Posada recalled. "We demonstrated the caliber of Cuban players. I think it was the balance that we had on all the clubs. It was a balance that whatever lineup you looked at there were players—I would say around 90 percent—on each team who had played or was playing in the Major Leagues. Just about all the players were from the Major Leagues."[49]

Almendares finished a game behind the Elephants, Habana was in third place by three games, and Marianao finished four games off the pace. "Until the [final] Friday—the season ended on Sunday—every team had a chance to win the championship that season," Habana second baseman Cookie Rojas said. "It was an extraordinary campaign."[50] Rojas, who had been traded from Cienfuegos to Habana during the season, led the league with a .332 batting average. "I just wanted to play so I could continue to develop in baseball," Rojas said. "Cienfuegos had [another] second baseman, and [manager] Tony Castaño naturally played him more. I talked to the team's owner about trading me. They traded me to the Habana team, and the way life works out, I won champion batter in the last season played in Cuba."[51]

Rojas, who went on to play sixteen seasons in the Majors with the Cincinnati Reds, Philadelphia Phillies, St. Louis Cardinals, and Kanas City Royals, still credits the role that Cuban League season played in his development. "For me it was one of the most important moments in my professional career because I established myself in baseball," said Rojas, who also had a long career as a Major League coach and managed the California Angels (1988) and Florida Marlins (1996), "and then the opportunities that opened for me in the Majors were much bigger."[52]

Bécquer didn't end up breaking the league record for home runs, finishing with 15 and a league-leading 50 RBI. Marianao teammate Zoilo Versalles was second with 14 homers. Almendares second baseman Tony Taylor led the league with 22 stolen bases, becoming the first player to steal as many as 20 bases in twenty-seven years. And Tiant compiled a 10-8 record with a 2.72 ERA to earn Rookie of the Year honors. "He was a tremendous pitcher," José Valdivielso said. "He was difficult to hit against. . . . When you connected with your bat it felt like it was a ball made of lead, hard, very difficult, very heavy."[53]

In being named the top rookie in the league, Tiant earned a

measure of vindication. "When you're a rookie, you don't know where you stand," he said. "You think one thing and the other people think something else. You have to take care of yourself and do your job the best you can. I did well. And the Cuban League, that was the biggest thing in baseball [in Cuba]. You have to feel good when your world opens up for you. Everything that I went through, the shit with them cutting me. They didn't want me here, they didn't want me there, until I arrived."[54]

Despite the exciting pennant race, there was reason for dread. "When Almendares and Cienfuegos played the final game of the 1960–61 season," historian Roberto González Echevarría wrote, "it was obvious to people running the Cuban League that there would not be a championship the next year."[55] In fact, González identified a bad omen just two days after the conclusion of the season, when Cuban baseball icon Agustín "Tinti" Molina died in Havana on February 10, 1961, at age eighty-six. "Molina had begun playing in his native Key West when the War of Independence was being organized, and had been a key performer, manager, and entrepreneur, both in Cuba and in the United States, where he ran the Cuban Stars (West) in the fledgling Negro leagues," González wrote. "It was as if the Cuban League was buried with him."[56]

State Department officials informed Major League teams on February 6 that they were free to make whatever arrangements were necessary to bring their Cuban players into the United States. But the severing of diplomatic ties with Cuba meant the U.S. embassy and consulate in Havana had closed. And with American consuls recalled, there was no way for Cuban players to obtain U.S. visas. That meant players would need to return to the U.S. by way of a third country. Mexico was believed to be their most likely route. "What they did was for us—the players in the two leagues—they sent us a contract saying we were going to play in Mexico," Miguel de la Hoz said. "It was something the big leagues did with the Mexican League, that they would send us a contract. And because Mexico and the United

States had normal relations there were no problems at all. I remember when my visa arrived at the Mexican consulate [in Havana]—I [think] it was 45 pesos because the visa had to be a work visa."[57]

Despite having visas to travel to Mexico, leaving Cuba was not without trepidations, as Miguel Fornieles learned. The inaugural winner of *The Sporting News'* Fireman of the Year award in 1960 with the Boston Red Sox was worried he might not get out of Cuba. "The only way I got out was to promise [the Castro regime] that I would come back," Fornieles admitted years later. "I told them, 'Sure I will,' but I knew at the time I wouldn't."[58] Allowed to take only $5 out of Cuba, Fornieles said he smuggled another $200 in the fingers of his baseball glove. Beyond whatever money he was forced to leave behind in Cuba, Fornieles also lost his family. His wife, whose family sympathized with the regime, later refused to join him in the United States.

A group of at least thirty players—De la Hoz, Peña, Valdivielso, Pascual, and Ramos, among them—left Havana on March 3, 1961. The flight stopped in Mexico's Yucatán peninsula before continuing to Mexico City, where they were taken to the Hotel Virreyes in downtown. "The next day we went to the American Embassy, and our visas were there," De la Hoz said. "And on the following day, everybody—because everyone was ready at that point with our tickets to where we had to go—we left. For example, I had to go—because I was with Cleveland [the Indians] at that point—to Tucson, Arizona [for spring training]. The players with Minnesota—Valdivielso, Camilo, Pedro—had to take a flight—they already had their tickets—to Florida. They trained in Orlando."[59] But what would the players do after the Major League season?

14

Casualty of the Revolution

A
l López-Chávez had gotten off the school bus near his Jersey City home when he ran into his father. "Oye, te enteraste?" ("Did you hear?"), the elder López-Chávez asked his son. "*Los Cubans* are looking for a batboy for this upcoming season."[1] It was the winter of 1961, less than four years since Al López-Chávez and his family had moved from Cuba to New Jersey. The sixteen-year-old student at St. Michaels High School in Union City, New Jersey, had been a huge baseball fan in Havana. He and his father had rooted for Almendares in Cuba.

López-Chávez knew the Sugar Kings had moved to his adoptive hometown the previous year but had not seen them play at Roosevelt Stadium in 1960. "As luck would have it, my family decided to drive from Jersey City to Key West [then travel] to Havana," he recalled. "We took the Pride of Havana ferry and spent the month of August in 1960 visiting family after the revolution. So, I was not able to go to any of the games."[2]

López-Chávez suddenly had an opportunity to not only see but also work for the former Sugar Kings, which still counted many Cuban players he had followed on its roster. "Of course, right away my interest is there," López-Chávez said. "My father says, 'Well, if you want to take advantage of that, you need to write a composition.' A composition? In English? Of course, I had not been in the country very long. . . . I went ahead and I wrote my composition in Spanish, and with the aid of a dictionary, I basically translated the whole thing, word for word."[3]

The composition was titled, "Why I Would Like to Be the Jerseys' Batboy." On March 9, the team narrowed the list of final-ists to ten, including López-Chávez. One would be chosen as the Jerseys' batboy, while a runner-up would work as the batboy for visiting clubs. The salaried position—it would pay three dollars per game—also would include one road trip during the sea-son. López-Chávez and the other nine candidates interviewed for the job March 8–14 at the team's Roosevelt Stadium offices.

On Friday, March 17, López-Chávez received a telegram informing him that he had won the contest. The team's news release described him as "possessing a baseball name if there ever was one," a reference to former Major League catcher and future Hall of Fame manager Al López. "As a fifteen-year-old being as fanatical about Cuban baseball and baseball in gen-eral because I did play in high school," López-Chávez said, "it could not have been a greater experience for a young boy to find himself in the United States and to have a chance to hang out, if you will, rub elbows with the players that he grew up idolizing."[4]

The Twins were wrapping up spring training on the road in West Palm Beach, Florida, when a story in the *Washington Post* indicated Pedro Ramos might return to Cuba "within a week or two" if anti-Castro forces were to launch a revolt in his home-land. The Twins' April 11 season opener against the New York Yankees—which Ramos was scheduled to start—was four days away. According to the story, Ramos had informed Minnesota manager Cookie Lavagetto that he had previously volunteered his services to the cause of toppling the Castro regime. And Lavag-etto was sufficiently concerned that Ramos was serious that the manager was "trying to talk the fast-balling right-hander out of the idea, but so far with indifferent success."[5]

Ramos made his 1961 debut as scheduled as the Twins (née Senators) made their debut in Minneapolis. Ramos limited the Yankees to three hits in a 6–0 victory against Whitey Ford. After the game, Ramos acknowledged his threat to join anti-Castro forces in Cuba was a joke. "I'm just kidding Cookie when I say I leave club to return to Cuba to fight Castro," *The Sporting News* quoted a winking Ramos as saying in broken English. "I baseball player, not fighter, great lover. I stick to baseball like Papa Joe [Cambria] told me. I no talk politics, baseball my game."[6]

Years later, Ramos denied even suggesting he might return to Cuba to fight Castro. "Reporters sometimes write things," Ramos said. "He asked me a question, and he chronicled it in his own way. I never said I was going to Cuba to fight anybody. . . . What happened was they asked a question. . . . Would I go to Cuba to fight against my brothers to liberate Cuba? I said, 'I'm not a soldier. I'm a ballplayer.' But the reporter wrote it in his own manner. . . . I wasn't a soldier or political. I only battled when I was on the mound."[7]

At the time, the notion of Ramos joining military operations against Castro seemed plausible because the prospect of Cuban exiles preparing to invade Cuba had been an open secret during the first few months of 1961. The previous March, Eisenhower had authorized the CIA to develop a covert plan to oust Castro. Operating with a $13 million budget, the CIA began recruiting Cuban exiles in April 1960, forming what became known as Brigade 2506, a force of fourteen hundred soldiers that trained on Useppa Island, a private island off the coast of Florida secretly leased by the CIA.

But in January 1961, Sergio Aparicio of the Democratic Revolutionary Front told the *New York Times* that the anti-Castro group was "building up and almost ready" to invade Cuba from "some place in the Western Hemisphere—definitely not in the United States."[8] Another report named Retalhuleu, Guatemala, as the site of a secret base used to train anti-Castro forces with U.S. help.[9]

By April 7, the *New York Times* reported that an army of five to six thousand Cuban exiles had been training for nearly nine months in parts of the United States and Central America. "Its purpose," Tad Szulc wrote, "is the liberation of Cuba from what it describes as the Communist rule of the Castro regime."[10] The next day, José Miró Cardona, the one-time Cuban prime minister and ambassador-designate to the United States who had defected from Cuba and was serving as president of the Cuban Revolutionary Council, predicted that a general revolt within Cuba was "imminent."[11]

An April 10 *New York Times* report no doubt explained the reason for Miró Cardona's prediction. Szulc reported that anti-Castro rebels had agreed on a strategy of using multiple guerrilla landings to infiltrate small commando units throughout Cuba to help coordinate uprisings and sabotage campaigns against the Castro regime. "Rebel sources," Szulc wrote, "have reported at least six landings in the last two weeks involving commando units instructed to establish contact with the underground in preparations for the uprisings."[12] Among those infiltrated into Cuba as a prelude to invasion was Ralph Ávila.

Ávila, who had managed to escape Cuba on New Year's Eve 1960, had returned to the island surreptitiously, arriving aboard a small plane in the early hours on *El Dia de los Reyes*, Three Kings Day on January 6, 1961. "I was with my brother-in-law in Miami when we went to see Miró Cardona about going to Quetzaltenango, Guatemala, for training," Ávila recalled. "Miró Cardona told me, 'It would be better for you to go to Cuba. You'll be able to do more there.' And then I returned to Cuba, infiltrated with a different name, a different passport.... The only ones on the plane were me and the pilot. We were supposed to leave at 8 [p.m.], but we left Miami around 12:30 [in the morning]. I got there, got a car and went to my house, and then I had to start running here, running there, going, coming. All those days ... when you're young, you have no idea what you're doing. I did it, and I did it in good faith."[13]

There was nothing left for Bobby Maduro in Cuba. He had already lost the Sugar Kings, and the future of the Cuban League was uncertain at best. His oldest son, Roberto Jr., was living in New York. His wife, Fufila, and their other six children had fled Cuba in October 1960 and were living in Philadelphia with family friends. Financially, the once wealthy businessman had lost nearly everything. "The family investments and business and lands had been systematically, if illegally, destroyed or grabbed by the lunatic revolutionist regime," *Rochester Democrat-Chronicle* columnist George Beahon wrote. "For more than a year, Maduro had hung on, hoping to salvage his last asset, the seaside home he built in 1958, against the day the Castro regime might be overturned. Now even that seemed hopeless."[14] It was time for Maduro to leave.

But in the chaotic bustle of José Martí International Airport, Maduro found himself detained on April 16. Although all his paperwork had been in order the previous day, government agents could not find his passport and they would not permit him to board his flight for the United States. According to his son Jorge, Maduro called Fidel's office: "Listen, I want to leave Cuba to go to the United States. I want to see my family. It's been a while since I've seen them."[15] In recounting the ordeal to Beahon, Maduro credited "friends" who "worked a miracle. They produced my papers and passport, somehow, and I boarded the plane at the last minute."[16]

It was the last flight out of Havana before an invasion force of Cuban exiles landed the next morning along the southern Cuban coast in what would become known as the Bay of Pigs Invasion. "For all I know," Maduro recounted years later, "they might have figured I had some advance information on that invasion."[17] Maduro would eventually find himself back at the helm of his team in Jersey City, but things would not be the same. "You can imagine," Jorge Maduro said. "Do you know what it is that after thousands and thousands and millions of dollars invested in this and then suddenly—it didn't just happen to my father; it happened to all Cubans—to have to start over? I can't comprehend how my father leaves Cuba without any money. . . . From what I've read he had six dollars in his pocket."[18]

A large sea inlet knifing some fourteen miles into the southern coast of Cuba, the Bay of Pigs draws its name from Conchillos,

the last name of an official in the Spanish bureaucracy in the six-
teenth century (cochinos means pigs in Spanish). West of the city
of Cienfuegos, the bay was surrounded by the Ciénaga de Zapata
(Zapata Swamp), the "largest expanse of wetlands in the Caribbean."[19] The bay itself is a tangle of mangroves and coral reefs, ill-
suited for establishing a military beachhead. Yet the Bay of Pigs,
specifically Playa Girón and Playa Larga—two beaches in name
only, one at the bay's mouth and the other deep in the inlet—
were chosen as the landing sites a month before the invasion.

Seeking to maintain plausible deniability for U.S. involvement, Kennedy had directed the CIA to change the invasion site
from Trinidad—less than one hundred miles east of the Bay of
Pigs—despite its advantages: an existing counterrevolutionary presence, a defensible beachhead, and a potential escape
route into the Escambray Mountains. Days before the invasion,
Kennedy pledged the United States would not intervene to help
bring down Castro's regime. "There will not be under any conditions, be an intervention in Cuba by the United States armed
forces," Kennedy said during an April 12 news conference. "[The
United States] can meet its responsibilities to make sure that
there are no Americans involved in any actions inside Cuba."[20]

The first phase of the invasion launched in the early morning
hours of Saturday, April 15. Almost nothing went as planned.
Before dawn, the freighter *La Playa* stopped near the mouth
of the Mocambo River in Oriente Province, about thirty miles
east of Guantanamo. The diversionary force of 164 men was
led by Major Higinio "Nino" Díaz, who had fought under Raúl
Castro in the Sierra Maestra but had turned against the revolution. Under the cover of darkness, nine men aboard an inflat-
able rubber raft ran reconnaissance within five hundred feet
of the rocky coast. They spotted two trucks and a jeep onshore.
Concluding the vehicles might be part of Cuban militia deployed
throughout the island in anticipation of an invasion, the raft
retreated to the freighter. A second attempt twenty-four hours
later also would fail, and the invasion never got its diversion.[21]

Ralph Ávila remembers being dispatched to greet Díaz's group.

"They sent me to wait for the invasion along the coast," he said. "Nino Díaz's boat, we could see it from the coast. It was out there. We could see the lights signaling."[22] From the shore, Ávila had a different prospective on Díaz's failure to make landfall. Radio Swan was transmitting to Cuba via short wave twice a day. According to Ávila, Cuban announcer Arturo Artalejo got ahead of himself. "We had a portable radio, and Artalejo said that commandant Nino Díaz had already disembarked and had advanced," Ávila said. "The boat had never disembarked. Nino heard all this stuff and thought it was *un gancho* [a trick], as we used to say. He turned back."

As dawn broke on Saturday, six B-26 bombers, designed to look like planes from Castro's Fuerza Aérea Revolucionaria (FAR) but flown by exile pilots, attacked several air bases, hoping to destroy the Revolutionary Air Force. The attack was staged to look as if were carried out by disgruntled FAR pilots who would then "defect" to the United States. One pilot flew a purposely bullet-riddled plane to Miami to sell the cover story of defectors carrying out the attacks. The air raids, however, failed to destroy all the planes in the Cuban Air Force.

Speaking at the Colón Cemetery on April 16, during a funeral for air force members killed in the air raids, Castro accused the United States of being directly responsible for the attacks. He also declared his revolution was "socialist" and carried out "right under the noses of the *Yanquis*."[23] Fearing the extent of U.S. involvement might be exposed, Kennedy late on the evening of April 16 cancelled the second phase: air strikes designed to take out what remained of the Cuban Air Force. It would prove to be a costly decision for the third and final phase: the amphibious landing at the Bay of Pigs on April 17.

Even before the landing, the air raids and other attacks— the destruction of sugar mills in Pinar del Rio and an explosion that blew up El Encanto, a huge department store in central Havana, among them—prompted Castro to order the preemptive rounding up of thousands of dissidents on the island. The CIA had hoped Monday's invasion would spark a popular uprising. But with so many anti-Castro Cubans herded into theaters, stadiums, and military bases, such a revolt never materialized. And the landing itself was a disaster.

An invasion force of about 1,500 members of Brigade 2506 began landing at Playa Girón and Playa Larga at 1 a.m. on April 17. But landfall was made difficult by the bay's coral reefs. By the time the Brigade made it ashore, it was outnumbered and outgunned by Cuban armed forces, including the remaining air force planes that could have been destroyed by the aborted air strikes. The rebels stood little chance of succeeding but managed to hold on for three days. In the end, some managed to escape, but more than 100 were killed and almost 1,200 were captured, including Ávila's brother-in-law, who hid in the Zapata Swamp before being discovered after twenty days. "It was a disaster what happened there," Ávila said. "My brother-in-law survived through a miracle of God."[24]

In the week following the failed invasion, the Castro regime rounded up 200,000 people across the island, including family members of anti-Castro leaders in the United States and American newspaper reporters, such as Henry Raymont of United Press International and Robert Berrellez of the Associated Press, who eventually were released and returned to the United States. Ávila managed to avoid the roundup and eventually escaped Cuba again "first through money and later through connections."[25] And his brother-in-law, along with the rest of the 1,179 prisoners, would be released and returned to the United States in December 1962 in exchange for $53 million worth of food and medicine.

The entire Bay of Pigs episode was a damaging embarrassment for the Kennedy administration. And instead of toppling Castro, the debacle only serviced to strengthen Castro's grip on power. In assessing the Cuban people's support of Castro, the *New York Times* quoted a Canadian businessman who had flown to New York on April 24 aboard the first commercial flight out of Havana after the failed invasion. "Before the bombing of Havana on April 15, it was 'yes' and 'no' with most of those we talked to," Henry Dolansky said. "After the bombing, and the invasion, all were for Castro."[26]

As the Brigade 2506 forces were getting routed for a second day, thirteen hundred miles away from the Bay of Pigs, Al López-Chávez and fellow batboy Roy Beeler reported for duty at Roosevelt Stadium. The Jersey City Jerseys were scheduled to open the 1961 season against the Buffalo Bisons on Tuesday, April 18. But rain postponed the start of the former Sugar Kings' second season in New Jersey until Thursday. Jersey City beat Buffalo 8–0 to open the season—albeit two days late—in front of a small crowd of 2,351. The inclement weather didn't dampen López-Chávez's enthusiasm. "It's sort of ironic that politics and history had me included in the mix," López-Chávez recalled. "So, I find myself reporting to the stadium, and I run into a lot of the players that were my favorite."[27]

Because he was Cuban, López-Chávez, whose given name is Alfonso, quickly became a favorite among players and coaches, who called him "Alfonsito." Manager Napoleón Reyes, in his deep baritone voice, called him "López López." It was a dream job for a baseball fan. López-Chávez helped take care of the team's equipment and uniforms. He learned how to use a mixture of clay and saliva to treat baseballs so they would have a firm grip. He even had his first taste of beer—at the suggestion of one player and with his father's blessing—while working as the Jerseys' batboy. When he was done with his duties, López-Chávez was free to join the players for infield practice and shagging fly balls. He often warmed up the pitchers and threw batting practice.

Miguel Cuéllar tried to teach López-Chávez the screwball that would help the future Baltimore Orioles All-Star win at least 18 games in consecutive seasons from 1969 to 1974. Despite being a first baseman, Borrego Álvarez taught López-Chávez how to throw a slider. That skill got the fifteen-year-old in trouble during one batting practice session midway through the season. "I was armed with a mean slider, which, to be honest with you, I truly had not perfected," López-Chávez said of tossing BP to future Senators pitcher Dave Stenhouse. "I decide to try Borrego's famous slider, and sure enough it gets away from me, and I hit Stenhouse on his right wrist. I see the ball fly off his wrist, and the bat goes flying up in the air. He yelled out, and the next thing I see—I'm still laughing remembering—I hear Napoleón Reyes come out of the dugout yelling, 'López López, get him out of there, get him out of there.' That was the end of my batting practice experience."[28]

López-Chávez's job as the Jerseys' batboy included one road trip with the team, which came August 22–25 to Richmond, Virginia, where Jersey City was scheduled to play a four-game series against the New York Yankees' Triple-A team. The trip would give López-Chávez the chance to play pepper with future Yankees All-Star Tom Tresh before one of the games at Parker Field. "I remember Tresh coming up to me basically behind home plate and saying, 'Hey kid, you want to play pepper?'" López-Chávez said. "I had no idea that he was [going to be] such a huge star."[29] The trip also gave López-Chávez his first experience with the Jim Crow South.

The Jerseys had left Newark International Airport the morning of August 22 aboard Eastern Airlines flight 341. Upon arriving in Richmond, members of the team were transported by a Virginia Transit Charter Bus to the Hotel Richmond in downtown, where López-Chávez was assigned to room with Cookie Rojas, who at twenty-two was only seven years older than the batboy. At a pregame dinner that first afternoon, López-Chávez innocently asked why Borrego wasn't at the table. "That's when I was told that we were in the South and that the black players were staying at another hotel," López-Chávez recalled. "I came from Cuba, where that was not an issue. It wasn't to me. In Jersey City, I never saw that to be an issue."[30]

Álvarez was one of the ten black players on the Jerseys—along with Zip Brooks, Yo-Yo Davalillo, Jim Pendleton, Andrés Ayón, Francisco Obregón, Daniel Morejón, Vic Davalillo, Marshall Bridges, and David Jiménez—who had to stay at Slaughter's Hotel. "Sure enough, traveling to Richmond, Virginia, it was an issue for black ballplayers," López-Chávez said. "So, when I further inspected this itinerary that I had gotten from the [team's] business manager, I see that the black ballplayers were staying at the Slaughter's Hotel. How apropos is that, when you think about it?"[31]

Bobby Maduro regained control of the team he had lost eleven months earlier, taking charge of the Jerseys on June 15. Since fleeing Cuba in April, Maduro had been living as a refugee with his family ninety miles away in Philadelphia, where he would continue to live during the season. "I will be a commuter and work without a title," said Maduro, who had lost more than $10 million of personal wealth because of the Castro regime's confiscation of all private business, land, and property. "The only money I have now is what I can earn."[32] But his was not entirely a triumphant return. He was in Buffalo, New York, for an emergency meeting to consider moving the Jerseys.

But a pledge from Jersey City mayor-elect Thomas Gangemi saved the club—for the moment. When Gangemi guaranteed he would form a local committee of industry and business leaders to support the team, directors of the International League voted against relocating the franchise during their four-hour session. Although there was no city available as an immediate relocation site, "we will have one or two cities available next year if we need them," league president Tommy Richardson said.[33] The Jerseys had struggled with attendance all season, and those troubles continued into July. One major factor was the team's proximity to the defending American League champion New York Yankees.

Jersey City was less than thirty miles from Yankee Stadium, so Bronx Bombers games were broadcast on local television. Why would fans go to watch a Minor League game at Roosevelt Stadium when they could visit The House That Ruth Built or watch the most-storied franchise in Major League history on WPIX Channel 11 from the comfort of their living rooms? "A trip to Yankee Stadium via the Hudson Tubes costs the Jersey City fan only a few cents more than a bus ride from Journal Square to Roosevelt Stadium," Howard M. Tuckner wrote in the *New York Times*. "For virtually the same price as a bleacher or general admission seat at Roosevelt Stadium, one can go to the Yankee playground and watch Mantle peg a strike to Cletis Boyer. . . . And no less significant, beer costs the same in both parks."[34]

It was no wonder that the Jerseys had drawn only 37,904 fans through the first twenty-eight home dates, an average of 1,354 per game. According to one club spokesman, the team would need to draw at least 225,000 fans—an average of 17,100—for the season to break even. "How much money can you throw out the window," the unnamed official said, "before you run out?"[35] Seeking financial relief, Maduro met with the newly elected Gangemi on July 17. He hoped to negotiate a new lease for Roosevelt Stadium that would reduce the rent from $15,000 to $1. But Gangemi refused to change the terms negotiated by the previous administration.

Facing the prospect of reportedly losing $100,000 for the season, Maduro on July 21 visited Jacksonville, Florida, which had been thwarted in three earlier attempts to land an International League franchise. On the trip, Maduro would say only that Jacksonville would get "sincere consideration" should he decide to move the Jerseys. One report said Maduro would seek to sell 49 percent of his stock for $125,000.[36] Amid those reports, Maduro made a public plea for support from Jersey City. "If a community spirit in the team can be created and the city gives us a helping hand, things might work out," he said. "I would be interested in selling stock in the club to local persons so that it would be a real home-town team. And the city fathers could help by reducing our annual rental from $15,000 to a token figure."[37]

Maduro's plea did not work, and developments on September 26 paved the way for the Jerseys' relocation to Jacksonville. The Houston Sports Association, which would run the Colt 45s National League expansion team in 1962, agreed to relinquish its territorial rights to Jacksonville in exchange for $10,895 and

Jim Pendleton, who batted .304 for the Jerseys. The same day, a ticket drive was launched with the hope of selling one hundred thousand tickets by December 1. "That's the deal of the International League meeting at the National Association Convention, which will be held in Tampa," Maduro said, "and we'll have to get league approval at that time."[38]

The International League didn't have to wait that long. With nearly sixty-nine thousand tickets bought during the first two weeks of the drive, the league's directors met in New York on October 3 and approved the Jerseys' move to Jacksonville. The team, which would enter the league in 1962 as the Jacksonville Suns, would serve as the Triple-A team for the Cleveland Indians. López-Chávez took the team's move in stride. "The team moves, and I guess I went about my business of being a high school student and playing baseball and basketball," López-Chávez said. "So, I didn't really react one way or the other. That's the way it was, and that was what was explained to me, that they moved on and that was it."[39]

As the Major League season rolled into July, about twenty Cuban players, including Orestes Miñoso (Chicago White Sox), Humberto Fernández (Detroit Tigers), Miguel de la Hoz (Cleveland Indians), Miguel Fornieles (Boston Red Sox), and Panchón Herrera and Tony González (Philadelphia Phillies), were among those making significant contributions to their teams. The Minnesota Twins had the largest contingent of Cubans with seven, including shortstop Zoilo Versalles and pitchers Camilo Pascual and Pedro Ramos. All were worried they would have a "serious problem" reentering the United States for next season because of circumstances in Cuba. Twins president Calvin Griffith described the situation as "a mess and we are right now trying to do something about it."[40]

Despite the severing of ties between Cuba and the United States, Cuban players were allowed to return to the United States for the 1961 season. Their temporary work visas were set to expire in October. "This agreement is out for next year,"

Griffith acknowledged. If they wanted to be assured of continuing their Major League careers, they might have to apply for U.S. citizenship and not return to Cuba. "The players are not sure they want to renounce their Cuban citizenship," Griffith said. "All have families there and are concerned over what would happen to them if they decided to remain in the U.S."[41]

The U.S. state department said there were no restrictions on Cubans entering the United States, but there would be no guarantee of players obtaining permission to leave Cuba in the future. "For every person that goes to Cuba, ten leave," a State Department spokesman said. "Airlines are booked through December." One of the Cuban players on the Twins told Washington sportswriter Morris Siegel, "They told us we would not get special treatment like this year. We must wait our turn to leave because so many want to leave the country. It is all very mixed up and very sad. We are baseball players, not fighters, not politicians. How come it has got to be like this?"[42]

In August 1961, the U.S. state department and Organized Baseball agreed to procedures for expediting reentry for the approximately two hundred Cubans in the Major and Minor Leagues. But the process included no assurance the Cuban government would allow the players to leave Cuba the following spring. As Cuban players weighed their options, the Cuban League was dealt its death blow. While in New York scouting for the Cleveland Indians, Almendares general manager Monchy de Arcos announced the team would withdraw from the Cuban League. The club's directors had met in Miami and voted to halt operations of one the league's founding teams "as long as Fidel Castro is in power."[43] The circuit did not open its season on October 20 as scheduled.

The Cuban League's destiny was a fait accompli almost the moment the previous season ended. In February, the Castro regime had created a new sports directorate, the Instituto Nacional de Deportes Educación Física y Recreación (National Institute of Sports, Physical Fitness, and Recreation). In March, INDER decreed the abolition of professional baseball, and held mass tryouts to quickly assemble a team to return to the Amateur World Series after an eight-year absence. Cuba, managed by former Almendares coach Sungo Carreras, swept the competition— Mexico, Venezuela, Panama, Guatemala, Nicaragua, the Dutch Antilles, and host Costa Rica—on April 7–12, days before Cuba repulsed the Bay of Pigs invasion.

When he returned to Mexico after the 1960–61 Cuban League season ended, Luis Tiant assumed he would be back in Cuba after the conclusion of the Mexican League season. While in Mexico, he wed Maria del Refugio Navarro on August 12, 1961. Tiant planned to take her to the Isle of Pines for their honeymoon after the season, but cancelled the trip. "A week before I was going there for my honeymoon with my wife, my father sent me a letter and told me not to come back," Tiant said. "There wasn't going to be anything professional, not baseball, not boxing. There wasn't going to be anything professional. He told me to stay and find somewhere else to play the winter."[44]

With the Cuban League shuttered, more than two dozen Cuban Major Leaguers ignored the Castro regime's threats it would seize their property if they failed to return to Cuba. Instead, they remained in the United States during the winter or spread throughout Latin America, playing in winter leagues in various countries. Miguel de la Hoz, Tony González, Orlando Peña, Leo Cárdenas, Román Mejías, Eduardo Bauta, and Tiant were among those who played in Puerto Rico. Panchón Herrera, Daniel Morejón, Diego Seguí, Julio Moreno, René Friol, Rodolfo Arias, and Sandy Valdespino joined the Panama-Nicaragua League. Leo Posada and José Azcue played in Venezuela. "I had my tickets to go back to Cuba," Posada said. "My father and my mother-in-law and all my family told me not to go back, that there wasn't going to be any baseball."[45]

Other Cuban players such as Orestes Miñoso, Camilo Pascual, Pedro Ramos, Humberto Fernández, Julio Bécquer, Carlos Paula, Zoilo Versalles, and Tony Taylor spent the winter in the United States rather than return to Cuba. "I decided to stay playing in the Major Leagues because I had a contract," Ramos said. "I didn't really think about if I could return, then leave or not leave [Cuba]. I made my decision based on the fact that I had a contract with [the Twins] and I stayed here."[46]

Said Taylor: "I decided to stay in the United States because in Cuba already there was nothing for the professional baseball player. There wasn't professional baseball, and there wasn't going to be professional baseball. The situation was very bad. I wasn't going to go back because of that man [Castro]."[47] Many of the Cuban players in the United States never returned to Cuba. "Long regarded as the game's winter mecca, Cuba's capital city of Havana stands deserted this fall as far as professional baseball activity is concerned," Clifford Kachline wrote in *The Sporting News*. "The Cuban Winter League has fallen victim to the Fidel Castro revolution."[48]

Epilogue

W hen Luis Tiant heeded his father's warning and chose not to return to Cuba in 1961, he could not have imagined it would take him forty-six years to again set foot on his native soil. But the twenty-one-year-old pitcher embarked upon the next phase of his life and baseball career with trepidation. "You feel uncomfortable, bad, because you don't know if you're really not going to be able to return," Tiant told me when I interviewed him over the telephone for this book. "Maybe you won't be able to see your mother and father again. Maybe that was the last time you saw them. You don't know what might happen. They could die or something could happen to them. You don't know. . . . And they didn't know either. They weren't young. They didn't know if they would ever see me again."

Tiant finally saw his parents again in 1975, when the Castro regime allowed them to come to the United States to visit their son, who at the time was pitching for the Boston Red Sox. They were in Fenway Park to watch Tiant toss a five-hit shutout against the Cincinnati Reds to win Game 1 of the World Series. Tiant's parents never returned to Cuba. They passed away, two days apart, after spending fifteen months with Tiant in the United States. Tiant eventually returned to Cuba in 2007 to visit family and friends, a story told in the 2009 documentary *The Lost Son of Havana*. "I prayed to God to let me see my homeland and see my family," Tiant said. "Many of my friends who played with me, that I knew, that we went to school together since we were kids, many died and were never able to return to their homeland. . . . You have to be Cuban to understand what we've been through."

My family understands. Many of them were among the more than one million Cubans who have migrated to the United States since the revolution. My uncle René and his wife fled Cuba for the United States in May 1962, by way of Jamaica. My parents applied for a visa to leave the country, only to have their efforts stalled when the Cuban Missile Crisis halted direct flights to the United States. Finally, on November 15, 1965—five months after I was born—my parents, paternal grandparents, and I were among the 2,979 refugees to leave Cuba aboard some 150 vessels during the Camarioca Boatlift. The port of Camarioca was shut down the day we left. The 2,014 who remained at the exit compound in Matanzas Province would later leave aboard chartered boats. In later years, other family members would follow—an aunt during the Freedom Flights of the 1970s, my maternal grandmother by way of Spain, an uncle with his wife and two children during the 1980 Mariel Boatlift. Some family members never left Cuba. And few of those who fled have ever returned.

That was the case as well for many of the Cuban players who opted to stay in the United States in 1961. Cuban League stars, such as Minnie Miñoso, Camilo Pascual, Pedro Ramos, Orlando Peña, Tony Taylor, Tony González, Leo Cárdenas, Cookie Rojas, and Mike Cuéllar, finished their careers in the Majors. Younger Cuban stars who found fame in the Majors, such as Tony Pérez, Tony Oliva, Bert Campaneris, and Jose Cardénal, never had the opportunity to play in the Cuban League. Despite a Hall of Fame career, Pérez still counts that as a chief regret. "I was raised watching Cuban baseball," he said in 2011, during the Cuban Cultural Center of New York's congress on Cuban baseball history. "I didn't dream of playing in the Majors. I didn't dream of playing in the United States. What I thought about was playing for one of the four teams that played at El Stadium in that era. . . . It's still one of the things that I carry with me. I couldn't play in front of my family."

After Bobby Maduro moved the former Sugar Kings from Jersey City to Jacksonville, Florida, the Jacksonville Suns enjoyed success in the team's first season in the Sunshine State. The Suns finished 94-60 to win the International League regular-season pennant in 1962 before losing in seven games to the Atlanta Crackers in the league playoffs. Maduro sold the club in 1963 but remained the team's general manager until he joined baseball commissioner William Eckert's staff in 1965 to direct the Office of Inter-American Relations, which coordinated efforts between Latin American leagues and Organized Baseball. Maduro, who founded the short-lived Inter-American League in 1979, died in Miami in 1986 at age seventy. "My father was an incredible fighter," Jorge Maduro said. "He always tried to turn a bad situation into a good one."

That's exactly what the Cuban players in exile did in establishing themselves and thriving in the Major Leagues. In the 1960s, most of the Latin American players in the Majors came from Cuba, with twenty-three on Major League forty-man rosters in 1969, compared to eighteen from both the Dominican Republic and Puerto Rico. With Major League access to Cuban talent closed off after Castro nationalized baseball on the island, the Dominican Republic and Venezuela began to easily overtake Cuba in producing Major League talent over the next several decades. In that time, many of Cuba's greatest postrevolution players, such as Omar Linares, Orestes Kindelán, and Víctor Mesa, never had the chance to play in the Majors.

Only those who managed to defect reached the Majors, beginning with Bárbaro Garbey, who was among the mass exodus of Cubans to reach the United States during the Mariel Boatlift. In the 1990s, what began slowly with the defections of players such as René Arocha (1991), Rey Ordóñez (1993), and Ariel Prieto (1995) soon led to a spate of escapes from the island. Pitchers such as Liván Hernández (1995), his half-brother Orlando "El Duque" Hernández (1997), and José Contreras (2002) were among the most successful.

As Major League Baseball moved into the twenty-first century, defections increased dramatically, bringing the likes of 2013 National League Rookie of the Year José Fernández, New York Yankees closer Aroldis Chapman, New York Mets slugger Yoenis Céspedes, Los Angeles Dodgers outfielder Yasiel Puig, Houston Astros first baseman Yuli Gurriel, and 2013 American League Rookie of the Year José Abreu. But the spate of defections also raised concerns and court cases over human trafficking. It also weakened the caliber of baseball in Cuba, draining talent from Cuba's Seria Nacional and the Cuban National Team, which had dominated international competitions for decades.

The twenty-first century also brought major shifts in Cuba's leadership and the country's relationship with the United States. After more than five decades in power, Fidel Castro stepped aside because of health issues, allowing his brother Raúl to succeed him as Cuba's president in 2011. Fidel died at age ninety in 2016, and Raúl stepped down as president in 2018, tabbing Miguel Díaz-Canel Bermúdez as his replacement. It marked the first time since 1959 a Castro was not running the country. When U.S president Barack Obama in 2014 restored diplomatic relations with Cuba for the first time in more than fifty years, it opened the possibility for discussions between Major League Baseball and Cuban officials. A group from MLB, including defectors Puig, Abreu, and Alexei Ramírez, went on a goodwill tour in Cuba in December 2015. The Tampa Bay Rays—with Obama sitting in the stands next to Cuban president Raúl Castro—played a spring training game against the Cuban National Team in 2016.

There have been talks between MLB and Cuban officials about possibly codifying a system by which Cubans players could once again participate in the Majors. And one group, the Caribbean Baseball Initiative, told the *New York Times* in 2015 of its efforts to eventually return a Minor League team to Havana. But in November 2017, the Donald Trump administration reversed Obama's policy by implementing tight new restrictions on American travel and trade with Cuba. It remains unclear how Trump's policy might impact the future of baseball in Cuba.

NOTES

1. The House That Bobby Built

1. René Brioso, interview by author, December 19, 2015.

2. Brioso, interview, December 19, 2015.

3. Brioso, interview, December 19, 2015.

4. "Extraordinario espectaculo se brindara esta noche en el nuevo stadium al inaugurarse La Liga Internacional," *Diario de la Marina*, April 20, 1954.

5. "Extraordinario espectaculo se brindara esta noche en el nuevo stadium."

6. "Extraordinario espectaculo se brindara esta noche en el nuevo stadium."

7. "Maduro Backs Havana Bid as Int. Loop Replacement," *The Sporting News*, November 4, 1953.

8. Rory Costello, "Bobby Maduro," in Bjarkman, *Cuban Baseball Legends*, 232.

9. Bjarkman, *Cuban Baseball Legends*, 233.

10. George Beahon, "Cuban Exile Maduro Basks in Suns' Success," *The Sporting News*, June 23, 1962.

11. Bjarkman, *Cuban Baseball Legends*, 233.

12. Jorge Maduro, interview by author, August 10, 2016.

13. Andrés Fleitas, interview by author, January 1997.

14. Ralph Ávila, interview by author, September 18, 2015.

15. González Echevarría, *Pride of Havana*, 409.

16. "Mike Gonzalez Becomes Sole Owner at Havana," *The Sporting News*, December 18, 1946.

17. Brian McKenna, "Joe Cambria," Society for American Baseball Research website, accessed November 10, 2016, http://sabr.org/bioproj/person/4e7d25a0.

18. McKenna, "Joe Cambria."

19. McKenna, "Joe Cambria."

20. "Salisbury Injuns on Market; Cambria Gets Bid to Move," *The Sporting News*, October 10, 1940.

21. Evelio Hernández, interview, by author, Septmeber 24, 2015.

22. Matt Welch, "The Cuban Senators," ESPN, accessed November 10, 2016, https://espn.go.com/page2/wash/s/2002/0311/1349361.html.

23. McKenna, "Joe Cambria."

24. Orlando Peña, interview by author, December 22, 2015.

25. McKenna, "Joe Cambria."

26. Clifford Kachline, "Higher Ratings Given Five Leagues by Minors," *The Sporting News*, December 13, 1945.

27. Figueredo, *Cuban Baseball*, 269.

28. Pedro Galiana, "Havana Will Install Lights for Debut in Organized Baseball," *The Sporting News*, February 7, 1946.

29. "Havana Upset in Synthetic Playoff, Muddles Florida-Int Title Picture," *The Sporting News*, September 25, 1946.

30. "Havana Upset in Synthetic Playoff."

31. "Washington Buys Control of Class C Havana Club," *The Sporting News*, July 31, 1946.

32. Luther Evans, "Cambria 'Scouting Expenses' under Probe in Florida-Int," *The Sporting News*, August 13, 1947.

33. Welch, "The Cuban Senators."

34. "O.B. Recognizes Griffith in Havana Club Dispute," *The Sporting News*, March 29, 1950.

35. "Row among Cuban Owners Won't Halt Club Operation," *The Sporting News*, April 5, 1950.

36. Jimmy Burns, "Griff to Fight Cuban Court Ruling Restoring Acosta as Havana Boss," *The Sporting News*, August 16, 1950.

37. Jimmy Burns, "Havana's F-1 Cubans Shift to Key West," *The Sporting News*, April 15, 1953.

38. Barney Waters, "'Passes by Dozens' Handicap Cubans," *The Sporting News*, August 9, 1950.

39. Waters, "'Passes by Dozens.'"

40. Jimmy Burns, "Havana in New Hands, Fla. Int Problem Ends," *The Sporting News*, May 13, 1953.

41. Burns, "Havana in New Hands."

42. Burns, "Havana in New Hands."

43. Costello, "Bobby Maduro."

44. Jimmy Burns, "Two Havana Clubs, Fla. Int Plan for '54," *The Sporting News*, August 26, 1953.

45. "Maduro Backs Havana Bid," *The Sporting News*. November 4, 1953.

46. Dan Daniel, "It's Official Now—Richmond and Havana Enter Int," *The Sporting News*, January 20, 1954.

47. Pedro Galiana, "Noble Tabbed as Havana Int Cleanup Hitter," *The Sporting News*, March 17, 1954.

48. Pedro Galiana, "Havana Ready for Fine Start in Int League," *The Sporting News*, March 31, 1954.

49. René Molina, "Ante una nueva etapa . . . Buena suerte Cubanos," *Diario de la Marina*, April 20, 1954.

50. Pedro Galiana, "Maduro Expects 20,000 Gate for Havana Int Bow," *The Sporting News*, April 14, 1954.

2. Winds of Change

1. González Echevarría, *Pride of Havana*, 90.

2. Pérez, "Between Baseball and Bullfighting," 493.

3. Cluster and Hernández, *History of Havana*, 93.

4. Pérez, "Between Baseball and Bullfighting," 505.

5. Gjelten, *Bacardi and The Long Fight for Cuba*, 30.

6. Gjelten, *Bacardi and The Long Fight for Cuba*, 30.

7. Gott, *Cuba*, 73.

8. Martí, *José Martí*, 9.

9. Antón and Hernández, *Cubans in America*, 63.

10. Antón and Hernández, *Cubans in America*, 64.

11. Pérez, *On Becoming Cuban*, 75.

12. Antón and Hernández, *Cubans in America*, 62.

13. Antón and Hernández, *Cubans in America*, 27.

14. Torres, *La leyenda del beisbol cubano*, 16.

15. Antón and Hernández, *Cubans in America*, 83.

16. Martí, *José Martí*, xxxi.

17. Tucker, *Encyclopedia*, 261.

18. Figueredo, *Cuban Baseball*, 31–33.

19. Martínez de Osaba y Goenaga, Alfonso López, and Porto Gómez, *Enciclopedia*, 153.

20. Casas, Alfonso, and Pestana, *Viva y en juego*, 18.

21. Casas, Alfonso, and Pestana, *Viva y en juego*, 27.

22. Martínez de Osaba y Goenaga, Alfonso López, and Porto Gómez, *Enciclopedia*, 153.

23. Casas, Alfonso, and Pestana, *Viva y en juego*, 18.

24. Martínez de Osaba y Goenaga, Alfonso López, and Porto Gómez, *Enciclopedia*, 153.

25. Casas, Alfonso, and Pestana, *Viva y en juego*, 18–20.

26. Figueredo, *Who's Who in Cuban Baseball*, 3.

27. Figueredo, *Who's Who in Cuban Baseball*, 3.

28. Casas, Alfonso, and Pestana, *Viva y en juego*, 20.

29. Cluster and Hernández, *History of Havana*, 101–2.

30. Crompton, *The Sinking of the USS Maine*, 39–40.

31. Cluster and Hernández, *History of Havana*, 101.

32. Charles Duval, "Evangelina Cisneros Rescued by the Journal," *New York Journal*, October 10, 1897.

33. Elias, *The Empire Strikes Out*, 37.

34. Gott, *Cuba*, 100.

35. Gott, *Cuba*, 97–98.

36. Tucker, *Encyclopedia*, 952.

37. Gott, *Cuba*, 111.

38. Gott, *Cuba*, 111.

39. Gott, *Cuba*, 120.

40. Gott, *Cuba*, 129.

41. Santana Alonso, *El inmortal del beisbol*, 42.

42. Santana Alonso, *El inmortal del beisbol*, 42.

43. Cluster and Hernández, *History of Havana*, 164–65.

44. Cluster and Hernández, *History of Havana*, 167.

45. Gott, *Cuba*, 139.

46. Argote-Freyre, *Fulgencio Batista*, 97.

47. Argote-Freyre, *Fulgencio Batista*, 99.

48. Argote-Freyre, *Fulgencio Batista*, 100–101.

49. Szulc, *Fidel*, 126.

50. Szulc, *Fidel*, 96–98.

51. Szulc, *Fidel*, 99.

52. Szulc, *Fidel*, 101, 103.

53. Szulc, *Fidel*, 109.

54. Szulc, *Fidel*, 120.

55. Pérez, *Cuba*, 220, 227.

56. Pérez, *Cuba*, 220.

57. Gott, *Cuba*, 144–45.

58. Pérez, *Cuba*, 222.

59. Szulc, *Fidel*, 137, 142.

60. Pérez, *Cuba*, 224.

61. Bonachea and San Martín, *The Cuban Insurrection*, 12.

62. Szulc, *Fidel*, 182.

63. Szulc, *Fidel*, 181–82.

64. Iber, *Neither Peace nor Freedom*, 122.

65. Ehrlich, *Eduardo Chibás*, 85.

66. Ehrlich, *Eduardo Chibás*, 228.

67. Ehrlich, *Eduardo Chibás*, 233.

68. Ehrlich, *Eduardo Chibás*, 233, 235.

69. Pérez, *Cuba*, 225.

70. Gott, *Cuba*, 145–46.

71. Gott, *Cuba*, 146.

72. Pérez, *Cuba*, 225.

73. Cluster and Hernández, *History of Havana*, 192.

74. Cluster and Hernández, *History of Havana*, 192.

75. Gott, *Cuba*, 147, 149.

76. Bonachea and San Martín, *The Cuban Insurrection*, 18–20.

77. Sweig, *Inside the Cuban Revolution*, 6.

78. Gott, *Cuba*, 150–51.

3. Golden Age

1. "Cuban Winter Loop Moves for Agreement with O.B," *The Sporting News*, April 16, 1947.

2. J. G. Taylor Spink, "Game Booming in Cuba Despite U.S. Slap," *The Sporting News*, January 22, 1947.

3. Vernon Tietjen, "Cards to Get Hotter, Others Cooler—Mike," *The Sporting News*, April 30, 1947.

4. Tietjen, "Cards to Get Hotter."

5. Dan Daniel, "Cuban League Makes Peace with U.S. Ball," *The Sporting News*, April 30, 1947.

6. J. G. Taylor Spink, "Cuban Pact to Spur Game in Latin-America," *The Sporting News*, July 16, 1947.

7. Spink, "Cuban Pact."

8. Spink, "Cuban Pact."

9. Spink, "Cuban Pact."

10. Pedro Galiana, "Clubs from Four Countries to Play Caribbean Series," *The Sporting News*, September 1, 1948.

11. Dennis Landry, "Venezuela Will Finish Season, Play in Series," *The Sporting News*, December 29, 1948.

12. Pedro Galiana, "Cuba Classic Assured with Venezuela In," *The Sporting News*, February 2, 1948.

13. Monte Irvin, interview by author, March 1999.

14. Monte Irvin, interview by author, April 1994.

15. Pedro Galiana, "'50 Caribbean Series to Puerto Rico; Bigger Split Arranged for Players," *The Sporting News*, March 9, 1949.

16. Pedro Galiana, "Irvin Sure-Shot in Triple-A Ball, Guerra Asserts," *The Sporting News*, February 23, 1949.

17. Samantha Burkett, "Remembering Monte Irvin," Baseball Hall of Fame website, January 12, 2016, accessed March 5, 2017, http://baseballhall.org/news/remembering -monte-irvin.

18. Irvin, interview, June 1993.

19. Irvin, interview, March 1999.

20. Cepeda and Fagen, *Baby Bull*, 13.

21. Pedro Galiana, "Meeting Called on Latin Series," *The Sporting News*, August 18, 1948.

22. Pedro Galiana, "Chandler Ban on Cuban Players Rapped by Havana Sports Paper," *The Sporting News*, March 2, 1949.

23. Associated Press, "Ban on Major Leaguers Who Jumped to Mexico Lifted by Chandler," *New York Times*, June 6, 1949.

24. "Cuba Cheers Ruling," *The Sporting News*, June 15, 1949.

25. Pedro Galiana, "Cuban Natives Spice Up Games after Chandler O.K. to Play in Winter League," *The Sporting News*, November 2, 1949.

26. Don Zimmer, interview, March 6, 2008.

27. Zimmer, interview.

28. Zimmer, interview.

29. Zimmer, interview.

30. Zimmer, interview.

31. Black and Schoffner, *Joe Black*, 171.

32. Grahame L. Jones, "Dodgers Fire Campanis over Racial Remarks," *Los Angeles Times*, April 9, 1987.

33. Bobby Bragan, interview by author, January, 1997.

34. Ralph Ávila, interview by author, October 5, 2016.

35. "Game on Video in Havana," *New York Times*, September 30, 1954.

36. "Plane Relays Pix to Cuba of First Overseas Telecast," *The Sporting News*, October 13, 1954.

37. Márquez-Sterling, *Cuba 1952–1959*, 19.

38. Márquez-Sterling, *Cuba 1952–1959*, 19.

39. Newcomb, *Encyclopedia of Television*, 635–36.

40. Márquez-Sterling, *Cuba 1952–1959*, 19.

41. "Cubans," *The Sporting News*, August 18, 1954.

42. "Chiefs Cop Fourth Place in Playoffs," *The Sporting News*, September 22, 1954.

43. "Obituary," *The Sporting News*, September 1, 1954.

44. "Obituary."

45. Maduro, interview.

46. Cluster and Hernández, *History of Havana*, 192.

47. Hank Messick, "Gangster's Molasses Paved His Way into the Big Time," *Miami Herald*, December 12, 1965.

48. Federal Bureau of Investigation, Freedom of Information Privacy Acts Release of Frank Sinatra, file no. 9-11775, part 2, 40.

49. "U.S. Ends Narcotic Sales to Cuba While Luciano Is Resident There," *New York Times*, February 22, 1947.

50. Associated Press, "Luciano Leaves Cuba," *New York Times*, March 21, 1947.

51. "Tight-Lipped Men Watch Lansky Sail," *New York Times*, June 29, 1949.

52. Federal Bureau of Investigation, Freedom of Information/Privacy Acts Section, Subject: Meyer Lansky, file no. 92-2831, sect. 13, 5.

53. Lester Velie, "Suckers in Paradise," *Saturday Evening Post*, March 28, 1953.

54. "Cuba Ousts 13 U.S. Gamblers," *New York Times*, March 31, 1953, special.

55. Lacey, *Little Man*, 1991, 227.

56. Cluster and Hernández, *History of Havana*, 193.

57. Bill Virdon, interview by author, March 1999.

58. Nicholas Gage, "Underworld Genius: How One Gang Leader Thrives While Others Fall by the Wayside," *Wall Street Journal*, November 19, 1969.

59. R. Hart Phillips, "Cuba Hopes for Peace and a Busy Winter," *New York Times*, November 3, 1957.

60. Cluster and Hernández, *History of Havana*, 193.

4. "This Was a Shipwreck"

1. Quirk, *Fidel Castro*, 66–67.

2. "Batista Decree Bans Criticism of Regime," *New York Times*, August 7, 1953.

3. "Batista Decree."

4. R. Hart Phillips, "Cubans Apathetic on Election Call," *New York Times*, November 1, 1953, 30.

5. "Cuban Ex-president Fined in Arms Plot," *New York Times*, September 8, 1954.

6. R. Hart Phillips, "Grau Quits Race in Cuba, Charging Vote Is Rigged," *New York Times*, October 31, 1954.

7. "Batista's Margin Is Placed at 6 to 1," *New York Times*, November 3, 1954.

8. Quirk, *Fidel Castro*, 79.

9. Szulc, *Fidel*, 312.

10. Wilson, *Early Latino Ballplayers in the United States*, 94.

11. Ávila, interview, September 18, 2015.

12. Hernández, *The Rise of the Latin American Baseball Leagues*, 142.

13. Dick Young, "Sanguily Blasts Native-Star Curb—'It's Killing Latin Loops,'" *The Sporting News*, February 23, 1955.

14. Dan Daniel, "Latin Loop Envoys Outline Problems in Confab with Frick," *The Sporting News*, July 27, 1955.

15. Bjarkman, "Pedro Ramos," in *Cuban Baseball Legends*, 349.

16. Hernández, interview.

17. Pedro Ramos, interview by author, December 15, 2017.

18. Ramos, interview.

19. Szulc, *Fidel*, 324.

20. Gott, *Cuba*, 152–53.

21. Gott, *Cuba*, 154.

22. Szulc, *Fidel*, 370, 372–74.

23. Szulc, *Fidel*, 375–76.

24. Szulc, *Fidel*, 378.

25. Szulc, *Fidel*, 381–82.

26. José Valdivielso, interview by author, January 30, 2015.

27. Rodolfo Arias, interview by author, October 30, 2016.

28. Gordon "Red" Marston, "Gates in Cuban Loop Hit by TV, Political Unrest," *The Sporting News*, January 2, 1957.

29. R. Hart Phillips, "Cuban Terrorism More Intense Despite Moves to Suppress It," *New York Times*, December 29, 1956.

30. Dolson, *Jim Bunning*, 34–35.

31. Valdivielso, interview.

32. Herbert L. Matthews, "Cuban Rebel Is Visited in Hideout," *New York Times*, February 24, 1957.

33. Matthews, "Cuban Rebel Is Visited in Hideout."

34. Antón and Hernández, *Cubans in America*, 136.

35. Matthews, "Cuban Rebel Is Visited in Hideout."

36. Teel, *Reporting the Cuban Revolution*, 40.

37. Teel, *Reporting the Cuban Revolution*, 26.

38. Associated Press, "Stories on Rebel Fiction, Cuba Says," *New York Times*, February 28, 1957.

39. R. Hart Phillips, "Batista Charges Castro Is a Red," *New York Times*, March 11, 1957.

40. Cluster and Hernández, *History of Havana*, 206.

41. "Batista Decries Killing of 'Fools,'" *New York Times*, March 14, 1957.

42. "Batista Decries Killing of 'Fools.'"

43. Frank Graham, "Adolfo Luque Is Dead?" *The Sporting News*, July 17, 1957.

44. González Echevarría, *Pride of Havana*, 260.

45. Maximo Sánchez, "Senor Bobby Bragan Highest Paid Pilot in Cuban History," *The Sporting News*, October 9, 1957.

46. Rubén Rodríguez, "Bragan Blues Rated as Flag Favorite in Cuban Winter Loop," *The Sporting News*, October 9, 1957.

47. Nelson Varela, "Exaltado Adolfo Luque a la 'Galaria de los Inmortales' del beisbol cubano," *Diario de la Marina*, December 31, 1957.

48. Maximo Sánchez, "Tempers Flare as Tension Rises in Tight Cuban Race," *The Sporting News*, January 29, 1958.

49. Rene Friol, interview by author, January 30, 2015.

50. Matt Kelly, "Winters in Cuba," National Baseball Hall of Fame website, accessed April 6, 2017, http://baseballhall.org/discover/hall-of-famers-played-in-cuban-winter-league.

51. "Cuban Rebels Raid Port Area; Citizens Reported Leaving City," *New York Times*, January 15, 1958.

52. Kelly, "Winters in Cuba."

5. Year of the Pitcher

1. J. G. Taylor Spink, "'Third Major Must Come Soon'—Rickey," *The Sporting News*, May 21, 1958.

2. Bob Wolf, "Perini Predicts Two Ten-Team Majors by '63," *The Sporting News*, March 26, 1958.

3. Neil MacCarl, "Shag Visits Havana, Denies Report Club May Be Shifted," *The Sporting News*, April 2, 1958.

4. Associated Press, "Cuban Rebels Seize Fangio, Auto Racer," *New York Times*, February 24, 1958.

5. R. Hart Phillips, "Kidnappers Kind, Fangio Asserts," *New York Times*, February 26, 1958.

6. "Mobsters Move in on Troubled Havana and Split Rich Gambling Profits with Batista," *Life*, March 10, 1958.

7. "Castro Proclaims All-Out Cuban War Starting on April 1," *New York Times*, March 18, 1958.

8. Cy Kritzer, "Uncertainty over Cuban Fighting Again Clouds Int Loop Opening," *The Sporting News*, April 16, 1958.

9. Kritzer, "Uncertainty over Cuban Fighting."

10. Cy Kritzer, "Shaughnessy Rides Out Storm, Bisons End Balk at Cuban Trip," *The Sporting News*, April 23, 1958.

11. Kritzer, "Shaughnessy Rides Out Storm."

12. Cy Kritzer, "Safety of Havana Proved to Bisons," *The Sporting News*, April 30, 1958.

13. Kritzer, "Safety of Havana Proved to Bisons."

14. Kritzer, "Safety of Havana Proved to Bisons."

15. "Cubans Int Club to Get Spink Trophy for Attendance Feat," *The Sporting News*, June 25, 1958.

16. Joe Alli, "Bisons All Shook Up by Bouncy Journey into Cuban Interior," *The Sporting News*, June 18, 1958.

17. Alli, "Bisons All Shook Up."

18. Maximo Sánchez, "Fans' Club Helps Sugar Kings Top '57 Gate Total by Early June," *The Sporting News*, July 2, 1958.

19. Jimmy Burns, "Unrestricted Draft Maduro's Choice as to Aid for Minors," *The Sporting News*, November 26, 1958.

20. "Marianao y Almendares abren el campeonato," *Diario de la Marina*, October 7, 1958.

21. Rubén Rodríguez, "Slow Hopper, Bad Toss Cost Cicotte $1,000 No-Hitter," *The Sporting News*, October 22, 1958.

22. Lasorda and Fisher, *The Artful Dodger*, 78.

23. Lasorda and Fisher, *The Artful Dodger*, 78.

24. "Ump Hurt in Fall, Running to Break Up Fight in Cuba," *The Sporting News*, January 16, 1958.

25. Peña, interview.

26. Eduardo Bauta, interview by author, September 24, 2015.

27. Werner Wiskari, "U.S. Embargo Set on Arms to Cuba; Shipment Halted," *New York Times*, April 3, 1958.

28. R. Hart Phillips, "Cuban Voting Set Amid Wide Curbs," *New York Times*, October 26, 1958.

29. Phillips, "Cuban Voting Set."

30. "Doubtful Future Confronts Cuba," *New York Times*, November 2, 1958.

31. "Fraud Is Charged in Cuba's Voting," *New York Times*, November 5, 1958.

32. Herb Heft, "Havana-Hater Cal Griffith No. 1 Booster after Visit," *The Sporting News*, November 12, 1958.

33. Tony Taylor, interview by author, July 2000.

34. Gott, *Cuba*, 163.

35. Gott, *Cuba*, 163.

36. Dorschner and Fabricio, *The Winds of December*, 22.

37. Dorschner and Fabricio, *The Winds of December*, 39.

38. Dorschner and Fabricio, *The Winds of December*, 190.

39. Dorschner and Fabricio, *The Winds of December*, 233.

40. Ávila, interview, October 5, 2016.

41. Dorschner and Fabricio, *The Winds of December*, 254.

42. Maximo Sánchez, "100 Per Cent for Winter Ball, Lane Assures Cuban Writers," *The Sporting News*, December 24, 1958.

43. Felo Ramírez, interview by author, February 5, 2015.

6. New Year's Revolution

1. Miguel de la Hoz, interview by author, August 11, 2016.

2. Dorschner and Fabricio, *The Winds of December*, 351, 356.

3. Dorschner and Fabricio, *The Winds of December*, 360.

4. Dorschner and Fabricio, *The Winds of December*, 377.

5. Dorschner and Fabricio, *The Winds of December*, 378–79.

6. Dorschner and Fabricio, *The Winds of December*, 383.

7. Lasorda and Fisher, *The Artful Dodger*, 81.

8. Valdivielso, interview.

9. De la Hoz, interview.

10. Dorschner and Fabricio, *The Winds of December*, 405.

11. Dorschner and Fabricio, *The Winds of December*, 412.

12. Johnny Goryl, interview by author, February 17, 2015.

13. Goryl, interview.

14. Associated Press, "Gamblers in Cuba Face Dim Future," *New York Times*, January 4, 1959.

15. Jo Lasorda, interview by author, January 15, 2015.

16. Ávila, interview, October 5, 2016.

17. Ávila, interview, October 5, 2016.

18. Ávila, interview, October 5, 2016.

19. "Players in Cuba Can Be Recalled," *New York Times*, January 3, 1959.

20. Bob Addie, "Nats Not Planning to Withdraw Players from Cuban League," *Washington Post*, January 3, 1959.

21. Addie, "Nats Not Planning to Withdraw Players."

22. "Rebel Soldiers Were Friendly to U.S. Players, Says Fowler," *The Sporting News*, January 14, 1959.

23. Lasorda, interview.

24. "Rebel Soldiers Were Friendly to U.S. Players."

25. Goryl, interview.

26. Dorschner and Fabricio, *The Winds of December*, 475.

27. Rubén Rodríguez, "League Resumes Action after Halt in Castro Revolt," *The Sporting News*, January 14, 1959.

28. Dorschner and Fabricio, *The Winds of December*, 488.

29. Hernández, interview.

30. Gonzalo "Cholly" Naranjo, interview by author, February 7, 2015.

31. Dorschner and Fabricio, *The Winds of December*, 491.

32. Dorschner and Fabricio, *The Winds of December*, 493.

33. Lasorda, interview.

34. Naranjo, interview.

35. Naranjo, interview.

36. "Recognition for Cuba," *New York Times*, January 9, 1959.

37. R. Hart Phillips, "Castro Declares Trials Will Go On," *New York Times*, January 14, 1959.

38. "Batista Denounces 'Barbarism' in Cuba," *New York Times*, January 16, 1959.

39. René Brioso, interview by author, January 2007.

7. Caribbean Spice

1. De la Hoz, interview.

2. Peña, interview.

3. De la Hoz, interview.

4. Leo Posada, interview by author, July 31, 2016.

5. Peña, interview.

6. De la Hoz, interview.

7. Leo Posada, "Cuban Players Panel," Society of American Baseball Research Convention, Miami, July 30, 2016.

8. "Cuba vs. Puerto Rico hoy en el juego inaugural," *Diario de la Marina*, February 10, 1959.

9. Peña, interview.

10. Peña, interview.

11. Eladio Secades, "Fowler, con una bonita exhibición dio a Cuba un gran triunfo sobre Venezuela," *Diario de la Marina*, February 13, 1959.

12. Secades, "Fowler, con una bonita exhibición."

13. Peña, interview.

14. Peña, interview.

15. M. J. Gorman Jr., "Almendares' Latin Crown Cuba's 4th in Row," *The Sporting News*, February 25, 1959.

16. Tad Szulc, "Fidel Castro's Years as a Secret Communist," *New York Times Magazine*, October 19, 1986.

17. Herbert L. Matthews, "Top Castro Aide Denies Red Tie; Leaders Say They 'Await Fidel,'" *New York Times*, January 4, 1959.

18. Szulc, "Fidel Castro's Years as a Secret Communist."

19. Szulc, "Fidel Castro's Years as a Secret Communist."

20. R. Hart Phillips, "Civil Prisoners Jam Cuban Jails," *New York Times*, February 20, 1959.

21. Robert Alden, "Cuban Rebels in City for Washington's Birthday Visit," *New York Times*, February 23, 1959.

22. "Cuban Elections Two Years Away," *New York Times*, March 1, 1959.

23. United Press International, "Executions in Cuba Rise to 483 Total," *New York Times*, March 20, 1959.

24. Arthur Daley, "The Rains Came," *New York Times*, March 20, 1959.

25. Earl Lawson, "Red-Dodger Cuban Junket Gives Run-Around to Rain," *The Sporting News*, April 1, 1959.

26. "Dodgers Flee to Havana," *San Bernardino County Sun*, March 20, 1959.

27. "Reds Fail to Gain Place in the Sun," *New York Times*, March 20, 1959.

28. Lawson, "Red-Dodger Cuban Junket Gives Run-Around to Rain."

29. "All Sports in Florida Washed Out," *Washington Post and Times Herald*, March 20, 1959.

30. Erskine, *Carl Erskine's Tales from the Dodger Dugout*, 10.

31. Lawson, "Red-Dodger Cuban Junket Gives Run-Around to Rain."

32. Pete Cava, "Ex-pitcher Remembers the Bullets and Baseball," *Indianapolis Star*, March 28, 1999.

33. González Echevarría, *Pride of Havana*, 64.

34. González Echevarría, *Pride of Havana*, 336.

35. Cava, "Ex-pitcher Remembers the Bullets and Baseball."

36. Frank Finch, "Dodgers Nose Out Cincinnati, 4 to 3," *Los Angeles Times*, March 22, 1959.

8. "Bullets Were Falling"

1. "Int Sets Up Havana Emergency Plan," *The Sporting News*, December 24, 1958.

2. "Maduro Sees Bright Future for Int Club with War Over," *The Sporting News*, January 14, 1959.

3. Cy Kritzer, "Havana Aglow, Hopes Include Crowd Trophy," *The Sporting News*, January 21, 1959.

4. Kritzer, "Havana Aglow."

5. A. L. Hardman, "Doherty Sees Only Danger in Cuba Trips," *The Sporting News*, February 4, 1959.

6. "'Never Treated Better Than in Cuba,' Lasorda Declares," *The Sporting News*, February 18, 1959.

7. Cy Kritzer, "Int Ball on Sounder Basis Than Ever in Cuba, Maduro Says," *The Sporting News*, February 11, 1959.

8. Kritzer, "Int Ball on Sounder Basis."

9. "Game Now Stronger in Cuba," *The Sporting News*, February 18, 1959.

10. Bob Addie, "Bob Addie's Column," *Washington Post and Times Herald*, March 8, 1959.

11. Bob Addie, "Bob Addie's ATOMS," *The Sporting News*, March 18, 1959.

12. "Castro, as Hurler, Had Good Control, 'Big League Spirit,'" *The Sporting News*, April 29, 1959.

13. Bjarkman, "Fidel Castro and Baseball," *Cuban Baseball Legends*, 32–33.

14. Bjarkman, *Cuban Baseball Legends*.

15. González Echevarría, *Pride of Havana*, 6.

16. Ávila, interview, October 5, 2016.

17. Jimmy Burns, "'Castro Genuine Fan, Havana Set for Big Season'—Maduro," *The Sporting News*, March 18, 1959.

18. Jimmy Burns, "'Cuban Ball Club Saved by Rebels' Victory'—Maduro," *The Sporting News*, April 22, 1959.

19. Eladio Secades, "Un jonrón de Héctor dentró del terreno decidio el inaugural: Gran concurrencia," *Diario de la Marina*, April 15, 1959.

20. "Crowd Hails Castro As He Reaches U.S. for an 11-Day Visit," *New York Times*, April 16, 1959.

21. "Castro Is Lunch Guest of Herter on First Day of Visit," *New York Times*, April 17, 1959.

22. E. W. Kenworthy, "Castro Declares Regime Is Free of Red Influence," *New York Times*, April 18, 1959.

23. E. W. Kenworthy, "Castro Visit Leaves Big Question Mark," *New York Times*, April 19, 1959.

24. Dana Adams Schmidt, "Castro Rules Out Role As Neutral; Opposes the Reds," *New York Times*, April 20, 1959.

25. Schmidt, "Castro Rules Out Role As Neutral."

26. Schmidt, "Castro Rules Out Role As Neutral."

27. Dana Adams Schmidt, "Castro Stresses Land Reform Aim," *New York Times*, April 21, 1959.

28. Philip Benjamin, "Castro Gets a Noisy Reception Here," *New York Times*, April 22, 1959.

29. Lindesay Parrott, "Castro Defends Election Delay," *New York Times*, April 23, 1959.

30. "Castro to Aid Plan to Keep Havana Club in Int League," *The Sporting News*, April 29, 1959.

31. "Havana Team to Stay," *New York Times*, April 24, 1959.

32. "With a Bomb Seized Near Castro at Rally in Park," *New York Times*, April 25, 1959.

33. Philip Benjamin, "Castro Departs to Joy of Police," *New York Times*, April 26, 1959.

34. R. Hart Phillips, "Reds' Alleged Role in Castro's Regime Alarming Havana," *New York Times*, April 24, 1959.

35. Ávila, interview, October 5, 2016.

36. R. Hart Phillips, "Cuba Will Take Over Airlines; Charges Batista Men Own Them," *New York Times*, May 24, 1959.

37. Allen Drury, "Ex-Aide Calls Castro a Red at Hearing of Senate Unit," *New York Times*, July 15, 1959.

38. Szulc, *Fidel*, 504.

39. "Castro Forces Out President," *Washington Post and Times Herald*, July 18, 1959.

40. R. Hart Phillips, "Castro Resumes the Premiership," *New York Times*, July 27, 1959.

41. Phillips, "Castro Resumes the Premiership."

42. Jimmy Burns, "Maduro Ready to Sell, Castro Offers New Aid," *The Sporting News*, July 29, 1959.

43. Burns, "Maduro Ready to Sell."

44. Burns, "Maduro Ready to Sell."

45. Burns, "Maduro Ready to Sell."

46. Luis Úbeda, "Lanzó el doctor Fidel Castro un inning y no permitió hits: Ganaron los Cubans," *Diario de la Marina*, July 25, 1959.

47. Greg Boeck, "Wings Saw Cuba Close," *Rochester Democrat and Chronicle*, May 8, 1977.

48. George Beahon, "Nightmare in Havana—Wings in Real Danger," *Rochester Democrat and Chronicle*, July 27, 1959.

49. Jimmy Burns, "Int Will Play Out Havana Sked, Despite Shooting, Shag Decides," *The Sporting News*, August 5, 1959.

50. Beahon, "Nightmare in Havana."

51. Cárdenas and Guckenberger, *Cuba's Campo Corto*. 35.

52. Boeck, "Wings Saw Cuba Close."

53. Beahon, "Nightmare in Havana."

54. Boeck, "Wings Saw Cuba Close."

55. Boeck, "Wings Saw Cuba Close."

56. Boeck, "Wings Saw Cuba Close."

57. Boeck, "Wings Saw Cuba Close."

58. "Game Called Due to Gunfire," *Montreal Gazette*, July 27, 1959.

59. Burns, "Int Will Play Out Havana Sked."

60. Burns, "Int Will Play Out Havana Sked."

9. Title Town

1. Rubén Rodríguez, "Int Sweet on Sugar Kings after Triumph in Playoffs," *The Sporting News*, September 30, 1959.

2. "'Happy Day for Cuba,' Castro Tells Club after Clincher," *The Sporting News*, September 30, 1959.

3. Halsey Hall, "Havana Pilot Once Cost Millers 2 Wins," *Minneapolis Star*, September 28, 1959.

4. Yastrzemski and Eskenazi, *Yaz*, 48.

5. Bob Beebe, "Doherty Hails Millers, Eyes 6th Straight AA Series Win," *Minneapolis Star*, September 26, 1959.

6. Beebe, "Doherty Hails Millers."

7. Jim Byrne, "Mauch, Spirit Hailed in Millers' Surge," *Minneapolis Star*, September 26, 1959.

8. Beebe, "Doherty Hails Millers."

9. Beebe, "Doherty Hails Millers."

10. Halsey, "Havana Pilot Once Cost Millers 2 Wins."

11. Bob Beebe, "Mauch Impressed, Not Scared," *Minneapolis Star*, September 28, 1959.

12. Beebe, "Mauch Impressed, Not Scared."

13. Beebe, "Mauch Impressed, Not Scared."

14. Goryl, interview.

15. Octavio "Cookie" Rojas, interview by author, February 3, 2015.

16. Bob Beebe, "Junior Series Moved to Havana Because of Weather," *Minneapolis Star*, September 29, 1959.

17. Beebe, "Junior Series Moved to Havana."

18. Rojas, interview.

19. Rojas, interview.

20. Bob Beebe, "Millers Shrug Off Cubans Home Edge," *Minneapolis Star*, September 30, 1959.

21. Beebe, "Millers Shrug Off Cubans Home Edge."

22. Goryl, interview.

23. Yastrzemski and Eskenazi, *Yaz*, 49.

24. Bob Beebe, "Castro, 20,000 Boost for Cubans," *Minneapolis Star*, October 1, 1959.

25. Goryl, interview.

26. Thornley, "Minneapolis Millers versus Havana Sugar Kings," 43.

27. Goryl, interview.

28. Thornley, 43.

29. Thornley, 44.

30. Bob Beebe, "Cuban Fans 'Win' in Top Series Battle," *Minneapolis Star*, October 2, 1959.

31. Yastrzemski and Eskenazi, *Yaz*, 51.

32. Yastrzemski and Eskenazi, *Yaz*, 49.

33. Eladio Secades, "Los Cubans y el milagro de las grandes concurrencias," *Diario de la Marina*, October 3, 1959.

34. Maduro, interview.

35. Bob Beebe, "Borland Will Start in Decider," *Minneapolis Star*, October 5, 1959.

36. Beebe, "Borland Will Start in Decider."

37. Beebe, "Borland Will Start in Decider."

38. "Millers, Havana Rained Out; Game Set Tonight," *Minneapolis Tribune*, October 6, 1959.

39. Bob Beebe, "Sugar Kings Cop Junior Series on Last-Ditch Rally," *The Sporting News*, October 14, 1959.

40. Yastrzemski and Eskenazi, *Yaz*, 52.

41. Luis Úbeda, "El final inolvidable ganaron los 'Cubans' la Pequeña Serie por un hit de Daniel Morejón," *Diario de la Marina*, October 7, 1959.

42. Úbeda, "El final inolvidable ganaron los 'Cubans' la Pequeña Serie."

43. Goryl, interview.

44. Goryl, interview.

45. Bob Beebe, "One Pitch Kills Millers in Cuba," *Minneapolis Star*, October 7, 1959.

46. Úbeda, "El final inolvidable ganaron los 'Cubans' la Pequeña Serie."

47. Leonardo Agüero, interview by author, March 1999.

48. Maduro, interview.

49. Úbeda, "El final inolvidable ganaron los 'Cubans' la Pequeña Serie."

50. Yastrzemski and Eskenazi, *Yaz*, 52.

51. Beebe, "One Pitch Kills Millers in Cuba."

52. Yastrzemski and Eskenazi, *Yaz*, 52.

53. Yastrzemski and Eskenazi, *Yaz*, 52–53.

54. Al López-Chávez, interview by author, January 8, 2016.

55. López-Chávez, interview.

10. Regarding Cienfuegos

1. Maximo Sánchez, "9 U.S. Stations Will Televise 26 Winter Contests," *Diario de la Marina*, October 21, 1959.

2. R. Hart Phillips, "Papers in Havana Retort to Castro," *New York Times*, October 1, 1959.

3. "Anti-Castro Planes 'Rail' Cuba Capital," *Washington Post and Times Herald*, October 22, 1959.

4. R. Hart Phillips, "Castro Charges Planes from U.S. Bombed Havana," *New York Times*, October 24, 1959.

5. Bonsal, *Cuba, Castro, and the United States*, 107.

6. R. Hart Phillips, "300,000 Rally to Back Castro; He Condemns 'Raids' from U.S.," *New York Times*, October 27, 1959.

7. Bonsal, *Cuba, Castro, and the United States*, 106.

8. Bonsal, *Cuba, Castro, and the United States*, 108.

9. Associated Press, "Darkness Halts Air Search in Cuba for Army Chief Missing," *Washington Post and Times Herald*, October 31, 1959.

10. Ávila, interview, October 5, 2016.

11. Hernández, *Memories of Winter Ball.*

12. Hernández, *Memories of Winter Ball.*

13. "Castro Broadcast Assails U.S. Again," *New York Times*, November 13, 1959.

14. Bonsal, *Cuba, Castro, and the United States*, 107.

15. Ruben Rodríguez, "Ailing Rodriguez Quits Job as Manager of Almendares," *The Sporting News*, November 11, 1959.

16. Rodríguez, "Ailing Rodriguez Quits Job."

17. Naranjo, interview.

18. Posada, "Cuban Players Panel."

19. Posada, "Cuban Players Panel."

20. R. Hart Phillips, "Leftist Named President of Cuba's National Bank," *New York Times*, November 27, 1959.

21. Phillips, "Leftist Named President of Cuba's National Bank."

22. Associated Press, "Matos Cites 'Differences' with Castro," *Washington Post and Times Herald*, December 12, 1959.

23. Associated Press, "Matos Cites 'Differences' with Castro."

24. Associated Press, "Castro Testifies in Matos Trial," *Washington Post and Times Herald*, December 15, 1959.

25. Associated Press, "Castro Testifies in Matos Trial."

26. United Press International, "Ex-hero Gets 20 Years; 2 Other Cubans to Die," *Washington Post and Times Herald*, December 16, 1959.

27. Geyer, *Guerrilla Prince*, 209.

28. Rojas, interview.

29. Costello, "Willy Miranda," *Cuban Baseball Legends*, 296.

30. Peña, interview.

31. Peña, interview.

32. Peña, interview.

33. Peña, interview.

34. Costello, "Willy Miranda," *Cuban Baseball Legends*, 296.

11. The Last Series

1. Bob Addie, "Nats Turn Down Million-Dollar Offer for Killebrew and Pascual," *Washington Post and Times Herald*, December 16, 1959.

2. Addie, "Nats Turn Down Million-Dollar Offer."

3. R. Hart Phillips, "Mikoyan Praises Castro Reforms," *New York Times*, February 10, 1960.

4. R. Hart Phillips, "Soviet Gives Cuba 100 Million Credit on Sale of Sugar," *New York Times*, February 14, 1960.

5. Peña, interview.

6. Peña, interview.

7. National Security Council, "Memorandum of Discussion at the 432d Meeting of the National Security Council, January 14, 1960, 9 a.m.," *Foreign Relations of the United States, 1958–60, Cuba*, volume 6, U.S. Department of State website, accessed October 3, 2017, https://history.state.gov/historicaldocuments/frus1958-60v06/d423.

8. National Security Council, "Memorandum of Discussion at the 432d Meeting of the National Security Council."

9. National Security Council, "Memorandum of Discussion at the 432d Meeting of the National Security Council."

10. Kinzer, *The Brothers*.

11. Gleijeses, *Conflicting Missions*.

12. "Eisenhower's Tour," *New York Times*, March 6, 1960.

13. Associated Press, "Dorticos See 'Cowardly Act,'" *New York Times*, March 5, 1960.

14. R. Hart Phillips, "Castro Links U.S. To Ship 'Sabotage,' Denial Is Swift," *New York Times*, March 6, 1960.

15. Associated Press, "Castro Makes Issue of the Maine's Loss," *New York Times*, March 6, 1960.

16. "U.S. Denies Insinuation," *New York Times*, March 6, 1960.

17. Department of State, *A Program of Covert Action against the Castro Regime*, paper by the 5412 Committee, Foreign Relations of the United States, 1958–60, Cuba, vol. 6, U.S. Department of State website, accessed October 3, 2017, https://history.state.gov/historicaldocuments/frus1958-60v06/d481.

18. Kinzer, *The Brothers*.

12. International Tensions

1. Jorge Zayas, "Castro Is Accused of Stifling Press," *New York Times*, January 24, 1960.

2. R. Hart Phillips, "Castro Criticizes Nixon's Comments," *New York Times*, January 19, 1960.

3. R. Hart Phillips, "Cubans Turn Ire On Eisenhower," *New York Times*, January 23, 1960.

4. William J. Jordan, "Cubans Vitriolic in Attacking U.S.," *New York Times*, January 27, 1960.

5. Cy Kritzer, "Int Okays Plan Allowing Quick Franchise Shift," *The Sporting News*, February 10, 1960.

6. Dan Daniel, "State Department Guides Latin-Ball Future," *The Sporting News*, February 24, 1960.

7. Daniel, "State Department Guides Latin-Ball Future."

8. Daniel, "State Department Guides Latin-Ball Future."

9. Doug Brown, "Cubans Clobber MacPhail for Canceling Havana Trip," *The Sporting News*, April 6, 1960.

10. Brown, "Cubans Clobber MacPhail."

11. Earl Lawson, "Paul Attempted to Persuade Orioles to Play Cuban Series," *The Sporting News*, April 6, 1960.

12. Brown, "Cubans Clobber MacPhail."

13. Brown, "Cubans Clobber MacPhail."

14. Brown, "Cubans Clobber MacPhail."

15. "Int Loop Scribes Receive Invitation to Visit Havana," *The Sporting News*, April 6, 1960.

16. Shelley Rolfe, "Man with Problems," *Richmond Times Dispatch*, April 11, 1960.

17. Earl Lawson, "Cuban Strong Boy No. 1 Red Picket Prize," *The Sporting News*, April 6, 1960.

18. Associated Press, "Predicen que los 'Cubans' se marcharan," *Diario de la Marina*, April 17, 1960.

19. United Press International, "'Se jugara en Cuba'—Simmons," *Diario de la Marina*, April 19, 1960.

20. Luis Úbeda, "Tras diez episodios perdieron anoche los Cubans el juego de inauguración," *Diario de la Marina*, April 21, 1960.

21. Luis Úbeda, "Barrió el Rochester con la serie y hoy reaparecerán los Bisontes de Buffalo," *Diario de la Marina*, April 23, 1960.

22. Associated Press, "Castro Assails Ike and Herter," *Washington Post and Herald Times*, April 23, 1960.

23. "250,000 in Havana Rail against U.S.," *New York Times*, May 2, 1960.

24. "¡Cubanos!" *Diario de la Marina*, May 12, 1960.

25. Associated Press, "Independent Paper Assailed in Havana," *New York Times*, March 24, 1960.

26. Elliston, *Psywar on Cuba*, 58.

27. Tad Szulc, "Cuban Anti-Red Exiles Set Up a Rebel Front against Castro," *New York Times*, June 10, 1960.

28. Tad Szulc, "Ex-Cuban Premier Quits Regime and Asks Asylum," *New York Times*, June 6, 1960.

29. Dan Daniel, "Cuba's Political Climate Is Not Healthy for O.B.," *The Sporting News*, July 6, 1960.

30. Cy Kritzer, "Sugar Kings, Dollar-Shy, Ask Loan, Clearing Way for Move," *The Sporting News*, July 6, 1960.

31. "Munitions Dump Explodes, Delaying Havana Twin-Bill," *The Sporting News*, July 6, 1960.

32. Associated Press, "Havana Will Lose Its Baseball Club," *New York Times*, July 8, 1960.

33. United Press International, "Havana Team Shift Called 'Big Mistake,'" *Washington Post and Times Herald*, July 9, 1960.

34. United Press International, "Havana Team Shift Calls 'Big Mistake.'"

35. Associated Press, "Order Havana Team Shift to Jersey City," *Asbury Park Press*, July 9, 1960.

36. United Press International, "Havana Team Shift Calls 'Big Mistake.'"

37. United Press International, "Havana Team Shift Calls 'Big Mistake.'"

38. López-Chávez, interview.

39. Associated Press, "Havana Franchise Seen Set for Jersey City," *Courier-Post* (Camden NJ), July 9, 1960.

40. Associated Press, "Havana Franchise Seen Set for Jersey City."

41. United Press International, "Cincinnati Will Operate Revoked Int. Franchise," *Courier-Post* (Camden NJ), July 11, 1960.

42. United Press International, "Cincinnati Will Operate Revoked Int. Franchise."

43. Associated Press, "Jersey City Team Needs Name, Boss," *Asbury Park Press*, July 13, 1960.

44. Rojas, interview.

45. Peña, interview.

46. Associated Press, "Jersey City's Cuban Pilot Called Traitor," *Washington Post and Times Herald*, July 16, 1960.

47. Joseph O. Haff, "Ex–Sugar Kings Get a Noisy Welcome in New Home," *New York Times*, July 16, 1960.

48. Haff, "Ex–Sugar Kings Get a Noisy Welcome."

49. Haff, "Ex–Sugar Kings Get a Noisy Welcome."

50. Howard M. Tuckner, "Columbus Wins, 8–3, as Crowd of 7,155 Has Big Night," *New York Times*, July 16, 1960.

51. Harold Rosenthal, "Cheering Jersey Fans Hail O.B. Return," *The Sporting News*, July 27, 1960.

52. Robert L. Teague, "Jerseys Lose But Fans Love 'Em," *New York Times*, July 17, 1960.

53. Tom Lauenstein, "TV Helped Jerseys Wind Up in Black," *The Sporting News*, September 21, 1960.

54. Rojas, interview.

13. The Last Season

1. Tiant and Fitzgerald, *El Tiante*, 10.

2. Tiant and Fitzgerald, *El Tiante*, 10.

3. Luis Tiant, interview by author, November 24, 2017.

4. Tiant and Fitzgerald, *El Tiante*, 10.

5. Tiant and Fitzgerald, *El Tiante*, 12.

6. Tiant, interview, November 24, 2017.

7. Luis Tiant, interview by author, November 29, 2017.

8. Tiant, interview, November 24, 2017.

9. Tiant, interview, November 24, 2017.

10. Dan Daniel, "Frick Declares Cuba Off Limits to U.S. Players," *The Sporting News*, September 7, 1960.

11. González Echevarría, *Pride of Havana*, 346.

12. Associated Press, "Three U.S. Banks Seized by Cubans," *New York Times*, September 18, 1960.

13. Associated Press, "Castro Moves Out of Hotel in Huff, Takes His Party to One in Harlem," *New York Times*, September 20, 1960.

14. Max Frankel, "Cuban Puts Case, Seeks World Support in a 4½-Hour Talk—Warns Other Lands," *New York Times*, September 27, 1960.

15. Associated Press, "Castro Considers Closing Down U.S. Base by 'International Law,'" *Washington Post and Times Herald*, September 27, 1960.

16. John M. Hightower, "U.S. Closing Its Big Cuban Nickel Plant," *Washington Post and Times Herald*, September 30, 1960.

17. Bernard D. Nossiter, "Cuba Trade Embargoed by U.S.," *Washington Post and Times Herald*, October 20, 1960.

18. E. W. Kenworthy, "U.S. Recalls Ambassador in Cuba for Extended Stay," *New York Times*, October 20, 1960.

19. United Press International, "Yankee 'Aggression' in Series Wins Cheers of Havana Fans," *New York Times*, October 8, 1960.

20. George Clifford, "Will Castro Bar Cubans from Playing in U.S.?" *The Sporting News*, October 12, 1960.

21. Tiant, interview, November 24, 2017.

22. "Ban on American Players Opens Door for Cuban Kids," *The Sporting News*, November 2, 1960.

23. Frederick G. Lieb, "Castro Sports Chief Promises Hands Off Cubans in U.S. Ball," *The Sporting News*, November 2, 1960.

24. Lieb, "Castro Sports Chief Promises Hands Off."

25. Shirley Povich, "New L.A. Franchise Seen for Washington If Nats Move in 1960," *Washington Post and Times Herald*, October 11, 1969.

26. Shirley Povich, "Griffith Moves Nats to Minneapolis; D.C. Gets New Club in 1961 Season," *Washington Post and Times Herald*, October 27, 1960.

27. Ávila, interview, September 18, 2015.

28. Andrés Fleitas, interview by author, March 1999.

29. R. Hart Phillips, "Baseball Is Dying in Castro's Cuba," *New York Times*, November 11, 1960.

30. "Cuban Players Slash Pay, Gate Dip Threatens Loop," *The Sporting News*, November 16, 1960.

31. Julio Bécquer, interview by author, January 31, 2015.

32. Dave Brady, "Ruling of State Department Helps Cubans to Obtain Balls," *The Sporting News*, November 16, 1960.

33. Phillips, "Baseball Is Dying in Castro's Cuba."

34. Max Frankel, "Cuba Doubts Kennedy Will Try to Alter Policy and Ease Crisis," *New York Times*, November 25, 1960.

35. Julius Duscha, "Kennedy Hits Nixon's Cuba Role," *Washington Post and Times Herald*, October 7, 1960.

36. Harrison E. Salisbury, "Nixon Says Kennedy Plan on Cuba Risks World War," *New York Time*, October 23, 1960.

37. Harold K. Milks, "Castro Assails Kennedy, Nixon; Suggests K for U.S. President," *Washington Post and Times Herald*, October 1, 1960.

38. Associated Press, "Castro Is Setting Up Party in the Communist Pattern," *New York Times*, December 3, 1960.

39. Department of State, "Dispatch from the Embassy in Cuba to the Department of State, Foreign Relations of the United States, 1958–1960," Cuba, vol. 6, https://history.state.gov/historicaldocuments/frus1958-60v06/d617.

40. Gay, *Leaving Cuba*, 26.

41. E. W. Kenworthy, "U.S. Breaks Its Diplomatic Ties with Cuba and Advises Americans to Leave Island; Eisenhower Cites 'Vilification' By Castro," *New York Times*, January 4, 1961.

42. Manuel J. Frau, "Frick Suggests Switching Site of Latin Series," *The Sporting News*, November 2, 1960.

43. John Drebinger, "Baseball Fears Action by Castro to Prevent Cubans from Playing in U.S.," *New York Times*, January 5, 1961.

44. Bob Addie, "Cubans Expected to Play," *Washington Post and Times Herald*, January 5, 1961.

45. United Press International, "Cuban Baseball Players Told They Can Join Teams in U.S.," *New York Times*, January 7, 1961.

46. Peña, interview.

47. De la Hoz, interview.

48. Ramos, interview.

49. Posada, interview.

50. Rojas, interview.

51. Rojas, interview.

52. Rojas, interview.

53. Valdivielso, interview.

54. Tiant, interview, November 29, 2017.

55. González Echevarría, *Pride of Havana*, 355.

56. González Echevarría, *Pride of Havana*, 351.

57. De la Hoz, interview.

58. Tom Long, "Miguel 'Mike' Fornieles, at 66; Left Cuba to Pitch for Red Sox," *Boston Globe*, February 14, 1998.

59. De la Hoz, interview.

14. Casualty of the Revolution

1. López-Chávez, interview.

2. López-Chávez, interview.

3. López-Chávez, interview.

4. López-Chávez, interview.

5. Associated Press, "Ramos May Leave Griffith's Twins to Join Cuban Anti-Castro Fighters," *Washington Post and Times Herald*, April 8, 1961.

6. Tom Briere, "'Twins' Ramos 'Just Kidding' in Threat to Fight in Cuba," *The Sporting News*, April 19, 1961.

7. Ramos, interview.

8. Peter Kihss, "Anti-Castro Group Is Termed 'Almost Ready' to Invade Cuba," *New York Times*, January 5, 1961.

9. Paul P. Kennedy, "U.S. Helps Train an Anti-Castro Force at Secret Guatemalan Air-Ground Base," *New York Times*, January 10, 1961.

10. Tad Szulc, "Anti-Castro Units Trained to Fight at Florida Bases," *New York Times*, April 7, 1961.

11. Sam Pope Brewer, "Castro Foe Says Uprising Is Near," *New York Times*, April 8, 1961.

12. Tad Szulc, "Castro Foes Map Multiple Forays with Guerrillas," *New York Times*, April 10, 1961.

13. Ávila, interview, October 5, 2016.

14. Beahon, "Cuban Exile Maduro Basks in Suns' Success."

15. Maduro, interview.

16. Beahon, "Cuban Exile Maduro Basks in Suns' Success."

17. Beahon, "Cuban Exile Maduro Basks in Suns' Success."

18. Maduro, interview.

19. Gott, *Cuba*, 193.

20. "Text of President Kennedy's News Conference on World and Domestic Affairs," *New York Times*, April 13, 1961.

21. Wyden, *Bay of Pigs*, 171–172.

22. Ávila, interview, October 5, 2016.

23. R. Hart Phillips, "Challenge by Castro," *New York Times*, April 17, 1961.

24. Ávila, interview, October 5, 2016.

25. Ávila, interview, October 5, 2016.

26. "Cubans' Support of Castro Noted," *New York Times*, April 25, 1961.

27. López-Chávez, interview.

28. López-Chávez, interview.

29. López-Chávez, interview.

30. López-Chávez, interview.

31. López-Chávez, interview.

32. Cy Kritzer, "Jersey Club Saved by Mayor's Pledge," *The Sporting News*, June 21, 1961.

33. Kritzer, "Jersey Club Saved by Mayor's Pledge."

34. Howard M. Tuckner, "Jersey City Facing Loss of Ball Team," *New York Times*, July 9, 1961.

35. Tuckner, "Jersey City Facing Loss of Ball Team."

36. Bob Price, "Jacksonville May Get an Int Franchise in '62," *The Sporting News*, August 2, 1961.

37. Tom Lauenstein, "Maduro Aims Plea at Jersey City Fans," *The Sporting News*, August 2, 1961.

38. Bob Price, "Colts Clear Path for Jacksonville to Land Int Club," *The Sporting News*, October 4, 1961.

39. López-Chávez, interview.

40. Morris Siegel, "Cubans Face Dim Chance for Return to U.S. in '62," *The Sporting News*, July 19, 1961.

41. Siegel, "Cubans Face Dim Chance for Return."

42. Siegel, "Cubans Face Dim Chance for Return."

43. "More Cuban League Troubles—Almendares Club Pulls Out," *The Sporting News*, October 4, 1961.

44. Tiant, interview, November 29, 2017.

45. Posada, interview.

46. Ramos, interview.

47. Taylor, interview.

48. Clifford Kachline, "Cuban Standouts Shun Own Land, Play Elsewhere," *The Sporting News*, November 29, 1961.

BIBLIOGRAPHY

Antón, Alex, and Roger E. Hernández. *Cubans in America: A Vibrant History of a People in Exile*. New York: Kensington Publishing, 2003.

Argote-Freyre, Frank. *Fulgencio Batista: From Revolutionary to Strongman*. New Brunswick NJ: Rutgers University Press, 2006.

Bjarkman, Peter C. *Baseball with a Latin Beat: A History of the Latin American Game*. Jefferson NC: McFarland, 1994.

———. *Diamonds around the Globe: The Encyclopedia of International Baseball*. Westport CT: Greenwood, 2005.

———. *A History of Cuban Baseball, 1864–2006*. Jefferson NC: McFarland, 2007.

Bjarkman, Peter C., ed. *Cuban Baseball Legends: Baseball's Alternative University*. Phoenix: Society for American Baseball Research, 2016.

Black, Martha Jo, and Chuck Schoffner. *Joe Black: More Than a Dodger*. Chicago: Academy Chicago Publishers, 2015.

Bonachea, Ramón L., and Marta San Martín. *The Cuban Insurrection, 1952–1959*. New Brunswick NJ: Transaction Publishers, 1974.

Bonsal, Philip W. *Cuba, Castro, and the United States*. Pittsburgh: University of Pittsburgh, 1972.

Brioso, César. *Havana Hardball: Spring Training, Jackie Robinson, and the Cuban League*. Gainesville: University Press of Florida, 2015.

Brown, Bruce. "Cuban Baseball." *Atlantic* 253, no. 6 (1984): 109–14.

Cárdenas, Leonardo Chico, and George Buzz Guckenberger. *Cuba's Campo Corto*. Cincinnati: Mott Studio, 2015.

Carter, Thomas F. *The Quality of Home Runs: The Passion, Politics, and Language of Cuban Baseball*. Durham NC: Duke University Press, 2008.

Casas, Edel, Jorge Alfonso, and Alberto Pestana. *Viva y en juego*. Havana: Editorial Científico-Técnica, 1986.

Cepeda, Orlando, and Herb Fagen. *Baby Bull: From Hardball to Hard Time and Back*. Dallas: Taylor, 1998.

Cluster, Dick, and Rafael Hernández. *The History of Havana*. New York: Palgrave Macmillan, 2006.

Crompton, Samuel Willard. *The Sinking of the USS Maine: Declaring War against Spain*. New York: Chelsea House, 2009.

Dolson, Frank. *Jim Bunning: Baseball and Beyond*. Philadelphia: Temple University Press, 1998.

Dorschner, John, Roberto Fabricio. *The Winds of December*. New York: Coward, McCann & Geoghegan, 1980.

Ehrlich, Ilan. *Eduardo Chibás: The Incorrigible Man of Cuban Politics*. Lanham: Rowman & Littlefield, 2015.

Elias, Robert. *The Empire Strikes Out: How Baseball Sold U.S. Foreign Policy and Promoted the American Way Abroad*. New York: New Press, 2010.

Elliston, Jon, ed. *Psywar on Cuba: The Declassified History of U.S. Anti-Castro Propaganda*. Melbourne: Ocean Press, 2005.

Erskine, Carl. *Carl Erskine's Tales from the Dodger Dugout: Extra Innings*. Champaign IL: Sports Publishing, 2004.

Figueredo, Jorge S. *Beisbol cubano: A un paso de las Grandes Ligas, 1878–1961*. Jefferson NC: McFarland, 2005.

———. *Cuban Baseball: A Statistical History, 1878–1961*. Jefferson NC: McFarland, 2003.

———. *Who's Who in Cuban Baseball, 1878–1961*. Jefferson NC: McFarland, 2003.

Fuentes, Norberto, and Larry Alson. *Hemingway in Cuba*. Secaucus NJ: L. Stuart, 1984.

Gay, Kathlyn. *Leaving Cuba: From Operation Pedro Pan to Elian*. Brookfield CT: Twenty-First Century, 2000.

Geyer, Georgie Anne. *Guerrilla Prince: The Untold Story of Fidel Castro*. Kansas City: Andrews McMeel, 1993.

Gjelten, Tom. *Bacardi and the Long Fight for Cuba*. New York: Penguin, 2008

Gleijeses, Piero. *Conflicting Missions: Havana, Washington, and Africa, 1959–1976*. Chapel Hill: University of North Carolina Press, 2009.

González Echevarría, Roberto. *The Pride of Havana: A History of Cuban Baseball*. New York: Oxford University Press, 1999.

Gott, Richard. *Cuba: A New History*. New Haven: Yale University Press, 2004.

Hernández, Lou. *Memories of Winter Ball: Interviews with Players in the Latin American Winter Leagues of the 1950s*. Jefferson NC: McFarland, 2013.

———. *The Rise of the Latin American Baseball Leagues, 1947–1961*. Jefferson NC: McFarland, 2011.

Iber, Patrick. *Neither Peace nor Freedom: The Cultural Cold War in Latin America*. Cambridge MA: Harvard University Press, 2015.

Kinzer, Stephen. *The Brothers: John Foster Dulles, Allen Dulles, and Their Secret World War*. New York: St. Martins' Griffin, 2014.

Lacey, Robert. *Little Man: Meyer Lansky and the Gangster Life*. Boston: Little, Brown, 1991.

Lasorda, Tommy, and David Fisher. *The Artful Dodger*. New York: Arbor House, 1985.

Márquez-Sterling, Manuel. *Cuba 1952–1959: The True Story of Castro's Rise to Power*. Wintergreen VA: Kleiopatria Digital Press, 2009.

Martí, José. *José Martí: Selected Writings*. Edited by Esther Allen and Roberto González Echevarría. New York: Penguin, 2002.

Martínez de Osaba y Goenaga, Juan A., Félix Julio Alfonso López, and Yasel Enrique Porto Gómez. *Enciclopedia biográfica del béisbol cubano*. Havana, Cuba: Editorial José Martí, 2015.

Miñoso, Minnie, and Herb Fagen. *Just Call Me Minnie: My Six Decades in Baseball*. Champaign IL: Sagamore, 1994.

Navarro, Antonio. *Tocayo: A Cuban Resistance Leader's True Story*. Westport CT: Sandown, 1981.

Newcomb, Horace, ed. *Encyclopedia of Television*. New York: Fitzroy Dearborn, 2004.

Pérez, Louis A. "Between Baseball and Bullfighting: The Quest for Nationality in Cuba, 1868–1898." *Journal of American History* 81, no. 2 (September 1994): 493–517.

———. *Cuba: Between Reform and Revolution.* New York: Oxford University Press, 2006.

———. *On Becoming Cuban: Identity, Nationality, and Culture.* Chapel Hill: University of North Carolina Press, 1999.

Pietrusza, David, Matthew Silverman, and Michael Gershman. *Baseball: The Biographical Encyclopedia.* Kingston NY: Total Sports Illustrated, 2000.

Quirk, Robert E. *Fidel Castro.* New York: W.W. Norton, 1993.

Rucker, Mark, and Peter C. Bjarkman. *Smoke: The Romance and Lore of Cuban Baseball.* Kingston NY: Total/Sports Illustrated, 1999.

Santana Alonso, Alfredo L. *El inmortal del beisbol: Martin Dihigo.* Havana, Cuba: Editorial Científico-Técnica, 2007.

Shetterly, Aran. *The Americano: Fighting with Castro for Cuba's Freedom.* Chapel Hill NC: Algonquin Press, 2007.

Smith, Wayne S. *The Closest of Enemies: A Personal and Diplomatic Account of U.S.-Cuba Relations since 1957.* New York: W.W. Norton, 1987.

Sweig, Julia. *Inside the Cuban Revolution: Fidel Castro and the Urban Underground.* Cambridge MA: Harvard University Press, 2002.

Szulc, Tad. *Fidel: A Critical Portrait.* New York: William Morrow, 1986.

———. "Fidel Castro's Years as a Secret Communist." *New York Times Magazine,* October 19, 1986.

Teel, Leonard Ray. *Reporting the Cuban Revolution: How Castro Manipulated American Journalists.* Baton Rouge: Louisiana State University Press, 2015.

Thornley, Stew. "Minneapolis Millers versus Havana Sugar Kings," *The National Pastime* 12 (1992): 43.

Tiant, Luis, and Joe Fitzgerald. *El Tiante, the Luis Tiant Story.* New York: Doubleday, 1976.

Torres, Angel. *La historia del beisbol cubano.* Los Angeles: Angel Torres, 1976.

———. *La leyenda del beisbol cubano, 1878–1996.* Miami FL: Review Printers, 1996.

Tucker, Spencer C., ed. *The Encyclopedia of the Spanish-American and Philippine-American Wars: A Political, Social, and Military History.* Santa Barbara: ABC-CLIO, 2009.

Welch, Richard E. *Response to Revolution: The United States and the Cuban Revolution, 1959–1961.* Chapel Hill: University of North Carolina Press, 1985.

Williams, Stephen. *Cuba: The Land, the History, the People, the Culture.* Philadelphia: Running, 1994.

Wilson, Nick. *Early Latino Ballplayers in the United States: Major, Minor and Negro Leagues, 1901–1949.* Jefferson NC: McFarland, 2005.

Wyden, Peter. *Bay of Pigs: The Untold Story.* New York: Simon and Schuster, 1980.

Yastrzemski, Carl, and Gerald Eskenazi. *Yaz: Baseball, the Wall, and Me.* New York: Warner, 1990.

INDEX